ALSO BY BRAD WARNER

Don't Be a Jerk

Hardcore Zen

It Came from Beyond Zen

Sex, Sin, and Zen

Sit Down and Shut Up

There Is No God and He Is Always with You

Zen Wrapped in Karma Dipped in Chocolate

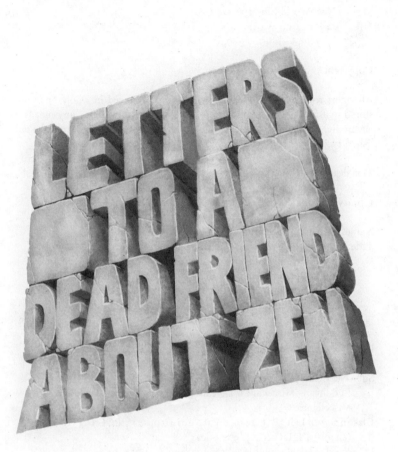

BRAD WARNER

New World Library
Novato, California

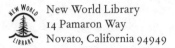 New World Library
14 Pamaron Way
Novato, California 94949

Text design by Tona Pearce Myers

Library of Congress Cataloging-in-Publication Data

Names: Warner, Brad, author.
Title: Letters to a dead friend about Zen / Brad Warner.
Description: Novato, California : New World Library, [2019] | Summary:
    "An introduction to Zen Buddhism for general readers, written as a
    series of imaginary letters from the author to a deceased friend; covers
    basic Zen concepts such as rebirth, karma, and mindfulness, while also
    examining the ethical challenges of living a Buddhist life in the modern
    world"-- Provided by publisher.
Identifiers: LCCN 2019022201 (print) | LCCN 2019981507 (ebook) |
    ISBN 9781608686018 | ISBN 9781608686025 (ebook)
Subjects: LCSH: Zen Buddhism--Miscellanea. | Religious life--Zen
    Buddhism--Miscellanea. | Death--Religious aspects--Buddhism--
    Miscellanea.
Classification: LCC BQ9265.4 .W356 2019 (print) | LCC BQ9265.4
    (ebook) | DDC 294.3/927--dc23
LC record available at https://lccn.loc.gov/2019022201
LC ebook record available at https://lccn.loc.gov/2019981507

First printing, October 2019
ISBN 978-1-60868-601-8
Ebook ISBN 978-1-60868-602-5

Printed in Canada on 100% postconsumer-waste recycled paper

 New World Library is proud to be a Gold Certified Environmen-
tally Responsible Publisher. Publisher certification awarded by
Green Press Initiative.

10   9   8   7   6   5   4   3   2   1

CONTENTS

1. CARVED INTO THE UNIVERSE

Dear Marky,

You're dead now, so I don't know if you'll get this letter.

I've just arrived in Hamburg, Germany, after bouncing around for five hours in the backseat of a Morris Mini up the autobahn from Bonn, where I was speaking to some nerds about Zen. That's what I do for a living. But you know that. Or you knew that before you died. Do you know anything anymore?

I'm sitting in a place called Pizza Pazza at the corner of Juliusstrasse and Schulterblatt, a couple of blocks from the place where I'm staying while I'm in Hamburg. The stocky Mediterranean-looking guy behind the counter was surly but figured out what I meant when I said, "Ein slice of funghi, bitte."

Just before I got to the counter, the guy in front of me was arguing with him about something. The guy grabbed a bunch of old magazines from the counter, slammed a coin down, and stalked out. The surly pizza man yelled after him, holding up the coin. The guy with the magazines was gone. The counter guy rolled his eyes and slid my slice into the oven.

The cobblestone streets outside are slick from the all-day clammy drizzle. Next door is the Rote Flora, a theater that first opened in 1888 and has been squatted since 1989. Now it mainly hosts punk-rock shows. It's huge and ancient, all covered with graffiti and old band flyers. You'd have liked it. The few people in Pizza Pazza look like they might have been at some show there earlier tonight. There's a hipster couple in one corner and a pair of blonde girls behind me talking intently in German about something apparently very important.

It's 9:40 PM, but somehow it feels like the middle of the night. Maybe that's because I just got the news that you died last night... or this morning... or sometime in the very recent past. I've traveled internationally since I was seven years old, and I can still never work out the time zones. Suffice it to say, dead is dead, no matter what time it happened.

Cancer. Age forty-eight. Jesus.

I'm in Hamburg to talk more about Zen to some other people tomorrow night. Maybe I'll get it together by then. But right now I don't want to talk about fucking Zen.

I want to be in Aberdeen, Washington, getting high with you, Marky, on the custom-grown weed your neighbor provided to help with your pain, like we did just a month or so ago when you were still alive. Watching stupid videos. I want to be back in Akron at the Clubhouse twenty-some years ago sitting on the bed with you and Lydia the Tattooed Lady eating Rasicci's Pizza, planning world conquest. Oh, the things we were gonna do.

When I arrived in Hamburg maybe an hour ago, I switched on my laptop and an email popped up from Lydia. She said you'd died a few hours earlier. I don't know what time it was back in the States, but Lydia was still up. We reminisced about the days you and I and she all lived in the Clubhouse — that dump in Akron where both our bands practiced. I think we both cried. Maybe that'll make you happy to hear. Everybody wants to imagine that people will cry after they die, right?

I'm staying in the apartment of a woman named Johanna who runs a tiny little Zen center out of her tiny little apartment. She made one of its two rooms into a zendo, which is what we Zen nerds call our meditation spaces, and that's where I'm going to be sleeping. If I can sleep tonight.

After I got the news of your death, I excused myself and went out to wander the streets of the city. I do that a lot when I'm on these European tours, drifting alone through strange cities, poking through dusty old record shops, when I can find them. You spent a lot of time in record stores too when you were alive. The record shops were all closed by the time I got to Hamburg, but I didn't know what else to do. Johanna and her roommate Julia were nice people, but I needed to be by myself.

You're not even the first person I know who died while I was on this tour. The day I arrived in Stockholm, the first stop on this tour, I got a call from my friend Melissa, who told me her brother Jeremy had passed away suddenly a few nights before. He was thirty-six. At least you lived a few years longer than him. Which is something, I guess.

What am I doing with my life? That's what I'm thinking as I sit here with my slice of pizza getting cold while I write this letter you'll never get. I'm supposed to be some kind of spiritual master. I write books about it, for God's sake!

People ask me questions all the time as if I have The Answer for them. I have no answer. I have thirty-odd years of looking at my own soul and finding there was nothing there to look at after all. I took a vow to save all beings. I couldn't even save you from being eaten alive by your own guts. And I never told you any of this. Until now, anyway. Now that it's too late to tell you anything.

Where are we going? Where do we come from? Why are we here? Does anybody care? I mean, do they? Honestly?

I guess your being dead is making me cynical right now. Not that I blame you for that. I've always had a cynical side. I'm skeptical of everything — including myself. Hell, I'm the last person I'd ever believe about anything!

What most people call "spirituality" is bullshit. And yet I have dedicated my life to something most people call "spiritual practice." Sometimes I wonder why I even do this. But other times I know exactly why.

Still, here I sit in a pizza shop in Hamburg, staring out the window through the drizzle sliding down the glass, making all the golden browns and reds and grays of this dirty city into a kind of abstract art piece, wondering how my friend died without my ever saying anything useful to him.

My old Zen teacher, who is also dead now, once told his student Jürgen Seggelke, "Every action you take in your life is carved into the universe."

My pizza. Carved into the universe.

Does anybody care? We careen into each other like bumper cars. We plow through fast-food suppers that were once cows living in mounds of shit before being dragged off to slaughterhouses, trusting their captors. Then we act as if it's all gonna last forever as we watch the next episode of *Duck-fucking-Dynasty*.

Slam! Bam! Crash! After a while we're just meandering into stores, shell-shocked at how it all passed us by, trying to find a bucket to barf in. Wondering where everything we understood went. Why are the children we raised on a steady diet of plastic garbage so resentful? Why does their music suck? Why doesn't anyone listen to me when I rage at the darkness that is another chain restaurant replacing the park where I first put my fingers inside someone and heard her whisper, "Oh God, please, yes"?

Why am I doing this at all? Riding foreign trains to places I can't even pronounce. Trying to figure out if the stuff in the fridge of the apartment someone let me stay in is hot sauce or toothpaste or some kind of butt ointment. At my level, I can't afford hotels. I ain't no Deepak Chopra! It's like those punk-rock tours our bands used to do.

Sitting. Sitting. Sitting. Meditating my life away as it all passes by. Lighting incense and candles. Bowing to nothing. Chanting the same stupid shit that they've chanted since forever ago because maybe this time it will work. That's how it feels tonight, anyway. I know there's more to it than that, but right now I just can't see it.

We're like icebergs, I told the folks at that Zen center in Bonn. What we know is only the little bit that shows above the water. The rest of us goes on forever below, unseen, unknowable. We can't understand it. We can only try to accord with it. Or we can pretend it doesn't exist and bang into all the other icebergs. They call that "winning."

You can make a statue of your little God and pray to it to spare you from the fate it has already decided for you. You can even ask it for money and sex and power and fame if you want.

When I walk into the meditation centers I speak at all over Europe and America, everyone looks at me. *He wrote that book!* Ugh. I mean, it's nice to be recognized, I guess. But usually it just makes me want to run away somewhere and hide.

Don't stare at me with those "There he is!" eyes, I'm thinking. I'm still trying to figure out what I want to be when I grow up.

You have made this world, I tell them. It's yours. All of it. And yet you're asking me to show you the way? What am I going to teach you? What you really need to know isn't something that I or anyone else can ever teach you.

Staring into the darkness of your own mind, what do you see? Are you afraid to look? Of course you are. I sure am. Every single time. And I've been doing it for decades.

Hell. I'm with you! Watching *Duck Dynasty* is a lot easier. There's a mountain of porn I could find on the phone in my pocket. There are things to buy on eBay. Why look into myself?

Carved into the universe. We don't admit it, but we are. I don't admit it, but I am.

We enhance our fairy tales about the hereafter with rituals and beautiful buildings and supposedly wise elders who can convince grown-ups to believe ancient lies. In some places there are punishments so that even those who cannot make themselves believe in those fairy tales will be afraid to say so.

Ever since I was a little kid I wanted to know the truth of this place where I found myself. This planet. This plane of existence. Whatever you want to call it. This *reality*.

You and I grew up in Wadsworth, Ohio. I was lucky enough to get out of that place for a good chunk of years when I was a kid. My dad worked at Firestone, like pretty much everybody in town's dad did in those days. They all worked for one of the tire companies or one of the companies that served the tire companies. At least before the tire companies all fled the country and left a giant gaping rust hole behind in northeast Ohio.

Firestone asked my dad if he'd go work in Nairobi, Kenya. He asked my mom. She said moving to Africa sounded like fun to her — even though I was seven and my sister was five at the time. That sounds like madness to me now.

After four years in Nairobi we came back to Wadsworth, and my questions had gotten even more intense. Churches were supposedly the places where you could find answers to those kinds of questions. So I went and sat in a few to hear what they had to say.

But all I got from the churches in Wadsworth were stories I couldn't believe, even when I tried to. I honestly made my best efforts to get my head around the idea of Jesus Christ coming to Earth to take on the sins of the world and then atone for them by sacrificing himself. But it made no sense. Couldn't an all-knowing, all-powerful, all-loving God come up with a better solution than that? Shit. Even *I* could come up with a better solution!

I looked into other religions too. But their stories weren't any better.

Plus, those religions all insisted that you had to *believe* their stories, or God wouldn't accept you. I remember thinking, Why would the creator of the entire universe, a being so infinite and powerful that he could see what was going on in a galaxy twelve-thousand light-years from Earth the same way I can examine a booger I just dug out of my nose, why would it bug him that I didn't believe in him when he didn't even have the decency to show himself?

Through sheer dumb luck I happened to encounter Zen Buddhism when I was a teenager. I didn't go looking for it. It was just there at exactly the time I needed it to be.

I don't believe in Buddhism either, by the way. It's not like I heard their fairy tales and figured they were better than anybody else's stories. The Buddhists have fairy tales too. The difference is that nobody cares if you believe them. They don't care whether you believe their stories because the very idea of a *you* who can believe in stories is something they also call into question.

Even so, I'm not all that interested in Buddhism. I'm much more interested in what is true. What I like about Buddhism is that the Buddhists are also interested in what is true. At least, most of them are.

I'm not sure if Zen Buddhism would have helped you or not, Marky. I never tried to sell it to you. You knew I was into it, but you never asked.

I never liked people who tried to sell me their religions. I know you didn't either, so I wasn't gonna do that to you. No one ever tried to sell me Zen Buddhism. If they had, I would have regarded them as people who were too insecure to believe in something unless a bunch of other people believed it too. I have no time for that.

But nowadays I'm a minor spiritual celebrity. I'm not as big as Deepak, but I'm big enough to make a living at it. Which was always a source of embarrassment whenever I interacted with you and still embarrasses me when I'm around friends who, like you, knew me long before I started doing what I do now.

I see spiritual celebrities as charlatans, as people who make their living selling empty promises that they themselves don't even believe. I swear that's not what I do. But I don't have anything against anyone who assumes the worst about me in that regard. Because that's probably what I'd assume about me if I wasn't me.

Spiritual celebs play the same stupid games as regular celebs. They, or maybe I should say *we*, validate each other the same way cheap nightclub singers do when they get on TV talk shows.

It's like there's a little Enlightened Beings Club. Here's how it works. Some guy says he's got enlightenment. He has a story to back him up about the wonderful day when he finally understood everything about everything. Another guy, his teacher, certified him as a member of the Enlightened Beings Club. And now he's ready to help you learn to be just like him.

You go to the enlightened guy, and he trains you to imitate the things he says. Or if he's real clever he teaches you how to rephrase his schtick in your own words. If your imitation meets his criteria, he gives you his seal of approval, and off you go. The industry is self-perpetuating. It's in your teacher's best interests to support your claims of enlightenment since you, in turn, are expected to support his. Without such support, the whole thing falls to pieces.

If someone comes along and says, "Ain't no such thang," it threatens the whole system since it is built on extremely shaky ground. Unless people believe in enlightenment, enlightenment cannot exist. The enlightenment they sell is nothing more than the belief in enlightenment.

This is the same deal with religions. Believing in God is not like believing in the existence of Mount St. Helens or something tangible like that. The difference is that you can question the existence of Mount St. Helens all you want, but it doesn't go away. But when someone questions the existence of God, the *very existence* of God is threatened, because that sort of God is nothing more than the belief in God.

And here's what's even weirder.

It turns out that enlightenment actually *is* real.

God actually *does* exist.

I don't know how you feel about my saying that now that you're dead, Marky. But I know that when you were alive you would have rolled your eyes at me. And I would not have blamed you.

There are a lot of things I wish I'd talked to you about. But I didn't. And so I'm writing you this letter. Maybe I'll write you a bunch of letters. There's a lot to say. I don't know if there's an afterlife and you can somehow read these letters, or if there's reincarnation and you're still a baby and can't read them, or if you just stay dead after you die, in which case you'll never even know of their existence. Maybe I'll write about that in another letter.

All I know is that whether or not you can receive what I'm saying doesn't change the fact that there are things I want to say. And so I'm going to say them.

But I'm going to have to say them later because right now there's nobody else in the Pizza Pazza and the surly guy behind the counter is giving me a funny look. So I'd better scarf down my cold pizza and go.

Stay cool down there!

Brad

2. REMEMBERING MARKY MOON

DEAR MARKY,

It's still drizzling in Hamburg, but the Hamburgers don't seem to mind. That's actually what you call someone from Hamburg in German — a Hamburger. Some folks took me out for ice cream after my talk last night. I got a flavor called *engelblau*. That means "angel blue," which sounds like it could be the name of a porn-video distributor. It tasted like the blue-moon-flavored ice cream they sold at Bidinger's Ice Cream Stand in Wadsworth.

I'm sad that you're gone. My God, am I sad!

People have some weird ideas about Buddhism. They think that Buddhists spend all their time trying to overcome attachment. They assume this means that we try to be as aloof and uncaring as possible, so that we never have any feelings toward anyone or anything and therefore we don't hurt when someone dies.

That's not what Buddhists mean when they talk about attachment.

The Sanskrit word that gets translated as "attachment" is *upadana*. It originally meant "fuel." Its use was later extended to mean anything that keeps some process going. Other English translations of *upadana* include "clinging" and "grasping."

It's about our desire to keep things the same and the mental fuel that keeps that process going. Change is unavoidable, but we don't like it. We want stability, dependability. It's natural to want such things. It's hard for any organism to adapt to change, and humans are no exception, even though, compared to most animals, we seem to do pretty well with change. Still, that doesn't mean we like it when something we rely on is no longer reliable or when something we value is no longer available. I valued the times we talked, and now I can talk to you but you can't respond. I don't like that.

In that sense, I was attached to our friendship in the form it had developed into by the time you died. I wanted that friendship to continue in that form. But it couldn't continue in that form because you died.

So in some sense, my grief is caused by my desire for things to be different from how they actually are. But does that mean that I would have been better off if I had never valued our friendship? Would I be happier now if I had been more aloof from you, if I hadn't cared about you?

I don't think so. Maybe I wouldn't feel any grief right now if I'd been like that. But in order to be the kind of person who could resist caring for people who were close to me, like you, I would have to be very hard and cold. I don't want to be hard and cold. That doesn't seem like a good way to live.

There's a term for using spirituality as an excuse for not feeling anything. People are calling it *spiritual bypassing*. I hate trendy terms like that, but the fact that someone made up a trendy term for it shows how pervasive it is. Lots of people seem to think that the way to be spiritual is to deny what they actually feel and pretend, instead, to be an aloof caricature of a spiritual person, like a phony Buddhist monk from a TV sitcom.

I don't go for that. Instead, when grief comes, I let it come. I feel it as fully as possible. But I try not to hang on to it. I try not to dwell in it. I refuse to define myself by it, even when I want to. Since you died, I've had moments when I've felt engulfed by grief. But these moments, like all moments, pass. I try not to be too attached to my grief.

Rather than dwelling on how sad I am that you're dead now, I've been thinking about what you were like when you were alive. I've been trying to recall whatever I could. I wanted to be able to see you as I wrote these letters to you. It seems important. So here goes.

When I first met you, you weren't even called Marky Moon. Your name at the time — the name your parents had given you — was Willard Marcus Clarkins. Some people called you Willy, which you hated. Others called you Will, which you tolerated but also hated. I wasn't surprised when you legally changed your name. I think it's one of the coolest punk-rock names I've ever come across. I always loved Television's 1977 debut album, *Marquee Moon*.

When you were still plain old Willy — sorry! — Will, you were the only black kid at Wadsworth High School. You were also painfully shy and kind of chubby, and you were two grades behind me. But more significant to me, you were one of the very few people in school who liked my band. I had the only punk-rock band in Wadsworth, Ohio, at the time. When our first drummer quit because he wanted us to play Foreigner songs and I refused, you stepped up to say you played drums and, for a while, you were the drummer in my band. The band only played five gigs together, and you were with us for four of them.

Back then you wore these aviator glasses that would probably look very cool and retro today, but in them days, they made you the target of lots of abuse — as if being the only black kid in the midst of so many racist assholes wasn't enough. The little striped sweater vests you wore all the time didn't help much either.

You might have been the very first fan I ever had of anything artistic I did. I used to make an amateur zine full of dumb jokes and bad cartoons called *The Reptile* that I printed up at the local Kinko's. You were one of the seven people who bought it.

I stopped making *The Reptile*, and you and a friend of yours started putting out your own zine called *The Amphibian*, which was actually a lot funnier and better produced than mine had been. At the time I thought it was really touching that you'd done that. But of course an eighteen-year-old boy is never going to say that out loud to a couple of sixteen-year-old friends.

Sometime toward the end of high school, and after our band went kaput, you started calling yourself Marky. You lost a bunch of weight and ditched the sweater vests for rock-and-roll T-shirts and tight black jeans. Once you got out of high school you started drumming in new-wave bands. You had this cool stage presence that made you stand out like a star, even behind the drum kit. Your being black went from being something you were hassled about in school to something that made you extra cool — at least within our mostly white punk scene.

My favorite of the bands you played in was this gothy group called the Zen Sex Butchers. They seemed like the perfect fit for your moody sexiness. Even I could tell you were sexy AF, as the kids say. The cutest girls on the scene all swooned for you, Marky, whereas they wouldn't have been caught anywhere near Willy. Or me, for that matter.

In the late eighties you worked it out so I could move into the Clubhouse, a rundown punk-rock house where you lived. The rent for a room was just $60 a month, which was about all I could afford. At that point you worked for the post office, while I did temp work for a variety of places. Both the Zen Sex Butchers and my band, Dimentia 13, practiced in the basement of the Clubhouse.

I spent lots of time in those days just hanging out with you and your girlfriend, Lydia, who we called Lydia the Tattooed Lady after a song Groucho Marx sang in the movie *At the Circus*. We'd sit on your bed and watch crappy horror movies on VHS. I remember one night there was a magnificent lightning storm, so we all went out on the porch to watch the show. The lightning strikes were coming so close that at one point we wondered if we'd get fried.

I'd been studying Zen for a while by the time I moved into the Clubhouse, but I don't think I ever told you very much about that side of my life. You were probably vaguely aware that I spent a lot of time at a place out in Kent called the Kent Zendo and that I meditated. I never made a big deal out of it.

Frankly, I was a little embarrassed to tell you — or any of our friends, for that matter — about that stuff. I figured you'd laugh at me. Because I know I would have laughed at someone who talked about meditation and spirituality. It was not punk-rock to meditate. It was old hippie bullshit, which we rightfully discarded along with all the other trash from the sixties that must have sounded groovy at the time but never worked out. I think we punkers were mostly right about meditation, at least when it came to how that stuff was interpreted by the West at the time.

While I was living at the Clubhouse, I applied for a teaching job in Japan and, much to my amazement, I got it. I wound up spending eleven years over there. I quit the teaching thing after a year and worked for a company called Tsuburaya Productions. They made cheesy monster movies just like the ones we used to watch with Lydia back at the Clubhouse.

When I moved to Japan, you and I lost touch for a while. Then, when the internet started getting up to speed, we found each other again. I always enjoyed chatting with you over the World Wide Web. I still find things I want to share with you there. Then I have to remind myself that you're dead and you probably won't get my emailed links any more than you'll get these letters.

I saw you a handful of times when I moved back to the United States because Tsuburaya Productions sent me to Los Angeles to run an international office there. That international office was a debacle, by the way. Whatever. Anyhow, eventually you ended up in Aberdeen, which seemed like a good place for you.

Then I got word that you had cancer. A friend of yours told me. I guess you didn't want to tell me yourself, which I totally understand.

I had no idea how bad it was until your friend told me your prognosis. They said you had less than a year left. You managed to hang on a bit longer than they said you would. But in the end, it was just too much for you.

I went and visited you twice during your illness.

The last time I was with you was a couple of months before my European tour started. You'd just made it through one of several bouts of pneumonia, a side effect of the disease that was killing you, and I wasn't sure how much longer you'd be with us.

The incident I remember best from those visits was when we were sitting on your couch one day watching a documentary on the life of Bob Guccione, founder of *Penthouse* magazine. Toward the end of the movie the narrator said that Guccione had died of cancer at age seventy-nine. Upon hearing that you said in a quiet deadpan, "That's not dying of cancer, when you die at seventy-nine!" We both laughed.

That's the kind of person you were. That's why I liked you.

When I left your place after that visit, I was pretty sure I'd never see you again, Marky. Your condition didn't seem all that bad at the time, but I heard from the friend who told me about your cancer that it was actually very serious. Still, you weren't bedridden. You could go out to places as long as the activity was pretty low-key, like playing the pinball machines at Boomtown Records. You even had lunch with me once, although you didn't finish your meal.

If you'd have asked me to talk with you about death, I would have talked about it. I told you this in an email. You thanked me, but you never asked anything. Sometimes I regret not pushing that point just a teeny bit harder. Maybe you wanted to talk but needed more encouragement. I'll never know. In any case, you know a hell of a lot more about death now than I do.

I would never assume that a person who knows he's dying wants to talk about death. When I'm dying, I hope nobody hits me up with their pet theories about death. I try to extend the same courtesy to others.

Sometimes, though, I wonder what I would have said to you if you'd asked me about death, Marky. Do I know anything about death that's worth telling a friend who is dying? Are the teachings of Zen Buddhism valuable to such a person? Would they have made a difference to the quality of your last days?

People who believe in religions generally assume the beliefs that have brought them comfort will bring comfort to anyone they share them with. Having been on the receiving end of such attempts at sharing, I can tell you that's not always the case. Usually, it's exactly the opposite.

I wasn't gonna be that guy to you, Marky. And yet there are times when I feel like if we had discussed it, maybe together we'd have come around to something valuable. I'm sad that I was too chickenshit to bring it up in person rather than just in an email.

So what I'm gonna do, starting with my next letter to you, is bring up everything I didn't bring up when I had the chance.

Until then, keep on smiling!

Brad

3. THE AKRON BOOK OF THE DEAD

Marky,

I'm in Berlin now. I'm leading a Zen retreat at a kung-fu studio with a skeleton hanging in one corner and punching bags and ropes suspended from the ceiling. Not really your standard Zen space. The folks who invited me to lead the retreat put me up in a room in the top floor of a five-story building in former East Berlin that had been squatted in for many years, although now I think they're actually paying rent. Or maybe they're not. I couldn't follow the explanation.

In any case, it's a total anarchist/hippie/punk/whatever building. Imagine the Clubhouse grown five stories high and placed in what used to be East Berlin. There's graffiti everywhere. Somebody has helpfully spray-painted Resist Xenophobia in giant neon-green letters on the door leading to the fourth floor, just in case anyone might forget to do that. This morning a resident was blasting hardcore punk at the communal breakfast table, where I was served a tasty but unidentifiable concoction that I was assured was vegan. It was sort of like stewed everything.

I'm using the room of a very tall guy named Oliver who sleeps on a mattress on top of a loft that you get to by climbing up a bookshelf. Every time I get up to use the toilet at night I'm convinced I'll break my neck. There's no heat in the place, but luckily it hasn't been that cold. Still, I bundled up and wore my hoodie to bed, wondering if the Dalai Lama sleeps in places like this.

I'M NOT REALLY COMPLAINING so much as realizing I may be getting too old for this sort of lifestyle. It's an interesting way to live. It's just that maybe I want to live in a more boring way nowadays. I did get to the Ramones Museum yesterday. You'd have liked that place. They had Dee Dee's actual Ampeg bass amps and one of Johnny's Mosrite guitars.

Have you met the Ramones yet in the afterlife, by the way? Speaking of dead people, I was about to say something about the Zen ideas concerning what happens after you die. I guess you know by now. Or maybe you don't know anything anymore. Either way, I'll tell you what Zen Buddhists have to say about death.

The best way to encapsulate Zen ideas about life after death is a joke often told at Zen places.

A guy walks up to a Zen master and says, "What happens after we die?"

The Zen master says, "I don't know."

The guy says, "What do you mean you don't know? You're a Zen master!"

The Zen master says, "Yeah, but I'm not a dead Zen master!"

One of the characteristics of Zen Buddhists is that we don't like to speculate. I should qualify that. Some of us actually do enjoy speculating. Just ask me for my thoughts on the possibility of intelligent life on other planets if you want to hear some speculating.

The problem is, when you start speculating about things you don't have any solid evidence for, all you're really doing is exercising your imagination. When it comes to death, there's no solid information those of us who are alive can call on other than the fact that it happens to everybody and that no one has ever come back to tell us what it's like.

I'm well aware that a lot of people *claim* to have come back. Or they claim that Jesus came back and told us all about it. I'm also aware of certain writings in the Buddhist tradition such as *The Tibetan Book of the Dead* that claim to tell us all about the afterlife.

The Tibetan Book of the Dead isn't part of the Zen tradition, by the way. It comes from a different branch of the Buddhist tree, one that split off well before Zen appeared. I tried reading it when I first started getting into Buddhism, but I got bored after a few chapters and never finished. I tried to read it again just before starting this tour, but the same thing happened.

Unless you believe that the person who wrote *The Tibetan Book of the Dead* actually had firsthand knowledge about death, it just reads like pointless speculation or like the regurgitation of religious ideas concocted by living people who also had no clue what death was actually like. Since I don't believe in living people who know what it's like to be dead, there was not much in the book to hold my interest.

A few general ideas about what happens after you die are fairly common throughout the Buddhist tradition. *The Tibetan Book of the Dead* presents one version, and it's not wildly different from some of the stuff you find certain Zen teachers saying. Even Dogen says a couple of things that are roughly similar to what's in *The Tibetan Book of the Dead*. Here's my version of what Dogen said.

Dogen, by the way, was a thirteenth-century Japanese Zen monk and author who went to China and brought back the form of Zen that I've practiced for thirty-odd years. He was a very down-to-earth, no-nonsense guy and not prone to wild speculations about other realms of existence. He famously said that we should have deep belief in cause and effect or, to put it another way, that we should be deeply suspicious of any claims of stuff that sounds supernatural. He also said, "Firewood becomes ash, it does not return to being firewood again. Similarly, after people die they do not return to life again."

And yet there is one place in Dogen's writings in which he

outlines the traditional Buddhist ideas about what happens after you die. In this passage, Dogen writes about something he calls Middle Existence that we enter at the moment of death. We stay there for seven days. Then we die in Middle Existence and get another body that also lasts seven days. With this body, Dogen says, we are able to see and hear everything in the whole universe with what he calls the Heavenly Eye. After seven days of this, we enter the Womb Store-house World. From here we enter into the womb of our mother to be in the next life and eventually get born once again into the material world.

Dogen probably learned these ideas when he studied Tendai Buddhism as a very young man before he entered into a Zen Buddhist temple as a teenager. Tendai Buddhism is a bit like Tibetan Buddhism in that it really gets into stuff like this.

Dogen only mentions this life-after-death stuff one time in all his voluminous writings, and even that mention appears in an essay that was unfinished at the time of his death. From the context of the piece in which this stuff appears it does not seem that Dogen is trying to convince his readers that this is what will happen to them. In fact, in all his thousands of pages of writing, Dogen never says what he thinks his readers should believe about what happens after we die.

Rather, he assumes they already believe this, and it seems he is using this preexisting belief to make a point about how important it is to revere the so-called Three Treasures of Buddhism, which are the Buddha, the dharma, and the sangha. Maybe I'll get into what those are a little later. Anyhow, in the piece in which Dogen mentions all this afterlife stuff, he's saying that the Three Treasures are so important that we should chant their praises even after we die, even when we find ourselves in the Middle Existence, even when we start seeing everything with the Heavenly Eye, and even when we are popping out of our next mother's womb.

I don't know if I'd have told you any of this as you sat there half stoned on the high-grade medical marijuana tincture you used to deal with the severe pain of your condition. If you seemed interested, I might have. It seems like the kind of thing a person might enjoy thinking about while high. But maybe not as they were dying. So I'd have tried to be careful with this stuff.

Personally, I've never had any real experiences indicating that there's any such thing as Middle Existence or Heavenly Eyes or reincarnation. Nor have I had any experiences that indicated there wasn't. So for me that all remains in the realm of speculation. And, as I said, Zen Buddhism frowns on speculation.

But I have had experiences that have made me cast great doubt on the standard way most of us conceive of the world. I no longer believe that I am an individual consciousness trapped inside a body whose existence will end as soon as this body stops functioning. The story that Dogen tells about the afterlife seems more plausible to me now than the idea that, at the moment of death, I'll just disappear. Although I still don't see how anyone could ever have known enough to be that specific about where exactly we go and how long it takes.

If I had said this to you, Marky, I'd probably have worried that you would think I was advocating a belief in the afterlife. If I had to answer yes or no to the question of whether I believed in life after death, I'd say no. I don't believe in life after death.

I guess that sounds like I'm contradicting what I just said about thinking I probably won't disappear the moment I croak.

I get that. The problem is that the categories of life and death as we tend to understand them are not quite right. There's an old Buddhist story in which a monk is with his teacher and they're visiting the home of a deceased member of the temple. The monk taps the coffin and asks his teacher, "Alive or dead?"

The teacher says, "I won't say alive. I won't say dead."

The monk says, "If you don't tell me, I'll smack you!"

The teacher says, "Smack me if you want, I still won't say!"

The monk smacks his teacher.

Years later, after his teacher has died, the monk tells another teacher this story and asks if his former teacher — the one he smacked — is alive or dead. That other teacher says, "I won't say alive. I won't say dead."

The monk asks this other teacher why he won't say. The teacher says, "I won't say! I won't say!"

On hearing this, the monk finally gets it.

I know. That just sounds weird.

We don't know any more details of this story than what I just told you, apart from the names of the people involved, which aren't really important. But my sense is that the monk finally understood the nature of the categories of "alive" and "dead" and saw that, like all categories made by human beings, these categories were flawed and incomplete.

What we call life may be an intrinsic property of everything in the universe, like electrical charge or mass. Maybe everything has a bit of life in it and the only difference is that certain assemblages of matter — like people or animals — are more aware of and able to express the life they possess than other assemblages, like rocks or puddles of water. This is a bit speculative, I guess. But after many years of meditation practice, this way of looking at things makes much more sense than the way I used to look at things.

In the past, I thought that the life I was experiencing was *my* life. I thought that my life was something that belonged to *me*. I thought that each person and thing that was alive had its own individual life.

I also believed there were lots of things that had no life at all. Things like rocks, or puddles, or elementary particles, or gasses. I thought those things were utterly different from me. They could not be said to be alive at all. Obviously, dead people like you could also not be alive. Unless maybe they had souls that left their bodies or something. But I didn't believe that.

After spending a whole lot of time sitting very still in the quiet, watching life do its thing, I began to see that I'd been mistaken. What

I thought of as *my* life wasn't mine at all. Life didn't belong to me. It was everywhere. Everything was alive. Everything was a manifestation of life.

Obviously, the life of a rock isn't the same as the life of a human being. But even saying that is kind of wrong. It's the same life. It just behaves very differently.

If you haven't seen this for yourself it just sounds like a pleasant theory. It did to me when I first encountered it in old Buddhist stories like the one I just told you. But if you keep practicing in the quiet, it becomes clearer and clearer, until the way you used to look at things seems doubtful and you eventually start to know for certain that you've been wrong about the nature of life.

This doesn't exactly erase the fear of death. Just hearing it from someone else probably won't help at all. Which is one of the reasons I didn't tell you all this when you were alive and dying. Even knowing it for certain doesn't make the fact that one of these days I'm gonna die that much easier to deal with. It's a little easier, I grant you. But it doesn't make the prospect of dying seem perfectly okay, that's for sure!

It does change things, though. And that change is significant. I no longer fear that I'll just blip out of existence one day and miss out on all the fun everyone else is having. That's a bit reassuring. On the other hand, I don't see any reason to believe that I'm going to live eternally, meaning that once this life is over, whatever is left to carry on won't be what I am now. So for all practical purposes I'll be gone for good. Or maybe not.

There's another couple of stories I might have told you if we'd had a talk about death and the afterlife. Here's one.

I knew this monk at San Francisco Zen Center named David Coady. I didn't know David very well. I only ever hung out with him two or three times. But he was one of those people you meet just a few times yet feel you've known all your life. It seems like everyone has people like this in their lives. Maybe you did too. I wonder why that is.

Anyhow, I felt a real bond with David in spite of how little we interacted. But David was a depressed guy. He'd already attempted suicide before I met him. And one day in July 2011 he attempted it again and succeeded.

I'd first met David at Tassajara Zen Mountain Center in Northern California, where he lived at the time. He'd moved out of Tassajara by 2011, so he didn't die there. But he loved Tassajara a lot. I'd already been scheduled to spend a few weeks at Tassajara in August of the year he died. So I went ahead with my plans and went, with a heavy heart since David would not be there, even for a visit. But actually, he was.

One afternoon I was supposed to lead a service at the zendo. It was blazing hot out, and my black robes made me feel like I was wrapped up in a pile of blankets as I stood out in the sun waiting for my cue to enter the zendo and perform my bit of the ceremony. I found a tiny patch of shade under a dried-out little tree and was hiding there from the heat, when all of a sudden, David Coady was there too.

I couldn't see him. So it wasn't like seeing a ghost. But I could feel his presence so strongly and clearly that it was undeniable. It was as if someone you knew very well came and stood behind you for a moment and you couldn't see him but you knew he was there. The feeling lasted for a few seconds — maybe a minute, but no more than that — and then he was gone.

I hadn't been thinking of David at all. I was only worried about getting out of the heat. It wasn't a memory. It was an encounter. I don't want to speculate on the nature of the encounter because I don't think I can make any sense of it. It was completely outside my belief system. And yet I can't deny that it happened and that it was as real as any encounter I've ever had with someone who was alive.

There have been other incidents like that. The most notable one for me was when my mom died in January 2007. I'd gone to visit her and my dad in Texas over Christmas. She was sixty-five years old and had been dealing with a terrible degenerative disease for about twenty years. It had been a few years since she'd even been able to walk on her own. She was in reasonably good spirits, although it had been a long time since she could say anything anyone could understand. But she smiled a lot, which was nice to see.

Somehow I knew I'd never see her alive again. I can't say why. I just did.

A few hours before dawn on the morning of January 12, 2007, I woke up with the John Lennon song "My Mummy's Dead" playing in my head. I could hear it almost as clearly as if I'd put a copy of Lennon's *Plastic Ono Band* album on and cued it up to the last song on side two. You loved that album too, Marky. That's something we bonded on. Anyhow, it wasn't like I was recalling the song or sort of playing it to myself in my mind. I could *hear* it, although not through my ears.

And I felt okay. It didn't scare me or weird me out. Which is strange since it really should have. Instead it felt familiar and nice. I soon went back to sleep. At about six o'clock my phone started ringing. It was my dad calling to tell me that my mom had passed away. He hadn't even noticed at first. They still slept together, although my mother had to be carried into bed. She always slept very still, so it took my dad a while to notice she wasn't breathing.

My mom had a weird sense of humor, and she knew how much I liked John Lennon. I'm certain this was her way of telling me she was gone but that things were all right even so.

Another thing about Zen Buddhists is they generally don't like to talk about the paranormal. But sometimes they do anyway. As I said, Dogen wrote an essay called "Deep Belief in Cause and Effect." In that essay, he says that everything in the universe is subject to the law of cause and effect. There is no such thing as the supernatural. Although there are plenty of things we can't yet adequately explain, that doesn't mean they happen without any cause. Even if you don't know the chain of cause and effect that produced a given event, you can be assured there is one and that it is perfectly rational.

Anyhow, that's probably what I'd have told you about death if you'd asked.

You never visited me after you died, Marky. Or if you did, I missed it. You should stop by sometime, if you can. Tell me about the Ramones! Maybe you could tell me what you think of all these dumb letters.

See you soon!

Brad

4. WILD BEAST JERKY

DEAR MARKY,

Let's get off the subject of death for a bit. Maybe I'll return to it later.

I first heard about how bad your condition was at the start of this tour, when I was in Helsinki. I knew things were rough for you before that, but that's when I got an email saying that you might go any day.

I was already having trouble sleeping, what with the way the sun never really sets up there this time of year. It gets a little dark, something like twilight anywhere else in the world, around midnight, but by about two in the morning it's full-on sunshine again. When you're already dealing with jet lag and a dying friend, that's just too much to take!

Finland was the first place in Europe that I ever got invited to speak about Zen. The first language that my book *Hardcore Zen* was translated into was Finnish. Up until I heard that news, all I knew about Finland was that it was way up north and that Monty Python had a song about it. I've been to Finland a whole bunch of times now, and I've really gotten to like the place. The Finns are crazy! But in a good way. They like to heat themselves up in saunas and then go jump into frozen lakes. I've seen 'em do it! At Zen retreats, no less!

Anyhow, after getting that news about you, I drowned my sorrows in pizza from the Foxy Bear Pizzeria near my friend Donny's place on the hills overlooking the city. Then my friend Essi took me to pay homage to the remains of the five-meter-tall gorilla made out of tires that used to stand on the campus of Helsinki University. Some asshole burned it down. After that, Essi drove me up to Turku, an hour or so west of Helsinki, where I spoke at a little café to a bunch of her Finnish Discordian buddies. Discordianism is this weird quasi religion that basically makes fun of other religions. I usually have a good time with the Finnish Discordians I know.

I can't really explain Discordianism, but maybe I can tell you about Zen. First, though, I have to give some caveats.

I have no idea what Zen is or how it should be done.

I don't know what a Zen priest is or how you should ordain one.

I don't know what it means to be a "Zen master" or even a Zen teacher.

I can't assess the relative value of one way of practicing over another, or the results of one form of practice over the results of another form. I can't see the point of trying.

I don't even know what it means to be a Zen student. This is why I get so confused when people ask if they can be my student. Maybe I'll talk about that later.

I suppose that sounds weird. But, honest to gosh, Marky, I'm not trying to be all tricky and "Zen" by saying this stuff. I am being completely, 100 percent, serious, straightforward, and unironic. I mean this. Absolutely. And yet I want to say some stuff anyway.

Even though I can't say anything definitive about Zen, I can say a little about what Zen means to me. To me Zen is like some kind of crazed wild beast with big fangs and slashing claws. The task I have set for myself is to try to somehow make friends with that beast so that I can sleep next to it in the warmth of its fur with a certain degree of confidence that it probably won't decide to tear me to pieces, disembowel me, and eat me.

This beast isn't a kitty cat or a puppy dog. It's not only not tame, it is deranged. Even if it doesn't kill me tonight, it could kill me tomorrow night. It's totally unpredictable.

The emerging consensus of American Zen, on the other hand, seems to me an attempt to capture that beast, anesthetize it, pull out its claws and teeth, and force it to breed tame, clawless, fangless offspring. These offspring will then be slaughtered, their bodies dried and salted, and then packed into plastic bags with a picture of the original beast on them and the words *Wild Beast Jerky* in flaming red and the slogan "Can you tame the wild beast?"

Not every teacher, every center, and every Zen experience that takes place within the fifty United States and its territories and possessions is like that. I just feel like it's trending in this direction.

Plenty of us are trying to resist this trend. But I feel like this is just what happens to any movement as it starts to become more mainstream. Punk got neutered into new wave to become trendy. Metal got anesthetized into hair bands to get onto MTV. But there's still real punk and real metal out there if you look for it. Same with Zen.

My understanding of the beginnings of what we now know as the monastic forms of Zen practice goes like this. It all started with Buddha — or *the* Buddha, if you like — in India about 2,500 years ago. He never claimed to be God or even the son of God. He didn't have superpowers. He was just a guy who meditated a lot and taught other people to meditate. I think I'll leave it for a later letter to get into the details of his personal background and all that. What I want to talk about right now is not Buddha himself but the community of folks who call themselves Buddhists — specifically Zen Buddhists.

After the Buddha started roaming through India talking about meditation, a group formed around him. Those were the first Buddhists. Some of what we do nowadays derives from what they did. Those guys made up their various forms and practices as they went along.

The Buddha was not the first person to attempt to discover the deepest truths of life by sitting quietly and observing them at work within himself. Lots of people had done that. The Buddha's great innovation was creating a way to teach others to do what he had done and transform what had been an individual practice into one that could be done in community with others.

It's important to remember that the Buddha didn't set out to form a religion or even a monastic order. He set out to find the truth *for himself.* After he felt that he had discovered that truth, he initially thought there was no point in even attempting to tell anyone about it. No one would get it. Legend has it that the god Indra asked him to teach others what he'd learned. I doubt that was what actually occurred, but for whatever reason, he decided to teach this meditation stuff to others.

Fast-forward a thousand years or so, and we get to Bodhidharma. Bodhidharma was this cranky Buddhist guy in northern India or perhaps Afghanistan, which at one time was home to lots of Buddhists. The Zen form of Buddhism is traditionally said to derive from the way Bodhidharma practiced. He just wanted to sit by himself and discover the truth. So he traveled from his homeland and found a cave somewhere in what we now call China. He sat in his cave for nine years, meditating alone.

Word got around about the weirdo sitting in the cave, and pretty soon four people — three men and one woman — decided to join Bodhidharma in his cave. I like to imagine them coming sheepishly, one by one, into the cave and asking if they could sit with him. Bodhidharma was probably all scowly and mean-looking, just like the caricatures and statues that depict him. He probably was all like, "Grrrr. All right. Just sit over there. And don't bug me, or I'll boot your ass out of here!" He probably made them clean up the place and do other stuff in exchange for allowing them to stay.

This is the bottom line for absolutely everything we do in Zen practice. All the stuff we do around meditation — the rituals, the chants, the costumes — exists just to make it possible to engage in a personal meditation practice within a group. Nothing else. Anything that looks like an attempt to standardize things is only there to make sure nobody's practice gets in the way of anyone else's. That's all. We are there to support each other and stay out of each other's way. The hierarchies that exist within Buddhist organizations are only there to make things run smoothly. If they do anything other than that, they're just causing needless interference.

No one can measure anyone else's practice. Well, they can try if they want, but that's a stupid waste of time and energy. Anyone who tells you your practice is better or worse than anyone else's has no idea what they're talking about. Anyone who tells you you've achieved something or solved something or failed to achieve or solve something is just messing with your head. There's no reason to listen to that kind of bullshit.

Zen teachers aren't even teachers in the sense that we usually understand the term. They're just people who've done this stuff a little longer. They're working on the same things you are. You can learn from them sometimes. And other times you'd be better off not doing it their way.

I never try to teach anyone Zen. Sure, I'll show them how to sit and I'll talk about the philosophical tradition. But after that there isn't a whole lot to teach. My approach is that I am trying to learn as much as I can about zazen. Playing the role of the guy who gives the talks and does the one-on-one meetings during retreats and the writing of books helps me do that. If other people benefit from watching that happen, great. That's beautiful. But I have no message for anyone. I'm not kidding about that either. I really mean it.

On the other hand, I know how good and useful this Zen stuff has been for me. And I know that I would never, ever, in a million years have picked up on Zen if all that had been available to me was the ritualized, institutionalized version favored by the large Zen Buddhist organizations now emerging in the United States. If my first introduction to Zen had been at, let's say, the San Francisco Zen Center or Zen Mountain Monastery in upstate New York, I'd have lasted a month or so before moving on to something else.

Luckily I got introduced to Zen by one of its wild men, a skinny weirdo named Tim McCarthy who had no use for big institutions or fancy titles or funny-looking robes. Then I met a teacher in Japan who had a similar disdain for the massive Vatican-like organization that pretends to be in charge of Zen over there. I got into it because of those guys, because I knew they were for real.

Reality is what's important, not religion, not ritual, not dogma and costumes. Reality.

That's yet another thing I wish I'd found a way to tell you when you were still alive.

I gotta go now. The people I'm staying with are yelling at me to get ready to sit in yet another tiny little car for another long trip up the autobahn.

Talk to you later!

Brad

5. BUDDHISMS: WHAT THEY AGREE ON

MARKY,

I'm in Bielefeld, Germany, today. Or maybe I'm not. You see, apparently back in the nineties some German jokesters made up a fake conspiracy theory that Bielefeld doesn't exist. But my German publishers are located in this city and it sure looks like it exists! It is kind of a boring town, though. Sort of like a slightly bigger Wadsworth, Ohio, but in Germany, if you can picture that. I can see why some people might think it doesn't exist.

Anyway, I've been chatting with people back in America about doing some kind of memorial service for you. You're going to have a proper funeral out in Aberdeen. But a bunch of your friends in Ohio want to get together to honor you too. I wish you could be there. It sounds like it'll be fun in its own weird way.

They want me to do some kind of official Buddhist-y thing and I said I would. My friend Melissa also wants me to do a little ceremony for her brother. I've still got several weeks of this tour to get through before any of that happens. Weeks traipsing through Europe, talking about what Buddhism is.

People often use the word *Buddhism* as if it's describing one, single, unified thing. It isn't one thing. No religion is.

Buddhism is around five hundred years older than Christianity.

33

Under the umbrella term *Christianity*, we find huge variations, from relatively orthodox versions like Roman Catholicism and the Church of England to somewhat less orthodox versions like the Mennonites and Quakers, all the way to versions that barely seem like Christianity at all — especially to members of the more orthodox churches — such as the Church of Jesus Christ of Latter-Day Saints (Mormons) and the Jehovah's Witnesses.

Along with those, we also have a whole lot of small fringe movements and straight-up cults that call themselves Christianity too. Buddhism has had five hundred more years to develop its own schisms and reimaginings. So there are at least as many varieties of Buddhism out there as there are varieties of Christianity. And some of them are just as fringe-y and cult-y as the wackiest of Christianities. In fact, some folks would even place Zen Buddhism in the category of outlying fringe-y forms of almost-but-not-quite Buddhism. There's even a popular reference book about Buddhism called *The Shambhala Dictionary of Buddhism and Zen*. That title tells you a lot about how Zen is viewed by many of the other forms of Buddhism.

In their excellent but far too expensive book *Buddhist Religions: A Historical Introduction*, Richard Robinson, Willard Johnson, and Thanisarro Bhikkhu (Geoffrey DeGraff) argue that "it seems better to regard the term Buddhism as describing a family of religions, each with its own integrity, much as monotheism covers a family of religions that are related but so inherently different that they cannot be reduced to a common core." This is from the introduction to the fifth edition, page xxi, if they have the book in the library wherever you ended up. In their estimation, Buddhism may belong to a category that supersedes the categories of individual religions. To them it's like a whole other phylum of religion rather than a mere species.

I'm not sure if I'd go quite that far. But those guys have studied more forms of Buddhism in a lot more depth than I have, so if they think so, I respect their opinion. Still, the question is, What makes something a form of Buddhism?

For that we have to go back to the guy who started it all, the man we know today as the Buddha. All forms of Buddhism that I'm aware of trace their origins to one person, variously known as Buddha, Gautama (or Gotama), Shakyamuni, and Siddhartha. I'll get into why he has so many names in a bit.

If you just make a blanket statement like "Buddhists don't regard Buddha as a god," you ought to qualify it because there are some Buddhists who kinda do think Buddha is a god. Most of them wouldn't put it in quite those terms. But if you poke into their belief systems a bit, you'll see that they regard Buddha as having all sorts of powers that we usually attribute to a god, or at least to something we'd call "supernatural." The Zen tradition tends to look on such claims with a lot of skepticism.

When people would ask Nishijima Roshi, my teacher in Japan, what Buddha was, he would say, "I think Buddha was a kind of genius." I think that's the best way to understand Buddha. That means he was sort of like a spiritual Albert Einstein or Stephen Hawking. We know that people like Einstein and Hawking are human beings like us. We don't think of them as having supernatural powers or having descended to our lowly planet from some higher spiritual realm. We don't pray to them. We don't imagine they have the power to reach down from heaven and save us. We don't think of them as infallible or incapable of error.

Furthermore, we understand that even the best theories of the greatest geniuses may be subject to revision. We understand that discoveries might be made in the future that expand on or even invalidate some of their ideas. But we also understand that most of us are not really qualified to question or revise the work of geniuses — though we could conceivably become qualified to do so *if we worked very hard at it.*

So who was Buddha?

Before you eat your meals at a Japanese Zen retreat, you do a chant that contains the following lines:

Busho kapira
Jodo makada
Seppo harana
Nyumetsu kuchira

That means, "Buddha was born in Kapilavastu, enlightened at Magada, taught in Varanasi, and entered Nirvana (died) in Kushinagara." That's the briefest outline of Buddha's life story that I know of. But I'll give you a few more details.

Historians tell us that Kapilavastu was a town near the present-day border of India and Nepal. Kapilavastu no longer exists, which is why we don't know precisely where it was. In the oldest sutras, the Buddha says he was born a member of the Shakya clan. The name Shakyamuni means "wise man of the Shakya clan." The Buddha also tells us that he was one of the Kshatriya, or warrior, caste. In the Indian caste system, the warrior caste is the second from the top of the four-level system. The top caste is the Brahmin caste, who were also the ones in charge of all things religious. So the fact that the Buddha was not from the Brahmin caste is significant. He was not from the caste of professional religious people.

The Buddha-to-be's parents named their child Siddhartha, which means "the one who has achieved his goal." The old sutras tell the story of his parents taking the infant to a soothsayer, who tells them that the child is destined to become either a great king or a great holy man.

A week after the boy was born, as the Buddha tells us in the sutras, his mother died. Siddhartha's dad then married Siddhartha's mother's sister, Mahapajapati. That would be really weird in our society, but in ancient India it was fairly common. It was from his mother's sister that he got the nickname Gautama, which means "the one who dispels darkness."

Historians tell us that Siddhartha came from a minor royal family. The sutras tend to play up the idea that he was a prince. But we now know it wasn't quite like he was, say, Prince William of England. His dad was the ruler of a small kingdom in the north near the Himalayas — more like a modern-day state governor than what we'd think of as a king.

Some legends say that Siddhartha's dad hid any and all indications of life's hardships from his son in order to make sure he grew up to be a king rather than a holy man. It's highly unlikely that this is literally true, but it's safe to assume that his father really did want him to become a king and that young Siddhartha had a pretty cushy life.

The stuff about the Buddha-to-be being a spoiled rich kid is pretty well attested to historically. The next bit isn't, but I'll tell it anyhow because you hear it a lot when people recount Buddha's life story.

The legend says that one day Siddhartha ordered his chariot driver to take him out to see the town they lived in, something the stories say he'd been forbidden to do. Once he was outside the palace he saw four people: an old person, a sick person, a dead person, and a wandering ascetic. Siddhartha's distress at seeing the first three of these people made him decide he wanted to find a way out of life's miseries, so he decided to leave the palace and become a wandering ascetic, a person who left home and family in order to discover the truth about reality.

In one of the oldest sutras, the Buddha tells this story, but not about himself. He says it happened to a prior Buddha. Buddhists generally believe that our historical Buddha wasn't the first Buddha but that there were several other Buddhas long before him and that there will be more Buddhas in the future.

However, about two centuries after the historical Buddha was dead and gone and couldn't make a fuss about it, this story was retold. But in the newer version it happened to Siddhartha rather than to a prior Buddha. These days most Buddhists don't know that.

In fact, I didn't even know it until I did a bit of research before writing this letter.

In any case, it's reasonable to think that, after living a cushy royal-type life, Siddhartha decided that material pleasures weren't all they were cracked up to be and that he needed to discover the deeper meaning of existence.

For a number of years, Siddhartha practiced a whole bunch of difficult activities that were supposed to free the soul from the fetters of the body and thus produce the experience of awakening to the truth. But even though he endured all kinds of hardships in his quest, Siddhartha never felt like he'd achieved the awakening he'd hoped for.

One day he was sitting on the side of the road. He'd starved himself nearly to death. He'd had a few moments of deep insight but wasn't really satisfied with them. They failed to address his main concern, which was why people suffer. Two of his meditation teachers had already offered to make him their successor because they felt he was more woke than they were. But he'd refused them both. And now here he was, nearly dead from all the work he had done to find the answer, having been lauded by lots of people, including his teachers, as a saint, and yet feeling like a total failure.

As he was sitting there emaciated and close to death, a little girl came by with a bowl of rice milk that she was going to place on an altar somewhere in the village. She was so moved by the sight of this poor starving guy that instead of taking the offering to the altar, she gave it to him. Up till then, Siddhartha would have refused such an offer. But now he accepted. From then on, he decided to just eat like a normal person. No more starvation diets!

Around this time, Siddhartha had been traveling with five companions who were also into this whole asceticism deal. When they saw Siddhartha eating, they branded him a sellout and stopped hanging around with him. He was on his own now.

Siddhartha decided to pursue what he later called the middle way, not too hard but not too easy. Sort of like Goldilocks. He remembered a time when he was a child and was sitting on a hill watching some workers plow his father's fields. He'd felt a deep sense of inner peace that day. So he decided to make that his new spiritual practice.

He got himself a rock, put a deerskin on top of it, put the rock under a tree, and plopped his ass down. The legend says he decided not to move from that spot until he had realized the truth. I'm sure he must have gotten up to pee and, since he was eating again, he must have taken breaks for that too. But essentially he made his whole life all about this one simple practice.

When Zen teachers tell this story, they often call what he did zazen. Of course, the word *zazen* didn't exist at that time. Siddhartha probably called his practice *dhyana*, which is usually translated as "meditation." The word *zazen* is Japanese. The *za* part means "sitting," and the *zen* part is a corruption of the word *dhyana*. They say Siddhartha sat under that tree for forty-nine days.

According to the sutras, while sitting all night on the forty-ninth day the Siddhartha had three great insights. First, he saw all his former lives and understood that they had been insubstantial, like dreams. Next, he acquired the Heavenly Eye, with which he could see everything in the universe throughout all time and space all at once — this is the same Heavenly Eye that Dogen talked about when he got into what supposedly happens after you die. Then the morning star rose, and when he looked at it, Siddhartha had his greatest insight of all. At last he had been awakened. He was thirty-five years old.

It's from this point on that we can start calling him the Buddha, which means "Awakened One." This is the name he bestowed on himself when asked if he was a god or a supernatural being. He said he was neither, just that he was one who had awakened. He also gave himself the name Tathagatha, which means "one who comes and goes just like this," another testament to his ordinariness.

The Buddha figured that his awakening was so vastly different from anything he had ever heard about before that nobody could possibly understand it. So at first he figured he'd just keep it to himself. But, as I said in a previous letter, legend has it that Indra, chief of all the Hindu gods, appeared before him and talked him into teaching the world what he had learned. As I said, I doubt that's how it went down, but for some reason the Buddha decided to teach.

First the Buddha looked for those two meditation teachers who'd offered to make him their successor. He figured that if anyone could understand what had happened to him, it would be those guys. But when he asked around, he learned that they'd both passed away. The only other people he could think of to tell this stuff to were those five traveling companions who'd branded him a sellout before.

He found out where they were staying and went there. At first those guys were gonna ignore him. But they looked at him, and something about the Buddha seemed different. So they decided to give him a chance and listen to what he had to say.

The sermon he delivered that day has come to be known as "The First Turning of the Dharma Wheel." In it the Buddha laid out two of his most important and enduring ideas, the Four Noble Truths and the Noble Eightfold Path. If I keep writing these letters, I'll get to what those are.

The Buddha then spent the next forty-five years going all over India teaching people how to meditate and how to follow the Noble Eightfold Path. He acquired a lot of followers. There were so many that he began deputizing his long-term students to teach on his behalf.

One of these long-term students was a guy named Mahakashyapa. Mahakashyapa became head of the Buddhist order after the Buddha died. The Zen tradition has a story about how that happened. Although variations of this story are used in other sects, it's the Zennies who make the most out of it. The story is probably not literally true since it doesn't appear in any of the accounts of the Buddha's life until several hundred years after they were first written down. But since it's so important to the Zen lineage, I'll tell you about it. Supposedly, one day the Buddha was scheduled to give a lecture. It's normal when a holy person speaks in India for there to be flowers set out all around the place where they're speaking and for some to be scattered on the ground as well.

In the story, the Buddha gets up on the stage but doesn't say a word. He just picks up one of the flowers, looks Mahakashyapa in the eye, and winks. This wink is regarded by Zennies as the moment when Buddha and Mahakashyapa both realized they had attained the same degree of enlightenment. It was the first instance of what the Zen folks call "dharma transmission." The Buddha supposedly said, "I possess the true Dharma eye, the marvelous mind of Nirvana, the true form of the formless, the subtle dharma gate that does not rest on words or letters but is a special transmission outside the scriptures. This I entrust to Mahakashyapa." This quote comes from a book called *Transmission of the Lamp*, which contains the stories of the great awakenings of teachers from the Buddhist lineage.

That's how the story goes. But chances are this never actually happened and the Buddha never really said any such thing since the book it appears in was written a long time after the Buddha died. The phrase is also loaded with buzzwords and special phrases from the Zen tradition. It was almost certainly the invention of a later writer from that tradition. It *is* well established that a guy named Mahakashyapa did take over the Buddhist order after the Buddha died. But it probably happened a lot differently.

Anyhow, a few years after this stuff with the flower that probably never happened, the Buddha died of food poisoning at age eighty. Some say he died from eating bad mushrooms; others say it was spoiled pork. Even so, the movement he started carried on without him. It became, for a time, the major religion throughout India and much of the surrounding region. It was huge in Afghanistan and even had a minor following in parts of Eastern Europe before it was stamped out by Christianity. It went on to be practiced all over Asia even after it was replaced in India first by Islam and then by a resurgence of Hinduism in a new form much influenced by Buddhism.

That's the short version of Buddha's life story. Pretty much all forms of Buddhism agree on at least this much of the story. There are loads of details they argue about, but not the main storyline I've given you here — besides the part about Mahakashyapa and the flower.

Next up, I want to get into what they don't agree on.

Almost as soon as Buddhism emerged, there were schisms. Initially there were eighteen different Buddhist monastic orders, each with their own version of the Buddha's teachings. Each of them claimed to be the one true authentic version. Because, of course they did.

For around two hundred years, these versions of Buddha's teachings were transmitted orally but never written down. Eventually, though, the various orders started writing down the teachings. The oldest version we have in complete form is the one written in Pali. Pali was not the language the Buddha spoke, but it's probably pretty close.

The two major divisions of Buddhism are Hinayana and Mahayana. *Hinayana* means "lesser vehicle" and was a term of insult coined by those who subscribed to the Mahayana forms of Buddhism. *Mahayana* means "great vehicle." Most forms of Buddhism that exist today are Mahayana. The only remaining Hinayana form of Buddhism is called Theravada. The *th* at the beginning is pronounced like a "t," followed by a little puff of air. It is not pronounced like Theraflu.

The Theravada folks accept only the oldest Buddhist scriptures as authentic. While the Mahayana folks have all sorts of other scriptures, often attributed to the historical Buddha, even though everybody knows they were written long after the Buddha died.

As for all those sects of Buddhism I mentioned, the main ones you'd have encountered while you were alive in the States are Zen, which I've talked about a bunch; Theravada, which I also talked about a little; as well as Tibetan Buddhism and Nichiren Buddhism. Tibetan Buddhism tends to be really colorful and ritualistic. When British scholars first encountered it, they thought it was Satan's corruption of the Catholic faith. Which I guess kind of makes sense if you come from that mind-set. The goings-on in Tibetan temples do look kind of like a Catholic Mass as envisioned by Martians.

Nichiren Buddhism was the invention of a monk named Nichiren who, like Dogen, lived in Japan in the thirteenth century. The O.G. Buddha, Siddhartha, supposedly predicted that another Buddha named Maitreya would come along after him, and Nichiren believed himself to be Maitreya. He taught his followers to chant *namu myoho renge kyo*, which means "homage to the Lotus Sutra." A subsect of the Nichiren lineage called Sokka Gakkai is pretty popular in the States these days. Members of that sect believe that chanting that little chant will bring them money, luck, and all kinds of nice things.

There are a few hundred other sects of Buddhism out there, but very few of them have made much impact on the West. None of these other sects are nearly as into meditation as the Zen folks are. Which is weird since meditation seems to have been the Buddha's main concern. But there you go.

So that's a brief primer on the Buddhisms of the world.

Don't take any wooden nickels!

Brad

6. IS ZEN BUDDHISM A RELIGION?

MARKY,

Sorry it's been a few days since I last wrote. But stuff's been happening.

One bit of news is that I don't have meningitis. That's good!

They gave me a spinal tap! And it went to 11 — on the pain scale.

Actually, it didn't hurt that bad. I'd heard it was one of the most painful medical procedures in the world. But I guess the doctor who did it must've been good. It hurt for sure. But only a little worse than a normal shot.

I did a talk a few nights ago at a little Buddhist bookshop in Hanover called Dharma Buchladen, but I was not feeling well. I figured I could handle it, though, because the place was just a two-minute walk from where I was staying — with a couple named Jan and Angela, who work at the bookstore. So I went over at the very last minute, talked for precisely the hour I was supposed to talk, and then went straight back to bed.

The next day I was feeling much worse, so Jan carted my ass to a nearby hospital. They took some blood and said I had a massive infection. Given my symptoms, they feared it might be meningitis, hence the spinal tap. The results came back negative. The doctor just basically shrugged and said the best thing to do was to take a bunch of antibiotics and see if that fixed it. So that's what I'm doing.

So here I sit again in bed at Jan and Angela's place writing you another letter. I think we were talking about some of the religious-seeming aspects of Zen. So let's go into that a bit more. You hated religions when you were alive. I never liked them either. I wonder how you feel about that now? Lots of religious people gleefully anticipate the day when those of us who resent religion will get our comeuppance in the afterlife and find out that their specific religion was actually the right one. Is that what happens?

My guess is no. But if you know otherwise, give me a sign, eh?

In any case, I want to get more into this question of whether or not Zen Buddhism is a religion. Some say yes. I generally say no. Maybe both answers are kinda right. It's complicated. So, to begin, what is religion?

The first definition the online version of *Webster's Dictionary* gives is "the service and worship of God or the supernatural" and the second is "a personal set or institutionalized system of religious attitudes, beliefs, and practices."

If we go by the first definition, then Zen Buddhism is not a religion. If we go by the second, it still probably isn't, but at least it's a bit closer. But dictionary definitions of words are often at odds with how those words are actually used.

As I said earlier, in some forms of Buddhism the Buddha is treated pretty much as a god, or even as *the* God, in an almost monotheistic sense. There are also forms of Buddhism in which belief in the supernatural is expected and encouraged. But in the Zen form of Buddhism, the Buddha is not thought of as a god, and belief in the supernatural is discouraged. From that point of view, then, you can't call Zen Buddhism a religion. (I should also note again here that in most forms of Buddhism, the Buddha is not regarded as a god, so Zen isn't unique in that regard.)

On the other hand, you could argue that Zen Buddhism does

have a set of attitudes, beliefs, and practices and that it does have institutions that promote these attitudes, beliefs, and practices. Then again, so do a lot of things that aren't religions — like the Elks Club or the Girl Scouts.

I think it's okay to say that there probably is a set of a few common beliefs that most Zen Buddhists agree with. It's also important to note, however, that belief is not central to Zen Buddhism the way it is to most religions. Your beliefs don't make you a Zen Buddhist.

Nishijima Roshi used to say, "I believe in the universe." He didn't believe in what he had not experienced for himself.

When it comes to beliefs about the historical Buddha, Zen Buddhists tend to believe he really existed. But they don't believe he was divine or even infallible. Being part of the Mahayana tradition, they tend to believe that there have been a lot of Buddhas and that Buddhas will continue to appear. They're not required to believe that, mind you. It's just that if you ask around, you'd probably find that most of us who practice Zen are at least open to the idea. Then again, most Buddhists believe in multiple Buddhas. The Mahayana Buddhists, however, tend to believe in more of them than the so-called Hinayana Buddhists.

Apart from that, there aren't a whole lot of beliefs you can say the majority of Zen Buddhists hold in common. Some are vegetarians, some aren't. Some believe in God, some don't. Some like the Smiths, while others, inexplicably, prefer the Cure.

It's not really about belief. It's more about attitudes and practices. So let's talk about attitudes and practices.

My ordaining teacher, Gudo Nishijima, dispensed with most of the elaborate ritual and symbolism of temple-based Zen practice. Yet he did the Buddhist meal chant before every meal I ever saw him eat — including when he got takeout sushi from convenience stores. The Buddhist meal chant basically goes, "Every bit of food I eat represents the work and sacrifice of others, including animals and plants that died so that I could eat. I vow to use the energy that this food gives me to do some good in the world." Nishijima Roshi also chanted a thing called the Verse for Opening the Sutras before every lecture he gave. This chant just says something like, "The Buddhist Sutras are really fab, let's read some of them." He chanted what's called the "Robe Verse" whenever he put on his robes. That one says something like, "Buddhist robes are the best kind of clothes, let's put one on." He bowed to the statue of the Buddha whenever he passed it while walking through the temple where we did our retreats. And he did a set of formal Buddhist prostrations to open and close his retreats. Those were the rituals he thought were essential. The rest he either dropped completely or did only on special occasions.

My first teacher, Tim McCarthy, was even more of a minimalist. Sometimes he did a few of the minor rituals during retreats. But outside of retreats, he pretty much stuck to zazen and nothing else.

I never even learned how to do most of the standard Zen Buddhist rituals until I started going to Tassajara, the monastic center established by the San Francisco Zen Center deep in the mountains of Northern California. And I had been doing zazen for well over two decades by then, including during my eleven years in Japan.

The rituals they do at Tassajara are much closer to what you'd find in most Zen Buddhist temples in Japan. Every morning they wake you up bright and early — 4:50 AM in the summer guest season and 3:50 AM in the spring and fall practice periods — and you're supposed to trot off to the zendo for an hour of zazen, followed by a chanting service that lasts about twenty minutes.

The chanting service is the part where it starts feeling pretty religious to me. It begins with a priest offering incense to a statue of the Buddha in the center of the room, followed by the whole group doing nine full-body prostrations. The standard practice is to do three prostrations. But apparently someone once complained to Suzuki Roshi, the founder of the San Francisco Zen Center, about too much bowing, so he added six more prostrations. Sometimes one guy ruins things for everybody!

After this, everyone chants the Heart Sutra together while the officiating priest does some more bows and offers some more incense. After the Heart Sutra, another sutra is chanted. After the second sutra is done, everybody chants the lineage of Buddhist ancestors, starting with the six legendary Buddhas who supposedly preceded Shakyamuni and ending with Suzuki Roshi, the temple's founder. Since historically in the Zen tradition only the names of male teachers are chanted, the folks up in San Francisco created a second lineage of female teachers. So after you chant the men's names, you chant the names of prominent female Buddhist masters. Then there's another incense offering and another set of three full-body prostrations, and only then is everyone allowed to leave and start the rest of their day.

In addition to all this stuff, lots of bells are rung to let everyone know when to bow and when to chant, some drums are beaten to keep time on certain chants, and the whole thing is conducted in a highly ritualized fashion in which everyone is expected to know more or less what to do and when and how to do it. It feels a lot like a Catholic Mass or some of the services you find at Orthodox synagogues.

It's completely understandable when people who've heard that Zen Buddhism isn't a religion encounter stuff like this and think they've been the victims of some kind of bait-and-switch tactic.

I get that. And if it really, really, really bugs you to do anything even the least bit religious seeming but you're still interested in Zen, you can probably find a place that suits you. I mean, you could if you were still alive, Marky. Anyhow, more and more of these ritual-free Zen places are popping up all the time. The solution I came up with for the Angel City Zen Center, the little place I established in Los Angeles, is to have certain days when we do some of the traditional rituals like chanting, bowing, and ringing bells and other days when we don't do any of that stuff.

It's my contention, however, that as religious as these rituals look, they really aren't *religious* rituals, even though they are rituals. Take the Heart Sutra — please! There's not much that's religious about that. Okay, it's addressed to Avaloketeshvara, who is a mythical being; some might even call her supernatural. But we're not worshipping her or even insisting she really exists. We're invoking the character of Avaloketeshvara, the Bodhisattva of Compassion, to emphasize that compassion is part of what we're talking about.

The rest of the Heart Sutra has nothing to do with religion or belief. It's a very philosophical treatise on emptiness. This same lack of religiousness holds for all the sutras I've ever heard, included in any Zen chanting services I've attended. They're never prayers to deities or hymns of worship to supernatural beings. The more religious-sounding Buddhist sutras generally are not used in Zen services.

The only exceptions I know of are things like well-being chants that you use to send healing to people who need it — I did a few of these for you when you were sick, for whatever that was worth — or the chants for the protection and preservation of the temple. Even when we do these, there is no insistence that they be taken literally.

The early Buddhists didn't write down the Buddha's teachings. Perhaps they were suspicious of the written word's ability to carry on the real spirit of the teaching. Or maybe it was because literacy wasn't so widespread then and they figured an oral transmission had a better chance of surviving. Whatever the reason, they kept their teacher's words alive by chanting them in groups. Our modern chanting rituals are a way of honoring this ancient practice.

Besides, people learn things better if they chant them. Philosopher and poet Alain de Botton, who wrote a book called *Religion for Atheists*, writes about how effective ritualized chanting can be if you want to really learn something deeply: "Rituals are...attempts to make vivid to us things we already know, but are likely to have forgotten. Religions are also keen to see us as more than just rational minds, we are emotional and physical creatures, and therefore, we need to be seduced via our bodies and our senses too." I found that quote in an interview with de Botton, which the *Daily Beast* website published on March 9, 2012. They titled it "Alain de Botton on the Benefits of Religion Without God."

The most overtly religious-seeming aspect of the standard Zen chanting service has to be when the priest offers incense to a statue of the Buddha and then bows down to it. So let's look at that.

The practice of offering incense also has a neat little backstory. The way I heard it was that in the Buddha's day, it was common practice to sacrifice animals to the Hindu gods and then burn their bodies on a pyre. The Buddha thought ritual animal sacrifice was cruel and needless. So instead of burning the bodies of animals, his followers burned scented wood. Pretty soon scented logs and branches gave way to smaller and smaller pieces, and eventually incense as we know it came to be.

So maybe burning incense is okay, but what about bowing to a statue of Buddha? That has to be a form of worship, right? I tend to look at it differently.

The most common explanation of why we bow down to statues of the Buddha is that we are honoring what within us is Buddha-like. We externalize it in the form of a statue, but we are not honoring the statue or even necessarily the person it's supposed to look like. We don't pretend the statue or the dead person it represents can somehow magically receive our worship. Rather, we honor what the statue stands for.

Personally, I don't think Zen Buddhism is a religion because it doesn't have a strict belief system and there isn't any compulsion for folks to accept the existence of anything supernatural. Still, I can understand why some of these other things I mentioned make people think of it as a religion.

I think I'd better sign off here and go back to sleep.

See you soon — maybe. Unless I get better.

Brad

7. TRUTH VS. BUDDHISM

MARKY,

I'm feeling a whole lot better now. Those German antibiotics worked like magic! But I gotta tell you how much I hate German trains. I mean, I love that you can get anywhere in Germany on a train and that the trains themselves are well taken care of and mostly run on time. But, my God! There is no possible way for me ever to find the correct seat. Even when I have an actual German person come onboard and show me to my seat, half the time they are wildly mistaken.

That's what happened again yesterday on the train to Groningen, which is in the Netherlands, which is where I'm speaking tonight. I was in the seat that a German friend told me with absolute assurance was the correct one, but when the conductor looked at my ticket, he said I was in the wrong car and that I'd need to drag my stuff three cars down. Nice.

Last night Lydia told me she consulted a psychic who said she was helping you cross to the other side and enter a place where spirits recover from traumatic deaths. Lydia seemed somewhat skeptical of whether what the psychic said was true, but she thought it couldn't hurt. It seems to have made her feel a little more at ease, which is nice. One of these days you'll have to tell me if it worked.

I think a lot about that word *true*, Marky. What does it mean? Does something have to be factually accurate to be true? I think there's a sense in which truth can transcend factuality. I mean, I don't believe in "alternative facts" or think things can be factually inaccurate and yet somehow morally true the way some politicians would have it. Those are dangerous notions, if you ask me. But novels and movies, for example, can express truths while still being works of fiction. Maybe some of the Mahayana sutras that purport to be the words of Buddha but were written hundreds of years after he died are also examples of being true while also being fictional.

But what is Truth with a capital *T*? What is Truth in the larger, more universal sense?

It seems just as absurd to me to insist that Buddhism has some kind of monopoly on the truth as it does to assert that Jesus Christ is our Lord and Savior, or that Krishna is the Supreme Personality of Godhead, or that Zeus, Apollo, or Thor is the one true and everlasting God. I don't see any reason that the truth should be Buddhist. Why would the universe be compelled to conform to the ideas of any human-concocted religion — or nonreligion, as the case may be?

When I was younger, I really wanted to believe. I tried my darndest to believe in Jesus, but I couldn't. Then I tried to believe in Krishna, but that didn't work either.

It is impossible for me to imagine a God who created this vast, vast universe and everything in it — billions of galaxies, each one containing billions of planets, probably countless forms of life, and endless ways of relating to God, all of it existing for billions of years — and then sending just one guy to one country on one planet, having him teach a handful of people for three years, and that's it. That's the version of God that absolutely every sentient being he created throughout all of time and space has to believe in. And if they don't believe, they burn in hell forever.

That just doesn't make any sense to me. It's like the aliens in old cheap science-fiction films who figure they'll conquer the Earth by sending one plastic-looking flying saucer piloted by two knuckle-heads equipped with ray guns. I cannot believe in a God who seems like something dreamed up by schlock film directors like Roger Corman or Ed Wood.

I can no more believe that God is a Buddhist than I can believe that God is a Christian or a Hindu or a Muslim or whatever. To me that seems obscene and deranged.

And yet here I am, a Buddhist. I ought to be an atheist, I suppose. But that didn't work for me either. The only rational option I have left, as far as I can see, is Buddhism. And not just any old type of Buddhism, but specifically Zen Buddhism.

Explaining why is gonna take a lot more letters. And I'm probably going to go off on a few tangents here and there. I'm sorry about that. But it's complicated! And you're dead anyhow, so what else do you have to do?

Still, I'll see if I can put it briefly here.

If Buddhism is true, it's true because it offers us a way to take a look at a truth that existed before there was any Buddhism. If it doesn't do that, then there is no reason to study Buddhism except, perhaps, as an academic discipline or a hobby. If Buddhism is all about believing in Buddhism, then Buddhism isn't worth believing in.

On the interwebs recently, I came across an argument that I think might have been put forth first by Ricky Gervais, the British comedian who created the TV show *The Office*. He posed a thought experiment in which he first asks us to imagine a world in which all forms of human knowledge are somehow wiped out. So math is gone, science is gone, philosophy is gone, and every religion that ever existed is gone too. He then asks if we can imagine any of the forms of knowledge that exist now somehow spontaneously reemerging.

Science would probably come back because it's a useful way of understanding cause-and-effect relationships in the physical world. Math would probably come back because it's useful to be able to calculate things. Lots of other forms of knowing would also return eventually.

Religion too might return because it seems to have some value to people. But would *Christianity* return? It seems unlikely because it's based on a very specific story about a certain guy who did and said certain things. Maybe some of Jesus's wise sayings would return in other forms. But Christianity probably would not. Although it's not hard to imagine that another wise person might be killed by the authorities for bucking the system and then later be regarded as a deity. Still, it wouldn't quite be Christianity even if that happened.

You could probably say the same thing about most other religions. Perhaps the wise things their founders said would come back in other forms. Maybe certain events would repeat in some way. But most of our religions are really specific. Jesus Christ is God's only begotten son, many Christians say. But if we somehow erased Jesus Christ from history, would some guy named Doug who got lynched after saying some wise stuff really be the same thing?

Thinking about that, I wondered if Buddhism would come back in such a scenario. I think it would depend on what you mean by Buddhism. If you mean the kind of Buddhism in which people worship the Buddha as a god and pray to him for stuff, then I'd say it probably wouldn't.

The Zen form of Buddhism isn't like that, though. It's called Buddhism because it derives from the seed planted by the historical Buddha 2,500 years ago. But it's not dependent on him. In fact, many Zen Buddhists aren't particularly well versed in the words of the historical Buddha. I'm certainly not! Nor do most Zen Buddhists believe in supernatural divinity of any kind, even when it comes to Buddha. Dogen for sure did not believe in the supernatural, although he did allow for the idea that there might be aspects of the natural world that we are incapable of ever fully understanding.

I think maybe something very like Zen Buddhism would come back if its current form were to somehow disappear from the world.

I think so because I believe that Zen Buddhism is a relationship to a truth that does not need to be called "Zen Buddhism" in order to be true. Let me see if I can unpack why I think that is.

When I was around nineteen years old, I was introduced to the central practice of Zen Buddhism, a style of meditation called zazen. More specifically, I was introduced to a type of zazen called *shikantaza*, which is a fancy Japanese word meaning "just sitting."

The *just* in *just sitting* is a strong *just*. It means doing nothing but *just* fully devoting yourself to the act of sitting rather than the kind of *just* you use when you say you're "just sitting around." In this style of meditation, you are not given any goal to pursue. You're not trying to gain insights. You're not trying to become mindful. You're not trying to make yourself a better person. You're not trying to have some kind of special experience.

Rather, you are trying to sit very, very still in order to fully experience the simple and real fact of just sitting very, very still.

That sounds easy, right? It did to me, anyway, when I first heard about it. And yet more than three decades later I'm still trying to get it right.

The reason I still do it, even after thirty-odd years of failure, is that it is the only method of engaging with the truth that makes any sense to me. Absent a letter from you postmarked from the Great Beyond or any other convincing evidence of eternal life, I am still far more interested in what *this* is — *this* world I am actually living in, *this* person I actually am. If I want to know what this life I am living right now actually is, then the only way to know that is to sit very quietly and watch it happen.

As far as I've been able to determine, zazen is the best and easiest way to do that. Not because it's extra holy or because it was delivered by an unquestionable divine authority, but because it makes so much more sense than anything else I have ever seen proposed. If there is a way to understand the truth about the life I am living right here and now, then zazen is the most viable candidate, as far as I can see.

I don't even take it for granted that zazen "works." And the reason I put "works" in scare quotes is that I want you to notice what that word implies. It implies that zazen will produce results, in this case the result of allowing you to see what life really is. But even that is not what it's for.

It's like baseball. The only thing you're guaranteed when you play baseball is that you'll be playing baseball. Both teams want to win, and maybe individuals on those teams have specific goals in mind for themselves, such as hitting home runs or whatever. But those things might not happen for those people. The only thing they're guaranteed is that they'll play some baseball.

It's not even a given that winning is the best possible thing to happen. This is probably hard to demonstrate in terms of baseball. But in terms of life, I think any of us can honestly examine our lives and see that lots of things turned out better for us because we did *not* get what we wanted.

For example, I graduated from a university with a degree in history and a teaching certificate. I went on a number of interviews to get a job as a history teacher in a bunch of high schools in small towns in Ohio. I got turned down every time. It turns out that high schools in Middle America don't hire history teachers. They hire coaches who can double as history teachers. At every interview I went to I was asked what sport I could coach. When I said I couldn't coach any sport, I could tell by the reactions I got that the interview was effectively over.

I was deeply disappointed each time I failed to get the job I wanted. But because I didn't get those jobs, I became desperate enough to go to Japan to teach English there, which in turn led to almost every significant thing I've done in my life. I got a cool job at a company that made Japanese monster movies. I met a Zen teacher who insisted on ordaining me, even though I had no interest in being a monk. That experience led to my writing a book, which then blossomed into a career. None of that would ever have happened if I'd gotten what I wanted and had been hired as a history teacher at a high school in Rittman, Ohio, or somewhere like that.

Each time I have some kind of disappointment, I remind myself of that time and of others when not getting what I wanted turned out to be the best thing.

And because I understand this, even though I do still have disappointments, I don't take my assessment of those disappointments very seriously anymore. When I get disappointed by some circumstance I find myself in I think, *Well, maybe I'm wrong.* Maybe I'm better off without whatever it was I wanted. Maybe I should be glad I didn't get it. And even if I don't exactly feel glad, the knowledge that my own assessment of the situation may be mistaken is of great comfort in those times.

Zazen may disappoint you. It certainly has disappointed me a lot. On the other hand, I can't think of any other activity I've engaged in that so consistently makes me feel better after having done it. Doing laundry and pooping come close. But most things that society holds up as being pleasurable and fun — like having sex, for example, or eating a delicious meal — are far less consistent.

The big hang-up with zazen is that it takes years of practice before most people notice anything like a "result."

You might ask me if, after thirty-plus years of doing it, zazen has at least given me the answers I sought when I first started doing it. I would certainly ask that of someone like me if I was considering whether or not to devote the necessary time, effort, and energy to a practice that doesn't even really begin to make sense until you've done it for at least five years — and more like ten or twenty in most cases.

I would say that it has. But those answers were not what I expected or what I wanted. In some ways, they were better than what I wanted. In other ways, they were not. I wanted the Big Answer to Everything. That never happened. Even though I did discover partial answers, and even though those partial answers were often astounding in their scope, the really big picture still eludes me and probably always will.

Maybe I'll talk about that in another letter, though. The point I want to make here is that I didn't convert to something called Buddhism. I don't believe in Buddhism. I don't feel any desire to spread the good word of Buddhism to the unfortunate people of the world.

Rather, the practice of Buddhism has allowed me to begin to understand a truth that does not belong to Buddhism. Buddhism provided an extremely useful set of tools for working on this. It's a method of looking for the answer rather than an answer in and of itself. In that way, it's hugely valuable, and I think a lot of people could benefit from it.

Zen Buddhism, to me, is an attitude. Maybe it's not the attitude most people associate with Zen Buddhism, which seems to be one of a passive acceptance and preternatural calm at all times. It's an attitude that strives for honesty and realism. It rejects superstition. It rejects any kind of rigid belief system. It strives to be ethical because it understands that we are all intimately connected with each other and that hurting others only hurts ourselves. It accepts that rituals are useful but doesn't believe any ritual has magic powers. There are other aspects to the Zen Buddhist attitude that I'll get to in other letters, but I feel like those are the most important.

But just as you don't have to call an apple a *ringo* if you're not Japanese or call it a *manzana* if you don't speak Spanish, you also don't have to call this attitude Zen Buddhism if you don't want to. Still, just as it's useful to have a word to call those crunchy, red, edible fruits that grow on trees, it's also useful to have a name for this attitude.

I call it Buddhism as an acknowledgment of where it came from. To get back to Ricky Gervais's thought experiment, maybe if you erased Gautama Buddha from history, someone else would come up with something very much like Buddhism. But that's not what happened. There really was a specific guy who started this stuff. And just like we give Einstein credit for the theory of relativity, so should we give the Buddha credit where credit is due. We understand that Einstein didn't create the relationship between matter and energy. But he found a way of describing it efficiently, and he put a lot of hard work into that discovery. He deserves to be acknowledged.

Furthermore, I think it's important not to pretend I invented something that I didn't. It wouldn't be right for me to just state a bunch of the things I've understood through the practice of Zen Buddhism without being honest about how I arrived at that understanding. That's part of the commitment to honesty that I learned from Zen Buddhist practice.

I also acknowledge other teachers, such as historical figures like Dogen or my own Zen teachers. This stuff didn't just pop out of my head. It has a history, and that history is important.

So I call this thing Zen Buddhism. But I know that it isn't really Zen Buddhism. If that makes any kind of sense.

Phew! That's enough for now.

Take care in the afterlife! Say hi to Phyllis Diller for me!

Brad

8. I'M JUST A ZEN BOZO

Dear Marky,

I'm writing this to you on another train, this one bound for Eindhoven, the Netherlands. I'm pretty sure I'm in the right seat this time. They're going to show the documentary that Pirooz Kalayeh made about me at a film festival there, and I got invited to be the special guest and do a Q&A after. That'll be a nice change after all the Zen audiences I've talked to.

The folks at Groningen last night were nice. We had a daylong retreat in the apartment of a professor at the local university. He has one large, mostly empty room, and we all sat in there. Then for lunch he arranged with a local restaurant to have us come in and do a silent meal while the place was closed to other customers. Again, this is not the standard way of doing things. But it worked out pretty nicely.

After the retreat they took me out to see a local punk-rock show. The club was immaculately clean, and there was a little machine near the stage that showed you the decibel level of the band, made up of neatly groomed teenagers playing shiny new guitars. It was a far cry from the kinds of dingy rat-infested hellholes where you and I have played!

Anyway, I said I'd write to you about Zen Buddhism, but I didn't really say a lot about what Zen Buddhism actually is in my last couple of letters. Are you interested? I guess I'll never know. But let me try to explain it anyhow. Maybe I can make some kind of sense out of it.

A lot of people assume they know what Zen means. To them, Zen means being chill and serene. The online *Urban Dictionary* defines Zen as follows:

Zen: n: a state of coolness only attained through a totally laid-back type of attitude. adj.: used to describe someone/something that has reached an uber state of coolness and inner peace. The examples they give for its use are "Nathan is so Zen," "Chilling out and wearing sunglasses all day makes me Zen," and "Can you pass the Zen, please?"

I live in Los Angeles, and that kind of "Zen" is all over this city. You should see it, Marky! Not only do people say things like this all the time, but there are Zen nail salons and Zen frozen yogurt shops, and I've seen ads for Zen and tonic liquor. I found a box of pills called Zen for sale at a truck stop on the I-5 freeway. They were supposed to enable you to "last all night in bed." I assume that means that you won't roll out of bed as you sleep, right? They also sold another pill called Zazen that was a sleep aid. Maybe you use them together? Within a few miles of where I live in Los Angeles, there's the Zen Bistro, Zen Sushi, and another sushi place called U-Zen. I've seen Zen Monkey cereal at the local hippie food shop. There's even a medical marijuana dispensary in West Hollywood called Zen, with a giant billboard of a fat, happy, stoned green Buddha.

And, of course, there was your band the Zen Sex Butchers. I can't forget that one! I always wondered if my interest in Zen had anything to do with the name of your band. I guess I'll never know.

In any case, if we Zennies got as easily offended as some other religious members, there'd be fatwas and protests every day of the week!

But back to the question at hand. What is Zen, really?

I was ordained as a Zen monk or priest or whatever in 1999 by

Gudo Nishijima Roshi in a short ceremony in Chiba, a city just out-side of Tokyo. So I ought to have some idea.

Let me start off by explaining what it means to be a Zen monk/priest/whatever. Even though Western Zen Buddhists use words like *monk* or *priest*, these words don't work very well to describe what I am. They're derived from the Catholic tradition in which they have a specific meaning and in which there is a clear difference between a priest and a monk.

In the Zen tradition there really isn't any distinction between a priest and a monk. There's just one designation that gets translated as "priest" or "monk," depending on who is translating it. The Japanese word for what I am is *bouzu*. That's not pronounced like bow-zoo, by the way. The *u* after the *o* just means you hold out the *o* sound a little longer. *Bouzu* sounds way too much like *bozo*, as in Bozo the Clown, for my liking. Although there are plenty of times when I feel like a bozo for having been ordained as one. So let's just call me what I really am: a Zen bozo.

There are several different ways to become a Zen bozo. If you get ordained through a large institution such as the Soto-shu in Japan or the San Francisco Zen Center in the USA, it's a very complicated process with numerous subrankings within the designation of Zen bozo. Some of the bozos in those traditions are more like priests, and some are more like monks. And, by the way, the Japanese word for a female Zen bozo is *nisou*, though often female monastics are also often called *bouzu*. So you might say some Zen bozos are nuns or priestesses, if you like those words.

Another way Zen bozos differ from priests, monks, and nuns in the Catholic tradition is that in the Japanese tradition, Zen bozos —both male and female — are not required to take a vow of celibacy. This has been the case since 1873. Before that, the Buddhist monas-tic vows were matters of law in Japan. So if a Zen bozo had sex or ate meat it wasn't just a transgression of the monastic rules; it was a crime that could land them in jail. A very long time ago it could even get them executed. In 1873 those laws were repealed. After the repeal, monasteries could have chosen to retain celibacy and vegetarianism as monastic rules, but they didn't. However, in most of the rest of Asia, Buddhist monastics are generally celibate and the bozos do not eat meat — though there are exceptions.

I've been using the word *monastics* here, which I should point out is also a bit misleading. Whereas a Catholic monk or nun generally lives in a monastery for life, Zen bozos usually do not. They train in a monastery for a while and then leave the monastic life either to run a temple of their own or sometimes to just go get a regular job.

The guy who ordained me didn't much care for the large Japanese Zen institutions or the way they handled things. He never bothered with any of the subrankings those guys like to use. In fact, he never bothered defining what *ordination* meant. It was up to the people he ordained to define it for themselves.

One time, shortly after my first ordination with him, I asked him, "Am I a monk now?"

He said, "Yes. You're a monk."

I could tell that the term didn't mean much to him. As far as he was concerned, *monk* was the word English speakers used for Zen bozos, and he was just confirming that my ordination was legit.

I'd been studying and practicing Zen for around twenty years by then. In fact, for most of the time we knew each other, Marky, I was doing this stuff. I started in the early eighties when I was a student at Kent State University, not too long after the band we were in together in high school broke up. Up until I got ordained, I never had any intention of becoming a monk — or a whatever. I just found Zen practice really useful. It was my Zen teacher in Japan's idea that I should become ordained. In some ways, I regret my decision to accept the ordination. I did it mostly because it seemed very important to him.

Nishijima Roshi didn't tell me I had to do anything specific after I got ordained as a bozo. It was completely up to me what I did with my ordination. Nishijima wasn't unique in that approach. Other teachers treat ordination very freely like that. But that's not the standard way of doing things.

Most other Zen teachers require those they ordain to do certain things as conditions of having been ordained. They might be required to always keep their head shaved, or to wear black robes as their main form of clothing, or to perform specific duties as a priest in a temple or monastery. The conditions vary from teacher to teacher. If a teacher is part of a bigger institution, the conditions are often set by the institution.

Nishijima Roshi himself always kept his head shaved, and I rarely saw him wearing anything but black robes. I asked him about this after he made me a bozo and he said that his clothing and hairstyle choices were just his "habit." He was into that look for himself, but he did not consider it necessary or even important for those he ordained to copy his habits.

To make matters even worse, Nishijima Roshi also did a second ordination with me in which he made me his dharma heir. This ceremony dates back to a legendary event in the life of Gautama Buddha, which I mentioned earlier. According to the traditional story, one day Gautama publicly recognized one of his students, a guy named Mahakashyapa, as having attained the same degree of insight as himself. After the Buddha died, Mahakashyapa recognized a guy named Ananda as also having attained this degree of insight. Then Ananda recognized a guy named Shonawashu, and so on and so on until the present day.

For the first few go-arounds there was only ever one dharma heir at a time. But later on, some teachers began recognizing multiple dharma heirs, and now there must be thousands of us running around who are recognized as equal to the Buddha — at least on paper.

One of the things I had to do during this second ordination was write out a list of all the dharma heirs who came before me. Then I had to connect them with a red line to my own name. Most historians think the whole deal of making up lineage lists of dharma heirs began in China hundreds of years after the Buddha died.

But although these lists of dharma heirs don't actually go back 2,500 years all the way to Buddha himself, many of them reliably go back more than a thousand years, which is pretty impressive. And there's good reason to believe that at least some of the connections on those lists go back even further. It's even possible that an actual lineage could be traced all the way back to the Buddha himself; it's just that we don't know the specific names any further back than about a thousand years.

Because I did that second ceremony, by some people's definition I could be called a Zen master. But that term is utterly ridiculous. I think anyone who calls themselves a Zen master or even allows others to call them that is silly. In the words of the great Zen master Kobun Chino Roshi, "Nobody masters Zen!"

The word *roshi*, by the way, just means "respected old teacher." In Japan roshi is not an official title or anything like that. Roshi is something other people can call you if they like you or if they want to blow smoke up your ass, but it's something you would never call yourself. Yet a lot of Zen teachers in the West use roshi as if it's a term of rank and apply it to themselves. I can speak Japanese, and every time I hear someone say something like, "Hi! I'm Ed Tarboosh Roshi!" it really grates on my eardrums. I use it when referring to teachers I respect. But I would never call myself roshi because that'd feel like calling myself Saint Brad or something.

So, anyway, that's what a Zen monk is.

As for what Zen is, the short answer goes something like this: Zen is a back-to-basics movement within Buddhism.

I've already gone over Buddha's life story in another letter, which I hope did not bore you silly. As far as we know, he was a real person who lived about 2,500 years ago and spent most of his life traveling around India teaching people to meditate. After his death, the movement he started continued to expand. As it did, it acquired a lot of rituals, dogma, and superstitions. Although the Buddha rejected being called divine during his lifetime, after he died he began to be worshipped by some almost as a god.

After a few hundred years of this, some people started saying that we should try to recover what Buddhism originally was all about, which was meditation. This back-to-meditation movement probably began in northern India, but it really took off when Buddhism started to be practiced in China. The Chinese word for meditation is *chan*, which is their mispronunciation of the Sanskrit word *dhyana*, which also means "meditation."

This movement made its way through a number of other Asian countries, including Japan. In Japan, they mispronounced the Chinese word *chan* as "zen." The movement later reached the West in the twentieth century, mainly through Japanese teachers, which is why we call it Zen over here.

So one way of interpreting the term *Zen Buddhism* is "meditation-based Buddhism." Since the historical Buddha apparently saw himself mainly as a teacher of meditation, you could argue that the only truly authentic forms of Buddhism are the ones whose main focus is meditation.

I saw an article in some Buddhist magazine not too long ago in which the author tried to dispel what he saw as the major misconceptions about Buddhism. One of the statements he labeled as a misconception was "all Buddhists meditate."

In one sense, he's right. There are a whole lot of people out there who see themselves as Buddhists but who have never meditated in their lives. In fact, I would guess that most of the people who consider themselves Buddhists do not meditate on a regular basis. Some of them even consider it arrogant for anyone but an ordained monk or nun to think they can meditate.

But to the people who started what we now know as Zen Buddhism, meditation was the core thing that the historical Buddha taught. And he didn't just teach it to certain special people, like the monks and nuns that he lived and traveled with. The Buddha offered meditation instruction to anyone who asked for it. And so, in the Zen tradition, meditation is taught to everyone without exception. Many in the Zen tradition would say that the statement "all Buddhists meditate" is not a misconception. For them, there is no Buddhism without meditation.

Maybe what I should talk about in my next letter is zazen.

Until then, keep Satan happy!

Brad

9. ZAZEN ISN'T JUST THE NAME OF A SLEEPING TABLET YOU CAN BUY AT TRUCK STOPS

Dear Marky,

A few minutes after I arrived in Amsterdam, my Dutch publishers called to say the speaking gig I was supposed to do here tomorrow had been canceled. So I have a couple of free days in Amsterdam, which is good. But I'm taking a hit as far as getting paid, which is not good. Most of my tours feel like I'm a member of Spinal Tap. Perhaps my appeal is becoming more selective, as their manager said when a bunch of their gigs were canceled. I guess I'll do something else today and tomorrow.

This is a fun city to be stuck in. Everybody knows about the legal weed and the legal prostitutes. But I'm not much interested in either. And anyway, Amsterdam is a lot more than that. For one thing, the best French fry shop in the world is just a couple of blocks from the main station. Plus, there are canals, and cool old churches, and several really good record shops. So I'm sure I'll be fine.

The movie screening at Eindhoven was groovy. A packed house! I was shocked! It was at a place called Natlab, which is in a building that was once part of the Philips Electronics factory. After the screening I did an interview with a guy named Henk van Straten for some Dutch Buddhist TV show. Henk is an important novelist over there, as well as a tattoo-covered ex–punk rocker. You'd have liked him, I think.

Anyway, I was gonna tell you about zazen.

When I started this Zen stuff I was a student at Kent State University, and I was still the bass player in the original line-up of Zero Defex. I'm not sure if you ever got to see us back then. We were the hardest-core hardcore punk band for miles around.

I had been vaguely interested in Eastern philosophies for some time. I guess I met you a couple of years after I returned from Nairobi, where I'd spent about four years of my childhood. I first saw Indian iconography there. My dad had a close friend named Ramesh who was from India and had pictures of Hindu gods at his house.

It was crazy-looking stuff to a kid who'd been raised up till then in Wadsworth, Ohio. As I know you will recall, back in those days Wadsworth was about the whitest place on Earth. Was yours the only black family in town then? It seems possible. Anyhow, the pictures on Ramesh's wall showed these blue-green dancing guys with four arms and stuff. I asked Ramesh what those pictures were and he said, "God." That was astounding to me. I had never imagined God looked anything like something out of the weird old science-fiction movies I loved so much!

That must have stuck with me because when I was a teenager I was still really interested in Indian religions. Like you, I was a real Beatles nerd in high school. George Harrison was into the Hare Krishnas. So I bought some books published by the Hare Krishnas at the Book Nook, that used bookstore that used to be downtown. But I mostly just looked at the pretty pictures.

When I was just starting in college, kind of on a whim I signed up for a class called Zen Buddhism. You know how you have a certain number of course hours you're supposed to take each semester or something? I just added it to my schedule to fill things out. It wasn't related to my major, which I switched several times anyway. That class totally changed my life and set the course for everything

I've done since then. It was completely unexpected. And yet I never told you or any of my other friends about this. I figured you'd think I'd gone off the deep end and joined a cult or something.

The course I took was taught by a guy named Tim McCarthy, who had studied with a Zen teacher named Kobun Chino, who I quoted in my previous letter. Kobun had come to America in the sixties to act as an assistant to Shunryu Suzuki, who ran the San Francisco Zen Center at the time. I found the philosophy, the way of life, and the attitude in Zen I learned about in that class to be incredibly sensible. Plus, I liked Tim a lot. He wasn't a guy everybody liked a lot. He was kind of a weird person. But I like weird people.

I knew Tim was not lying to me. That was the key thing. Every other religious teacher I'd met or seen on TV up till then seemed like they were full of shit. They seemed incredibly insecure about their faith too, like if you questioned their God he would disappear. How could I believe in a God that couldn't stand up to questioning, a God that retreated from reason and science? How "all-powerful" is that?

But Tim didn't fear science or reason or questions. He wasn't afraid to admit he didn't know everything. He wasn't scared that if others didn't believe what he believed it would all fall apart. He talked about a religion that wasn't a religion, a religion that didn't fear science and logic. Like me, he was interested in discovering reality, not submitting to a fixed belief system.

I decided that, based on his recommendation, I was going to do this crazy zazen thing every day. I really wanted to understand what it was about. He said you need to do it every day, even if it's just for "five lousy minutes." So I decided that I could manage to squeeze it in.

The practice I learned from Tim was based on the instructions of a guy named Dogen, who I mentioned a few letters ago. He was a thirteenth-century Japanese Zen teacher who wrote a lot about how to practice Zen. One of his most important writings is "Fukan

Zazengi," which means something like "Recommending Zazen to Everybody."

In "Fukan Zazengi" he says, "At your sitting place spread out a thick mat and put a cushion on it. Sit either in the full lotus or half-lotus position. In the full lotus position first place your right foot on your left thigh; then place your left foot on your right thigh. In the half-lotus position simply place your left foot on your right thigh. Tie your robes loosely and arrange them neatly. Then place your right hand on your left foot and your left hand on your right palm, thumb tips touching lightly." I'm using the English translation done by Nishijima Roshi and his student Mike Cross. Dogen actually wrote in Japanese. I'm assuming you didn't magically learn every earthly language after you died, so I'm sticking with English.

Anyway, then Dogen says, "Straighten your body and sit upright, leaning neither left nor right, neither forward nor backward. Align your ears with your shoulders and your nose with your navel. Rest the tip of your tongue against the roof of your mouth with the teeth together and lips shut. Always keep your eyes open and breathe softly through your nose. Once you have adjusted your posture, take a breath and exhale fully. Rock your body right and left and settle into steady immovable sitting. Think of not thinking. Not thinking? What kind of thinking is that? Non-thinking. This is the essential art of zazen."

And that's pretty much all there is to it. Lesson one is exactly the same as lesson three million and one. You just keep doing this simple thing over and over.

A zafu is a round cushion made for sitting. You can buy them all over the place these days. You usually put a mat underneath called a zabuton. *Zafu* is just a Japanese word that means "sitting cushion," and *zabuton* means "sitting futon." *Za* means "sit" and the *buton* part of it is the word *futon* you're familiar with from going to Bed Bath & Beyond — before you went to the Great Beyond, that is. Japanese futons come in many different sizes.

When I first started doing zazen you could not get zafus and zabutons very easily. At least not in Ohio! I was a broke-ass college student, subsisting on whatever I got in my work as a part-time dishwasher. I didn't have $60 to order a zafu from the one place I found that made them, plus another $60 for the zabuton. So when I lived with you and Lydia I used a variety of different things.

I used chair cushions or couch cushions. Or I used rolled-up towels mashed up into a vaguely zafu-like shape. I sometimes used my jacket, folded up. Bed pillows were not so good because they tend to be a little too smooshy. When I travel I often still use these sorts of things. You can always work out something. It doesn't have to be the official regulation item. The Buddha sat on a rock with a straw mat on top of it.

When I sit I do the posture pretty much as Dogen recommends. I usually sit in a half-lotus myself. I used to do full lotus, but then my knees started complaining about it, so I now do half-lotus. Or what I call "half-assed lotus," which is what we used to call "sitting Indian style." Hipster Buddhists call this Burmese position.

I think proper posture is important in Zen practice, and I say that a lot. When I say it on the internet I always get a bunch of angry people making comments that I'm being cruel to people who have bad legs and bad knees and so forth. But actually the leg position is not the most crucial part of the posture. There are lots of ways for people with bad legs to deal with that aspect.

When I talk about proper posture I'm referring to the whole body being in the proper alignment the way Dogen describes it, the spine straight, the nose aligned with navel, and all that. The leg position just acts as a base for that.

I'm not a big fan of trying to do zazen practice on chairs. I think if it's the absolute last resort and you can't do it any other way, then it's better to do it on a chair than not do it at all. People who have serious, debilitating conditions but really want to do zazen can always find a way to make it work. I once told a guy who had advanced MS that if he had to do zazen lying down on his back, that was better than not doing it at all.

But I don't recommend that able-bodied people do it in chairs or lying on their backs. These are workarounds for people who have no other choice.

Zen practice is as much a physical practice as yoga. Bending over slightly is not the same as doing downward-facing dog. There is a posture for doing zazen, but kind of leaning back in your armchair is not it. I once read a study that concluded that relaxing in an easy chair was exactly the same as meditating. I don't know what criteria they used to determine that. But I've done both activities plenty of times, and they are not the same!

For those who have to sit on a chair I usually say to try not to use the back of the chair, because chairs are funny in that they force your body into a specific position that we imagine is natural. But it's not really natural because the hips like to be tilted forward a little so that the upper body can balance itself. When you're on a chair, that tilt is gone. Your butt is flat, which means you're tilted slightly backward as far as the rest of your body is concerned, and so you need the back of the chair to keep you steady. Sitting on a cushion gives you the forward hip tilt that helps you keep your spine balanced on top of your hips. Sometimes you can achieve this by putting a little cushion on top of the chair.

The reason for this is that the really crucial thing is your spine. We human beings are unique in the animal kingdom. No other animal that we know of — at least on this planet — stands erect like we do. The other two-legged animals like birds walk in a way that keeps their spines nearly parallel to the ground. The other great apes walk on their knuckles most of the time and only stand on two legs occasionally. Kangaroos use their tails for balance. The center of gravity of these animals is very different from ours. But we walk upright with this odd posture. In zazen we are settling into this uniquely human posture that is our birthright.

What you're trying to do is to balance your upper body on your hips so that you are not using a lot of effort but you are not also being lazy. It's a position between being effortful and being effortless. It's a balance pose like the tree pose or one of those other balance poses in yoga.

And the best thing to do if your mind gets foggy is to adjust your posture. I heard this from Nishijima Roshi. About a year after I moved to Japan I started studying with him, and he said that if your mind is cloudy, adjust your posture. I remember distinctly that when I heard that I thought, "What a load of crap! That's not going to do anything." I've been sitting pretty much every day for the twenty-plus years since I first heard that advice, and there has never been a moment when I was deep in thought or otherwise preoccupied and still maintained good posture.

But the thing that hangs people up most in Dogen's instructions is that bit about thinking the thought of not-thinking, and how it's different from thinking. There is a peculiar idea that Zen practice or meditation practice in general is about emptying your mind.

This is where zazen differs from meditation. Meditation is often about trying to empty your mind. Zazen is not.

Kodo Sawaki, who was one of Gudo Nishijima's teachers, said that the only time you have a completely empty mind is when you're dead. Is that true, Marky? I guess if anyone would know, it'd be you.

In any case, when you do zazen you can allow thoughts to just happen without stopping them. A Zen teacher named Kosho Uchiyama had a really nice way of expressing what thoughts are. In his book *Opening the Hand of Thought* he said, "Thoughts are the secretions of your brain the same as stomach acid is the secretions of your stomach." I don't know what page he said this on; it seemed he repeated it several times throughout the book as well as in his other books. Anyhow, your stomach usually sits there in the middle of your body, secreting stomach acid and just doing its business, which is digesting the things that you ate. Your brain is also doing its business, which is digesting what you've put into it during the day or during the week or during the month.

Thinking just happens. That's not good or bad. There's no need to stop it. In fact, I would say it's probably unhealthy to try to stop thoughts from happening, the same way that trying to make your stomach stop secreting stomach acid would be unhealthy. You don't want to stop the secretions of your stomach, and you don't want to stop the secretions of your brain.

It doesn't even really matter what the thoughts are. Sometimes people imagine that certain thoughts are better or worse than others. In the conventional sense that may be true, since thoughts often lead to action. But in zazen it doesn't matter. Just allow all thoughts to arise and allow all thoughts to pass away. You don't need to judge any of them as being better than others. Whenever I brought up some thought that was distracting my zazen practice to my teacher he'd say, "That's just the contents of your zazen."

Dogen uses two words in the Japanese version of this to describe his ideas about what to do with thoughts: *fushiryo* and *hishiryo*. The root word *shiryo* is not the usual Japanese word for thinking. *Shiryo* is actually more like "consideration." The prefixes *fu* and *hi* are negations; *fu* is a mild negation and *hi* is a stronger one. So what Dogen is pointing to here is not the automatic bubbling up of images into the head but deliberate consideration of those images. He's not advising us to make our minds blank. He's advising us not to chase around the images that come up in our heads. Just allow them to be.

At first this is extremely difficult, because you're not used to it. But that's okay. This practice is difficult for anyone who does it. That's why they build giant statues to people whose only claim to fame is that they could sit still for a long time, because sitting still and being quiet and facing yourself is a difficult task.

Charles Tart, author of several books on transpersonal psychology and parapsychology, is quoted in *Zig Zag Zen*, a book putting forth the idea that psychedelic drugs are as valid a path toward enlightenment as meditation. Which is a dumb idea, but maybe I'll get to that in another letter.

Anyhow, on page 168 of *Zig Zag Zen*, Mr. Tart says, "Meditation was far more difficult than I imagined, and a lot of meditating was spent daydreaming, rebuking myself for daydreaming, and getting nowhere. It's clear that many of us westerners have such hyperactive minds and complex psychological dynamics that it is very difficult to quiet and discipline our minds enough to make any real progress along the meditative path."

Everybody feels that way. The idea that Asians somehow have it easy while Westerners have more complex minds and therefore have a hard time meditating is racist nonsense. In fact, eight hundred years ago Dogen complained that people in Japan liked to say that Chinese people could meditate but Japanese people were incapable of it. He called bullshit on that. And I'm calling bullshit on the Western idea that Japanese people and other Asians have it easier than us when it comes to meditating.

Everybody is lousy at meditating when they start off. There's nothing particular to the so-called modern Western mind that makes it any more difficult. It was difficult for Buddha 2,500 years ago, and it's going to be difficult for you, but that just means it's a worthwhile practice.

So you just sit down and shut up. That's pretty much it. The type of zazen that I learned is called *shikantaza*, which means "just sitting." We went over that in an earlier letter. You're attempting to just sit with no goal in mind or no object that you're trying to focus on.

You are seriously *just* sitting with no goal or objective other than to sit. This idea of goallessness is difficult. There's an old argument that I hear a lot that some people seem to think trumps everything. They say, "Well, if your goal is to be goalless then that's a goal too. Ha ha! Gotcha!" To which I say, yes and no.

Yes, semantically you can say that the goal of having no goal is also a goal. But in real life, the practice of setting your sights on not having a goal is actually something you can do. You're making goal-less practice your aim rather than your goal. It's like you're pointing an arrow and hoping that it hits somewhere near the target, but you're not too concerned about the target. You're more concerned about the aim — the way certain people who lived at the Clubhouse were not when it came to using the toilet. But I shouldn't speak ill of the dead.

Anyhow, that's enough for this letter. I'll talk more about aims and goals in another letter.

Stay cool in the heat down there, buddy!

Brad

10. THE GOAL OF HAVING NO GOALS

Dear Marky,

The Dutch sure love their bicycles. I'm not in Amsterdam anymore. Last night I spoke in Utrecht. About half an hour before I was supposed to go on, I noticed I'd forgotten the little recorder I carry to record my talks. I mentioned this to Francine, the person who hosted the talks, and she said, "No problem! Let's go get it!"

I was staying at the house of a lady who'd been at one of my events in Germany a few weeks earlier. It was about two miles away. So Francine had me get on the back of her bicycle and kind of stand on the little protrusions where the axle of the back wheel sticks out from the sides. Then she proceeded to race down the streets dodging other bikes as well as pedestrians and cars with me hanging on for dear life — in the rain, mind you!

We survived a mad trip through the narrow winding streets and into a park, then got the recorder and made it back with minutes to spare. We'd achieved our goal. We set out with the intention to get the voice recorder, put in the hard work necessary to retrieve it, then made it back with the recorder in hand.

One of the hardest things to do at the retreats I lead is explain to the participants that zazen doesn't work like that. There is no goal to Zen practice. It's hard to explain to people that if they don't achieve whatever they set out to achieve by doing zazen, that doesn't mean they're doing it wrong.

Here's another difficult question related to that. A friend who doesn't meditate once asked, "If nothing happens when you do zazen, what's the point?" That's kind of the crucial question if you're doing this type of meditation. If you are not seeking anything it's very easy to say, "Well, why do it at all?"

Earlier I mentioned Kodo Sawaki, my teacher Gudo Nishijima's teacher. Sawaki was a Zen teacher who traveled around Japan teaching zazen at various temples. He didn't have a temple of his own like most Zen teachers. So he was nicknamed "Homeless Kodo."

Sawaki was orphaned when he was quite young and sent to live with a variety of fairly nasty relatives. They weren't abusive so much as they were neglectful. They didn't want to be burdened with a kid. This set Sawaki on a rather unique path in life. When he was a teenager, he left the home of this uncle — who was a professional gambler — and walked all the way across Japan from somewhere near Yokohama to Eihei-ji, the temple founded by Dogen in the thirteenth century.

That's more than four hundred kilometers, or around 250 miles. It's a long way to walk. There is a mountain range in between, so a lot of it is uphill in rugged terrain. It would be the equivalent of walking across California from west to east. This was not a guy who merely saw being "into Zen" as a lifestyle enhancement.

Sawaki became a monk at Eihei-ji when he was sixteen. He soon became convinced that one of the biggest problems in Japanese Zen was that the teachers and the monks and the priests were not very concerned with zazen practice — they'd lost the plot.

In Japan in Sawaki's time — and these days too — the way most people got to be Zen priests was by being the eldest son of a Zen priest. Occasionally the eldest daughter gets saddled with this nowadays. They have an obligation to run the family temple, much like anyone else who inherits a family business. I don't know if they have movies where you are, but there's a Japanese movie called *Fancy Dance* that's all about this. The protagonist is a ska musician who inherits his dad's Zen temple and has to go train to be a monk.

Most of the people Sawaki trained with at Eihei-ji didn't want to be there. They had no real commitment to the philosophy and practice of Zen. For them it was kind of like how boot camp must be for someone who gets drafted into the army. It was brutal training for a career they had not chosen.

Sawaki, on the other hand, was highly committed to Zen practice and teaching. So he made it his life's work to try to reform Zen in Japan.

After his training was complete, Sawaki started leading zazen-only retreats. These were unusual sorts of Zen retreats in which there was no chanting or rituals, just lots and lots of zazen.

Anyway, getting back to the question of "why do zazen at all," one of Sawaki's famous phrases is, "Zazen is good for nothing." The full quote goes like this: "What is zazen good for? Good for nothing. As long as this good-for-nothing practice does not penetrate our bones and as long as we don't really practice what is good for nothing, it won't be good for anything." I got that quote from a Xeroxed compilation of Sawaki's writings for magazines and newspapers that I found at the library at Tassajara. To put that quotation in other words, if the practice is not good for nothing, it won't be good for anything. I think that's an interesting way to express it.

Zazen practice is good for nothing, meaning it's not for establishing something else apart from itself. It is for getting into your true experience; it is for learning how to not be chasing after something other than where you are right now.

Any time you have a goal, even if that goal seems very lofty and beautiful, like gaining enlightenment or becoming a better person, this is a construct in your mind. It's something you've invented. You have an idea of what enlightenment should be or of what being a better person should be or what being spiritual should be, or whatever it is. There are all sorts of goals you can put in there, but whatever the goal is, it's not what's going on at this moment; it's something that's off in the future or embodied in someone else.

What we're trying to do in zazen practice is to get into our real experience unadorned — as it is — and see it for what it is. What happens when you do that is surprising. For me, when I finally started to understand what my own life really was, I discovered that my ordinary, mundane life was much subtler and more beautiful and important than I ever could have imagined.

I don't mean that I had some grand experience in meditation. I had a few of those too. But that wasn't the point at all. In fact, it was a distraction. What I'm talking about here are things like the experience of sitting on the subway and hearing someone burp real loud — even *that* is a subtle and grand experience. It's important. Every experience we have is cosmic in its scope. Because it's real, whereas all the loftier things we imagine are just ideas. That's what "good-for-nothing" is about.

Here's another quote from Sawaki from that same set of Xeroxed writings: "Practicing what is good for nothing with confidence, isn't it worth a try?" I like that. I'll just leave that as is.

Here's one more Sawaki quote from that same source: "You say you would like to try zazen in order to become a better person. Become a better person by doing zazen? How stupid. How could a person ever become something better in the first place?" Becoming a better person is a very popular meditation goal.

As I said, goals are always in the distance. That's what makes them goals. Scoring a goal in soccer or football is only exciting because the goal is far away and surrounded by all kinds of obstacles, like other players whose job it is to keep you from reaching the goal.

The other problem with focusing on goals is that in doing so we create habits that pull us away from our real lives here and now. These habits are very hard to undo. In fact, the more goal oriented your life becomes, the harder it will be to get out of that goal-seeking mentality.

The goal-seeking mentality can drive you to achieve things, like getting rich or famous or whatever it is you've decided will make you happy. The problem becomes glaringly apparent once any goal is achieved. Achieving goals only makes us happy in the short term.

If you have created a habit of always seeking something better, you have a permanent problem. Once you've achieved whatever you set out to achieve, you may be happy for a little while, but this state always goes away. This is because you've become acclimated to seeking. Your habit of seeking something better will turn anything you achieve into something that must now be improved or replaced. No matter what it is. Even if it's enlightenment.

This is why the richest and most powerful people are often so deeply unhappy. They've driven themselves to acquire things. If they get really good at it, eventually they have everything they ever wanted, at least among the things one is able to achieve through wealth and power. I live in Los Angeles among a whole lot of people who have achieved all their wildest dreams and yet are still deeply unhappy. Many people who live within a few miles of my apartment back in LA are so super rich they can literally buy anything that's for sale.

You may imagine people in that position can simply relax and enjoy the fruits they've strived for. But that rarely happens. In fact, I'd venture to say that it never happens. The same restlessness that drove these folks to acquire their riches continues to drive them, even when there's nothing left to acquire.

In driving ourselves to acquire those things that are far away from us, we miss out on what is very near. We miss out on our real lives here and now. And that's the saddest thing that can possibly happen. Because your real life right here and right now is the most precious thing you could ever have.

I guess you probably know how precious life is, Marky. So

forgive me if I'm life-splaining something every dead person already understands.

The very simple solution to this dilemma was something Buddha noticed 2,500 years ago. That is to forget all goals. Just throw them away. There is nothing at all to achieve. There is nothing at all to strive for. In this very moment you can give up all hope for the future and in so doing, you can fully enjoy the present just as it is.

This does not mean being complacent. Part of living in the present moment is doing what needs to be done right here and right now to make this moment better. If there are things in your real life that need fixing, there is nothing wrong with attending to that stuff and trying to make it better. There's not even anything particularly problematic with doing things now to improve your future. We all do that — even Buddhists. But a Buddhist is likely to be more involved with what she is doing right now to improve her future rather than with her hypothetical future.

Throwing away your goals is easier said than done. In fact, it's probably the single most difficult aspect of Zen practice. It's so difficult that even within the world of Zen, truly goalless practice is rare.

When I think about the goals I've had in the past, I can ask myself some questions. Which of these goals have I accomplished? Did they solve the problems I thought they'd solve? What new problems arose as a result of achieving those goals? Did achieving those goals make me as happy as I expected? In what ways were the goals I achieved like what I expected them to be? In what way were things different?

Back in 1754 Jean Jacques Rousseau, in his *Discourse on Inequality*, said, "Conveniences by becoming habitual had almost entirely ceased to be enjoyable, and at the same time degenerated into true needs, it became much more cruel to be deprived of them than to possess them was sweet, and men were unhappy to lose them without being happy to possess them."

Almost as soon as we get or achieve something it starts to seem ordinary to us. No matter what it is. We start to seem to "need" things that we lived perfectly fine without before we got them. Achieving a goal or getting what we want never seems to solve the problem of suffering.

This is precisely what the Buddha discovered about a thousand years before Rousseau, although he didn't articulate it in quite the same way. When the Buddha said, "The cause of suffering is desire," he wasn't talking about desire as a far-off thing. He was saying that believing that some other place is better than this one, or that some other state is better than the one you are in, causes suffering.

Of course, there's suffering and there's suffering. What you went through in the months before you died, my god, *that* was suffering. I don't want to minimize that or pretend that you could have been perfectly content going through all that agony if you'd only had the right attitude. That's obviously not true.

But the sad thing is the way most of us suffer needlessly in situations that we could be enjoying or at least learning from.

We tend to compare ourselves to others or to what we think we ought to be or what we think other people think we should be, and all that other stuff. But that just takes us away from reality. In Zen practice, we're trying to get at what we are right now. So becoming a better person, maybe that'll happen gradually, but you become a better person by not wanting to become a better person, ironically.

This happens all the time: someone sends me a long email listing various distractions that happen while doing zazen followed by, "Am I doing it right?" I had this exact same question when I started practicing. So I don't consider it a dumb thing to ask. It took me a long time to learn what I'm going to tell you very quickly.

Every one of us who meditates thinks that our particular brand of distraction is somehow unique or is evidence that we're doing it wrong, and so on, but it's not. On the one hand, because you are a unique human being, your sort of distraction is different from anybody else's.

There are certain categories of distraction, like the sex distraction or the possession distraction, the thing you want to get or the thing you must avoid at all costs. Sometimes the distraction is abstract. You see weird colors or patterns on the wall in front of you. Whatever the distraction is, it's all kind of the same damn thing. As Nishijima Roshi said every time I asked about stuff like this, "That's just the content of your zazen." I think I told you that in another letter, but it bears repeating.

Whatever you put into your mind during the rest of the day is going to manifest itself in your meditation. This is why I used that quote from Kosho Uchiyama in an earlier letter, the one where he said that the secretions of your mind are like the secretions of your stomach. You've put things in there. You've had experiences, conversations, random things you saw while surfing the internets, and so on.

They're all in there. So when you sit, these things will start to bubble up. In and of itself, it doesn't matter if it's sex, if it's money, if it's whatever. Just keep sitting. My usual go-to solution is to adjust my posture. It doesn't fix everything instantly, but it helps.

Here's another Sawaki quote from that set of Xeroxed articles I found at Tassajara: "You think that things are supposed to become better because you practice zazen. No. Zazen means to forget about better and worse." This is his way of saying one of the same things that Dogen says in "Fukan Zazengi": "If the least like or dislike arises, the mind is lost in confusion."

Even so, just because the mind is lost in confusion, that doesn't mean you're doing it wrong. It just means the mind is lost in confusion. Keep sitting.

Like and dislike are very powerful things because we need to be able to distinguish between what's good for us and what's bad. We are hardwired to do that. Throughout the day we're making comparisons, like, "Am I doing this right?" "Am I doing it wrong?" In life, you need that. You need to know what the red light means and what the green light means. You need to know that yellow snow isn't the same as lemon-flavored Hawaiian ice. You have to discriminate. Yet when you do zazen, there isn't a right or wrong.

Okay, I take that back. There's a right or wrong in terms of posture. But beyond that, if you're actually doing it, you're probably doing it right. There is almost no way you can screw up zazen. You just keep on doing zazen — and the fact that it isn't what you think it ought to be is not evidence that you're doing it wrong. It's just something else you're sitting with.

So you just sit with the thought that says, "This is not right. I hate this." I can't tell you how many times I have sat zazen, especially in long retreats, where the main thought on my mind was, "I got to get out of here. I *have to.* This is not working." But I found in retrospect that the ability to sit through that kind of thing has been incredibly useful.

It's useful because no one can put anything into your head that's worse than what you can put into it. All anyone can ever do is push the buttons you already have. But if you just sit there, letting all your thoughts and feelings happen, and you stay still and refuse to react, then you can do exactly the same thing the next time an asshole boss or a malignant relative or a toxic neighbor pushes your buttons by trying to put their thoughts and feelings into your head. When that happens to me, I think, "If they imagine they can do worse to me than I can do to me, let 'em try! Ha! It ain't gonna happen."

So those are a few of the reasons why we Zennies set the goal of having no goals.

See you on the flip side!

Brad

11. THE FOUR NO-BULL TRUTHS

Dear Marky,

It's getting close to Halloween. Halloween is a very American thing, but they do it up a little over here in Europe too. Some of the folks from the retreat I'm leading in Utrecht took me to a Halloween party after the talk last night. You paid three euros to get in, which got you a complimentary blue drink served in a test tube. I think mine had dissolved marshmallows in it. It was really sweet. I'm not a drinker, so I had only one test tube.

There were all kinds of people dressed up as all kinds of crazy things. A bunch of Dutch dudes were dressed as an American football team, and their girlfriends were dressed as cheerleaders. You gotta admire the effort at coordination. But my favorite was the guy who showed up dressed as himself. I don't mean he just dressed normal. No. He had a beard, so he made a fake beard and stuck that over his real one. He wore fake glasses on top of his real glasses. He even made a fake version of his favorite T-shirt. I thought that was clever.

I'm starting a two-day retreat this afternoon, so no more parties until that's over. Still, it was fun to get out for a night. People who come to Buddhist retreats are, naturally, usually people who are really interested in Buddhism. So I'm sure I'll meet a lot of people at the retreat who are really into Buddhism. Sometimes I don't understand why people get into this stuff. In order to understand them I have to start thinking about what got me interested in it.

If you had ever asked me about why I got into Buddhism, I'd have probably said that it just made sense. It wasn't bullshit. Maybe I should tell you about some of the things that made sense to me and why I thought they were sensible. So let's talk about the Four No-Bull Truths, or, as normal Buddhists like to call them, the Four Noble Truths. Do they like terrible puns wherever you are? If it's the Bad Place, I guess they probably like bad jokes...

Legend has it that the very first sermon the Buddha gave after his experience of enlightenment was about the Four Noble Truths. If you take a comparative religions course, they'll tell you that the Buddha's first words to his first students in his first-ever talk about his philosophy of life was, "All life is suffering. The cause of suffering is desire. By eliminating desire, you eliminate suffering. The best way to eliminate desire is to follow the Eightfold Path." The eight folds of the path are right view, right intention, right speech, right action, right livelihood, right effort, right mindfulness, and right concentration.

You know, I can recite the names of Santa's eight reindeer from memory, but even after thirty-some years of working with Buddhism I have never been able to recite the eight noble folds of the Noble Eightfold Path without looking them up.

Nishijima Roshi hated that interpretation of the Four Noble Truths, by the way. In a pamphlet called "The Buddhist Precepts" — which you can find online if you have internet access wherever you are — he wrote, "If all things and events in this world are suffering, then Buddhism can be at best a dogmatic and pessimistic religion. If all suffering results from human desire, then Buddhism can be no more than asceticism. If the idea of destroying all our desires was a Buddhist idea, then Buddhism must be a religion which advocates what is impossible; for it is utterly impossible for us to destroy our desires. Desire is the basis of our human existence itself."

He presented a different interpretation of the Four Noble Truths. He said it's better to think of them as the Truth of Idealism, the Truth of Materialism, the Truth of Action, and the Truth of Reality.

A lot of people use the word *idealism* as a synonym for *optimism*, but that's not what Nishijima Roshi meant. By *idealism* he meant philosophical idealism. Philosophical idealism holds that the world of matter is either unreal or at best a pale shadow of an unseen immaterial ideal world. Most religions preach some version of this. To lots of the Christians in the town where we grew up, for example, heaven was far more important than this world. To idealists, the only things that really matter are the things that happen in our minds, or in our souls, if you want to use that word.

A lot of people use the word *materialism* as a synonym for *greed*. The belief in philosophical materialism is often used as a justification for greed, as in the whole "greed is good" thing that was in fashion in the '80s. But when Nishijima talked about materialism he meant the philosophy of materialism. The philosophy of materialism just says that the world of matter is the whole of reality — or at least it's the only part that matters. Materialism holds that everything is the result of material forces. Even our subjective experience of consciousness is nothing more than a side effect of the interactions of chemicals and the transfer of energy.

Before we get to the other two Noble Truths, and before I go into more detail about Nishijima's version, let's talk some more about the first two Noble Truths.

You were like me, I think, Marky — basically a pessimist. My basic belief before I got into Zen was that life was shitty. Pessimistic people like us are prone to depression and don't have too much trouble with the standard version of Noble Truth number one. When I heard that Buddhists believed that all life was suffering, I was like, *right on!* I mean, even when things are going really well, it never lasts and there's always this nagging feeling about what comes next. Like maybe you could get a terminal disease just when you were finally starting to get a grip on life.

The idea that the cause of suffering is desire wasn't too difficult for me to accept either. Every time you desire for things to be different it means you don't like the way things are now, which means you're suffering. From that, it's easy enough to extrapolate that the cause of all suffering might be some kind of desire.

The standard version of Noble Truth number three follows easily from that. If you stop desiring, you stop suffering. If you can accept number two, you'll probably accept number three. That's how most people I run into in Buddhist places seem to deal with it.

The standard version of truth number four is a little harder to accept. At least it is for me. Why would doing all those things help me end my desires? And what on Earth is meant by "right" livelihood? Or "right" effort? Who says what's right and what's not? How would you know if your livelihood was "right"? I remember when you used to tend bar at a strip club down on Furnace Street, Marky. Are you now damned for all eternity for what lots of people would consider "wrong" livelihood?

Furthermore, I have to agree with my teacher that desire is a fundamental fact of life. Maybe you'd stop suffering if you stopped desiring, but who the hell can do that? If you were to overcome your desire to eat or your desire to breathe, you'd die. Even if you excluded those desires that are necessary for survival, how on God's green Earth are you supposed to never want anything at all? It's ridiculous.

This is where my teacher's reimagining of the Four Noble Truths comes in.

My teacher used to say that idealism and materialism were the two fundamental ways people look at the world. Most people are never fully in one camp or the other. They vacillate between the two. But most individuals do have a strong tendency to stay with one side more than the other.

Religious people are idealists most of the time. Materialistic people are materialists most of the time — obviously. All the world's philosophies, my teacher said, belong to one of these camps or the other. Marxism, for example, is overtly materialistic. Contemporary Western society tends to be materialistic, even when it's not Marxist and even when many of the people within it are religious.

Religions, on the other hand, are based on idealism. They say that the spiritual world, which has no material existence, is where all the really important things happen. There are also plenty of secular philosophies that are idealistic.

The only philosophy that doesn't fit into one or the other of these two camps is Buddhism, Nishijima Roshi said.

The problem with trying to look at the world through either the materialistic lens or the idealistic lens is that every action we take has an idealistic component and a materialistic component. The idealistic component is your subjective experience of whatever you're doing. The materialistic component is the physical part of that action.

But every action you take includes both sides. If your hands feel cold, like mine do right now as I type this, there's the idealistic aspect of that experience, which is the subjective sensation of cold and the subjective sense that this is occurring in your hands. Then there's the materialistic component, which is your actual hands themselves, the air temperature in the room, the nerves that transmit temperature information to your brain, and so on.

As I type this letter to you, both halves are fully and inseparably engaged in that action.

So, when doing action, we transcend materialism and idealism. And we do this literally all the time. This was how Nishijima Roshi defined the Third Noble Truth, which he said was action.

Action takes place within reality because, as Woody Allen said, "I hate reality but it's still the best place to get a good steak." Or to take nude photos of your ex-girlfriend's adopted daughter, apparently. But that's a whole other story. Still, I think Woody was right, at least about the steak.

I like my teacher's version of the Four Noble Truths a lot better than the standard version. He says he got this version by reading between the lines in Dogen's writings. So far, though, he is the only person I know of who explained them this way.

Still, I think my teacher may not be the only one who questions the standard version of the Four Noble Truths. For example, I can't think of even one reference to what has become the standard version of the Four Noble Truths in any of Dogen's writings. Lots of other Zen teachers just kind of ignore it too. They might refer to it in passing, but they don't get really into it. Maybe they don't agree with it either.

The July 18, 2014, issue of the *New York Times* featured an article by Arthur C. Brooks called "Love People, Not Pleasure." I'm guessing you weren't in any mood to read newspapers at that point since by that time you were pretty sick. But a three-paragraph section of that article may help shed some light on the matter of desire a little better than the standard comparative-religions-class version of the Buddha's Noble Truths:

> From an evolutionary perspective, it makes sense that we are wired to seek fame, wealth and sexual variety. These things make us more likely to pass on our DNA. Had your cave-man ancestors not acquired some version of these things (a fine reputation for being a great rock sharpener; multiple animal skins), they might not have found enough mating partners to create your lineage.
>
> But here's where the evolutionary cables have crossed: We assume that things we are attracted to will relieve our suffering and raise our happiness. My brain says, "Get famous." It also says, "Unhappiness is lousy." I conflate the two, getting, "Get famous and you'll be less unhappy."
>
> But that is Mother Nature's cruel hoax. She doesn't really

care either way whether you are unhappy — she just wants you to want to pass on your genetic material. If you conflate intergenerational survival with well-being, that's your problem, not nature's. And matters are hardly helped by nature's useful idiots in society, who propagate a popular piece of life-ruining advice: "If it feels good, do it." Unless you share the same existential goals as protozoa, this is often flat-out wrong.

Desire, the seeking behavior the author refers to, is built into our physical nature. The human body can only live if it consumes food for energy. So we are designed to desire food. The human species only survives by procreating. So we are designed to desire sex. If you try to battle it out with those desires, you're going to lose.

What about desires for things that aren't so necessary? What about the desire for a shiny new car, or my personal desire for that sexy-looking bass that Danelectro just put on the market? What about the desire not simply for food but for that one specific burger they only sell in Kalamazoo, Michigan? What about the desire not just for sex but for finding your perfect soul mate who will stay with you forever and never change?

As the author of that article hints at, the real problem may be that we think desire relates to happiness.

Let's start simply. You have natural desires. For example, your bodily energy runs low. This makes you grumpy, unhappy. You feel hungry. You desire food. You grab a cherry Pop Tart, toast it up, and eat it. You feel happy because you are no longer hungry, at least for the time being.

From this you learn that satisfying a desire brings you happiness.

Because there are a lot of cases in which satisfying a desire makes us feel happy, we begin to believe that if only we could satisfy *every* desire, we would feel happy all the time.

Very few of us would actually be so dopey as to say this out loud. In fact, we'd probably say just the opposite. We know very well that we can never get everything we want and that even if we did, it still would not create perfect happiness.

And yet when we find ourselves feeling unhappy, we generally attribute that feeling to some desire that has not been fulfilled. I've even found myself doing this while doing zazen.

Everyone who meditates has some desires about their meditation practice, as well as some kind of idea about how their practice relates to their happiness. Maybe you think your mind is too full of noise and you want it to stop because you think a less noisy mind would make you happy. Or maybe you've heard about enlightenment and you think that if you get enlightened, you'll be happy. Or maybe you're too stressed and you've heard that meditation will fix that. There are loads of reasons why people meditate. I had reasons when I started too. So did everyone — even the Buddha.

The Buddha started on his quest when he discovered the same thing Kurt Cobain would discover a couple of thousand years later — that even a wealthy person with all the advantages power and privilege have to offer suffers. But instead of blowing his brains out with a shotgun, the Buddha reacted differently. He desired to find a way out of suffering and into the opposite of suffering — contentment, happiness. He lived in a culture that already had the idea that meditation will bring you happiness. So he meditated. Several hundred years later in Japan, Dogen had lost both his parents by the time he was seven years old. It was that suffering that led him to try meditation. Search the biography of any great meditation master, and you will find a similar story.

Meditating doesn't always make me feel happy. Often the noise in my head continues. Or my emotions overwhelm me — like they did every time I did zazen while you were dying. But most of the time when I meditate I don't feel too different from how I feel the rest of the time.

All of us who meditate sometimes desire a different experience in meditation from the one we are actually having. Without ever saying so, even to ourselves, we imagine that if we could feel the way we wanted to feel, then we would finally be happy. If only we could eliminate the things that disturb our meditation, then we'd be able to do it right.

In an essay called "Flowers in Space," which appears in volume three of the Gudo Nishijima and Chodo Cross translation of *Shobogenzo*, Dogen famously said this about trying to eliminate disturbances: "The very moment itself of eliminating is inevitably disturbance. They are simultaneous and are beyond simultaneousness. Disturbances always include the fact of [trying to] eliminate them."

You can't fight your desires and ever hope to win that fight. However, you can come to a different understanding of desire and happiness, thereby finding a new way to respond to desire.

The thing that makes zazen very different from most other forms of meditation is that in zazen you are not trying to change anything or improve anything or achieve anything. You sit for the sake of sitting itself. I know I keep saying this, but it bears repeating.

In other words, zazen practice is not related to any outcome. Zazen practice is not related to happiness. That's why it's goalless.

Anyhow, my teacher said that the First Noble Truth — the one that's often phrased "All life is suffering" — is the Truth of Idealism. When we look at things in an idealistic way, all life seems to be suffering because our real lives can never match our ideals about how our lives ought to be. This goes for anyone, no matter how rich or famous they are or how close their lives match the prevailing societal definition of fabulous.

My teacher said that the Second Noble Truth — the one usually phrased as "The cause of suffering is desire" — was the Truth of Materialism, or the Truth of Accumulation. To understand this interpretation, it may be useful to look at the Second Noble Truth in terms of goals.

As long as you have a goal that has not yet been met, you suffer. There is dissonance between you as you are right now and you as you think you'll be once your desire is met. You feel incomplete. It's like being hungry. You think you need to accumulate or acquire whatever you desire in order to complete yourself.

But you're wrong if you think satisfying a desire will complete you. You are complete as you are right now — no matter what you think you lack. It's not that your life couldn't improve if you got that thing you want. Maybe it could. And maybe you really do need to acquire whatever that object might be. More than likely, though, if you examine it clearly, you'll see that you don't really need that object after all. Still, even when you do need whatever it is, that isn't the problem.

The problem is when you allow the idea that fulfilling a desire will make you happy to dominate your experience. The bare fact that you have desires and goals is not a problem in itself. It's perfectly normal. You couldn't rid yourself of them if you tried. So there's no point in trying.

When practicing zazen, you put your desires aside. Any idea you have about wanting your practice to be anything other than what it actually is, is just another thought. It's no more worthy of attention than, say, a random thought about pink potato chips or suddenly remembering the name of your second-grade teacher. As you would with any other thought, you put aside the thought that your practice ought to be clearer, calmer, more insightful, or whatever you think it should be.

Desires are just thoughts that occur in our brains. Some are useful, some aren't. What messes us up is the way we identify with our desires. We have a desirous thought, and then we attempt to own that thought. And because it is now *my* desire, I think I must do something to satisfy it.

Once you learn to stop this process of identifying yourself with your thoughts, you find that desires don't really have much of a hold on you. They're just more thoughts your brain generates. Just more brain secretions.

According to a scientific study I once read, we have around fifty thoughts each minute. I'm not sure how they tabulated that. But I've watched my own brain do its thing during meditation long enough to see that the number of thoughts I generate throughout the day must run into the millions.

Most of these thoughts we simply ignore. We barely notice them at all. They're subtle and fleeting. Other thoughts are a bit more concrete and stick around a while longer. Yet we still dismiss them.

Some thoughts appear to be tagged for immediate dismissal by some sort of habit-based mechanism in the brain. These are our supposedly "evil" thoughts, the thoughts we've been taught since childhood are not to be allowed. Each one of us has a different set of these. But we all have them. Sometimes if we become aware of such thoughts, we get deeply disturbed by the fact that they even appear in our minds.

But we shouldn't, because the mere fact that such "evil" thoughts appear in the mind doesn't mean anything in and of itself. The brain is just firing away, doing what it needs to do, and some of that random activity is perceived as thought. As long as we don't act on the kinds of thoughts we know we shouldn't act on, we're fine. I mean, it's probably not a good idea to linger too long on the worst of our thoughts. But it's not a big deal just to have them.

Other thoughts, though, are attractive. When they appear in our minds, we begin to play with them, like a little kid playing with a lump of dirt. We manipulate them, we caress them, we pull them apart and put them together in new ways. And these thoughts often turn into desires and goals.

All we need to do is learn how to allow such thoughts to dissipate and vanish the way we allow most of our other thoughts to dissipate and vanish. Which is easier said than done.

When we identify with these thoughts, that is, when we imagine that something called "me" is generating these thoughts, that's when we get into trouble. One of the key ways we define who we are is to state what we desire. For example, I'm Brad Warner and I want to be a bestselling author. What I want is, to a large extent, who I am.

So we fear that if we were to let go of our desires, we would be letting go of who we are.

But I've found that this really isn't the case. I've discovered, through a long and often very difficult meditative practice, that I am not my desires at all. I can let them go — all of them — and still retain my core being.

When you do zazen, you sit there and you meet your desires moment by moment. And you don't do anything at all to satisfy even the easiest ones to satisfy. You'd rather be checking Facebook, but you don't. You want to scratch, but you don't. Or at least you put it off for a while. You want this meditation session to be full of peaceful feelings and bliss, but you stick with it even when it's full of conflict and distractions. You just sit still.

This usually causes desire to redouble its efforts. Rather than getting more blissful and full of peace, you might get positively enraged. It's not an easy practice, however simple it seems. It never was. Not for anyone.

This is one of the reasons why methods that are advertised as quick and easy ways of experiencing spiritual bliss or achieving altered states of awareness are ultimately damaging and a colossal waste of time and effort.

Achieving spiritual bliss and altered states of awareness are just more ways of giving in to desire. Your desire for bliss or altered states is satiated for a little while, but then it comes back again even stronger, and you have to make even greater efforts to achieve more bliss or states even more altered than the ones you've achieved, or else simply suffer for the lack of them. This is how the folks who sell those methods of meditation keep you coming back for more, by the way.

But bliss will always make you feel like shit after a while.

When people come to meditation because they want bliss, they generally want mind-blowing and spectacular experiences. And those really do sometimes happen to people who meditate. But they're actually kind of a problem. This is because they can't last forever; they cannot be permanent.

The very nature of bliss is impermanence. As *Stumbling on Happiness* author Daniel Gilbert pointed out, no matter what state you find yourself in, you acclimate to it after a while and it starts becoming normal — even a state of spiritual rapture or bliss.

Once that happens you start to need another fix. A bigger one! The very same mechanism that drives rich people to want even more riches and famous people to want even more fame works on meditators too. Often people who meditate get caught up in craving more and more and more beautiful meditative experiences.

I know because this is exactly what happened to me. I had a few very exciting experiences in my meditation that ended in feelings of deep depression because I couldn't get them back. I had to learn to let those beautiful experiences go before I could be happy with my regular life again. It was tough because some of those experiences were incredibly wonderful.

The experiences I'm talking about were exactly the kinds of things you read about in misguided books describing what they say ought to happen when you meditate deeply and correctly — bliss, rapture, insight, the whole bit. But none of those blissful experiences ever stayed.

If you think you felt bad when the boy/girl/none-of-the-above of your dreams dumped you, imagine how it feels when God dumps you. Imagine how it feels when the bliss you've been chasing for years finally appears and fills your whole being with abundance and light and then after a little while just packs its bags and goes back to live with its mother — or wherever such things go. It's tough. Believe me.

People who've never had those experiences envy those who have. In fact, lots of people who've had them seem to make careers out of getting others to envy them. You can make loads of money getting people to envy your meditative accomplishments.

What we're working on when we do zazen is the exact opposite of "following our bliss." We are following our lack of bliss, following our lack of satisfaction. Paul Westerberg of the Replacements was right when he said in the song "Unsatisfied," "Everything goes / Well, anything goes all the time / Everything you dream of is right in front of you / And everything is a lie."

But the fact that everything is a lie is okay. What that *New York Times* article calls "nature's useful idiots in society" lie to you and say that the best thing you can do is satisfy your desires. They do so in the hope of satisfying their own desires with the money and fame they take away from you. But in the end they fail.

We Zennies don't confront desire in order to be all austere and severe with ourselves. We do so in order to find real happiness. If Buddhism wasn't about finding happiness, it wouldn't even be worth talking about.

Real happiness doesn't come from satisfying our desires. Real happiness is to be found in dissatisfaction itself.

That's enough for one letter, I think!

Tell Jesus I said hi!

Brad

12. WHEN YOU'RE DEAD YOU'VE GOT NO SELF

MARKY,

The Utrecht retreat is finished, and now I'm on a Jet 2 Airlines plane bound for Leeds, England. I'm going to get picked up in Leeds by Rebecca from Hebden Bridge, which is the "lesbian capitol of Great Britain," according to the internet. It's a former mill town in the rolling hills between Manchester and Leeds that has rebranded itself as a sort of artists' colony.

The lady who was in charge of one of the retreats I led in the Netherlands and whose house I stayed at while I was there said that I didn't thank the people who made the retreat possible. I thought I had done that in my first lecture at that retreat — I listened to the recording just now and sure enough, I did. But maybe I didn't make a big enough deal out of it? Who knows? I've never been very good with social niceties. The truth is, I am eternally super grateful to be able to do what I do, and I know that it's made possible by people who buy my books, watch my videos, and support me financially. I probably don't say that often enough or loudly enough. But it's a fact, and I know it and I am thankful.

The people who buy my books and who book me on retreats make it possible for me to lead the kind of life I always wanted to, as an independent artist who doesn't have to work a day job to make

101

my rent. And yet, who I am to those people is so different from who I think I am that...well, it's weird. They see me as one thing. I see myself as quite another. I'm not certain who is right. But then again, I don't even think I have a true self.

Which is what I want to write to you about this time. It's the number one most misunderstood topic in all of Buddhism: the idea that there is no such thing as self.

I've published six books about Zen and long ago lost count of how many articles, blog posts, lectures, and videos I've done on the subject of no-self. In every book I've written and, I'd say about 20 percent or more of the other writings, speeches, and videos I've done, I've tried to say something understandable about this subject. I've also read a lot of other people's attempts to grapple with the issue.

It took me at least a decade of living with the idea of the non-existence of self before I felt like I really understood it. I know it's a tough nut to crack. But I'm going to try to write you, my dead friend, a letter about it that I think you might have understood when you were alive and you were my living friend. Wish me luck!

According to Buddha you have no self. And not just you because you're dead. You didn't have a self when you were alive either, and neither do I.

Most people who hear this idea think it's weird.

To most of us, there couldn't be anything more obvious than the fact that self exists. René Descartes famously said, "I think; therefore I am." Nothing could be plainer than that.

When your doctor diagnosed you with cancer *someone* felt shock and confusion at being told he was gonna die much sooner than he expected. *Who* was gonna die? *You* were. Who can I no longer talk to about Ren & Stimpy or weird mash-ups of Danzig songs on You-Tube? *You*.

So obviously you had a self. Maybe you still do. I don't know.

But you definitely had one when you were alive. And so do I, at least for now. Right?

Because if there's no self, then who is talking about there being no self? Right?

But the Buddha wasn't saying that you don't exist. He wasn't saying that you don't feel pain when someone you care about dies. He wasn't saying we're mistaken in thinking we are real.

He was saying that the *concept of self* as a way of explaining these real phenomena is completely mistaken. It's the wrong way to understand reality. It holds us back. It doesn't allow us to see the truth of what we actually are.

The idea of the self implies that we are one thing and one thing only, and that the core of that thing never changes. It implies that the self is always the same core thing, no matter what happens to it.

But we know that nothing stays the same forever. You sure didn't! You went from being the nerdiest kid in school to being one of the coolest guys in town. Your whole attitude changed. Mine did too, in different ways. I'm sure as hell not the same person I was when I was going to Wadsworth High School. Everyone changes.

But what about the core something in the center of it all?

I mean, obviously there's some kind of continuity. I learned to play bass guitar when I was in high school and I can still play it now. So I am a thing that once couldn't play bass and now can.

Back when I was learning to play bass I used to watch the *Big Chuck and Lil' John Show* late on Friday nights on Channel 8, where they would show old horror movies and play funny skits during the commercial breaks. I got some DVDs of those shows recently, and it's cool to see them again because of all the memories they bring back. Those DVDs are something I'd definitely share with you if you were still around. Anyway, I must be the same person I was in high school, or how could I remember those shows?

So it can't be entirely wrong to say that I'm the same person I was back then. I have the same name, after all. You changed your name from Willy (sorry!) to Marky. But you can still say the name change happened to one distinct person, even if that person had different names. Even if someone is transgender and has surgery and hormone therapy, we still say that Caitlin is the same core person as Bruce.

Most people would say that changes like that happen to the self. First there's a self who can't play bass, and then the same self can play it. First there's a self who hasn't seen the latest *Star Wars* movie, and then two hours later, the same self regrets having wasted his money on it.

It is perfectly self-evident to us that each person is a discrete and independent unit. Therefore, I have a self, you have — or at least had — a self, Glen Danzig has a self, Henry Rollins has a self, and so on. There are more than seven billion selves just among humans on this planet alone. Lots of us assume animals have a self too, so add a few billion more if you believe that. And who knows how many other selves might exist on other planets?

Buddhists don't deny that things sure seem this way. They don't even deny that, for conventional purposes, we can act as if this is true. When my dad farts, I shouldn't get blamed for the smell. Not even a Buddhist would do that.

So you might be asking, If the Buddhists deny that there are selves at the core of all this, then what do they say is really going on?

The oldest forms of Buddhism say that rather than a self, what we are is a coming together of five skandhas. The word *skandha* just means "heap," or if you want to be fancier, "aggregates." These five heaps/aggregates are form, feeling, perceptions, impulses, and consciousness.

In the Zen form of Buddhism you don't hear a whole lot about the skandhas. Indian Buddhists loved to make lists and analyze things. When Buddhism got to China, most of that stuff got lost. The Chinese weren't into all those lists, and neither were the Japanese, who inherited the Chinese Zen tradition.

What you do hear about a lot in the Zen tradition is the idea of emptiness. For example, there is a line in the Heart Sutra about the skandhas. The Heart Sutra is pretty much the main scripture in Zen Buddhism — if you can even call anything in the Zen tradition a "scripture." In that sutra we are told that all five skandhas are empty. So basically it's saying that the self is empty. Then the same sutra says that form is emptiness and emptiness is form.

But what the holy heck does that even mean? It sounds like we're back to the idea that you don't exist, which would be absurd. But that's not what it means.

In a book called *The Wisdom of Insecurity*, Alan Watts says,

> While you are watching this present experience, are you aware of *someone* watching it? Can you find, in addition to the experience itself, an experiencer? Can you, at the same time, read *this* sentence and think about yourself reading it? You will find that, to think about yourself reading it, you must for a brief second stop reading. The first experience is reading. The second experience is the thought, "I am reading." Can you find any thinker who is thinking the thought, "I am reading?" In other words, when present experience is the thought, "I am reading," can you think about yourself thinking this thought?

You can't know what you are in an objective sense because you can't step outside your self and observe your self. You're always in the way of your own understanding of who you are. So you might as well call any idea you have of your self "empty" because it's just speculation at best.

But it goes further than that. Because the self is empty of any unchanging, permanent core substance, that also means it's completely free. If you can let go of *you*, then you can let go of anything.

But we're then back to the question of who is doing this letting go.

The best answer is, I don't know. Which seems like a cop-out, I guess. But knowing that I don't know who or what I am has made me less concerned about a lot of things I think most people are deeply concerned with.

There is no self that I have to defend when someone insults me. There is no self I feel compelled to make better than anyone else's self. There is no self to feel pity for. There is no self I need to enhance. There is no self I must work hard to keep defining over and over again in my head by remembering my past pains and past triumphs.

That last one has been really important to me. I'm not sure how exactly to explain it. Here goes, anyhow.

At some point in my practice of zazen, I noticed that I spent an awful lot of energy trying to define myself to myself. Things would happen, and I'd have to work out an opinion of them. I'd have to, for example, figure out whether or not I was in favor of the current president of the United States. And I'd want to be consistent.

Like, I could change my mind about the president, just to stick with that example. But I'd need to work out a consistent reasoning for why I disliked the president at one time and then liked the president, or vice versa. It would all have to refer back to a thing called "me" that made some sort of sense. At least to me.

That's just one small example. I noticed I was doing this all the goddamn time. Like, every minute of every day, or even every second of every minute, or every nanosecond of...Well, I think you get the picture.

I never really noticed how much effort this took because I'd just sort of done it all my life. I didn't even think of it as effort because it just seemed to kind of happen. It didn't appear to be deliberate.

In fact, it seemed to happen even when I didn't want it to. Like, I can remember staying awake all night sometimes because someone had done something to me that threatened my sense of who I was. Like maybe someone broke up with me and thereby threatened my image of myself as someone who was worthy of being loved. That happened a few times at the Clubhouse when you were around, and you may remember me whining about it.

All kinds of things could send my brain into this horrific mass of spinning thoughts and emotions, all based on this core sense of who I was.

Of course, I didn't understand it this way at first. I'd be all like, "I can't stop thinking about [fill in the blank]!" Because that truly seemed to be the case. Try as I might, the thoughts would keep popping up. There seemed to be no way to make them quit.

These thoughts seemed to be produced by and experienced by a core *something* that I called "me." There was a sense that these were almost two distinct entities — one that produced all these thoughts and emotions and another that received and experienced them. It was like I had two selves and one was really bothering the other and wouldn't just shut the hell up so that the other one could get some rest.

But that makes no sense, because I also seem to be just one self, for all the reasons I outlined earlier in this letter. There can't be two of me!

Yet, in a way, this idea of two selves might be a tool for getting a grip on why Buddhists say there is no self.

In an essay called "Universal Guide to the Standard Method of Zazen" ("Fukan Zazengi"), Dogen described doing zazen as "taking a backwards step and turning the light around to shine it inwards." When you do zazen, it's quiet and you are very still. You do it in a place where you can reasonably expect not to have to deal with outside distractions.

It's not easy to find such a space. This is why zendos were constructed and communities of meditators were established. The zendo is a physical space that's conducive to keeping the people inside it free of distractions. Decorations are kept to a minimum. Noises are kept out. Often they're far away from cities and towns. The community also acts as a buffer. There's usually someone whose job it is to forego meditating in order to do the other stuff that needs doing, like cooking or dealing with visitors. These jobs rotate so that everyone gets a chance to meditate as much as possible.

The meditators also try not to become distractions to each other or to themselves. This is why it's forbidden to use drugs or alcohol in the meditation space. Dope and liquor stimulate your brain in unpredictable ways, thus providing an internal distraction. You're also not allowed to talk. In most zendos there's a dress code. Sometimes it's really strict and everyone has to wear black monk's robes. Other times they just tell you not to wear anything too colorful or flashy.

Once you're in this quiet space you have a chance to observe yourself in ways that are not possible when you have a lot of distractions to deal with. This allows you to step back, metaphorically speaking, and shine the light of awareness inward on your own mind rather than outward like we usually do.

When you do that, awareness can take the mind as its object. It's a little like when you are bothered by thoughts that you cannot stop thinking. As I said, it feels like there's one silent self and it's observing another noisily chattering self that it can't make shut up. You often become even more aware of just how much your mind is chattering all the time. It can feel like things have gotten worse rather than better. That's just a trick, though. Things are just as they always were, but now you notice it.

Gradually, as less and less stuff is introduced to the mind during the period you've set aside to do zazen, it starts to settle down. Once the noise and chatter of the mind begin to subside, you start to become more aware of the other self, the one that's observing all that chatter and noise.

Dogen said, "To study the self is to forget the self." As you study this silently observing self, then the other sense of self — the chattering, talkative self — starts to become less important. You watch yourself explaining and defining yourself to yourself and become aware that you don't really need to do that. Rehashing your own opinions becomes incredibly boring and you notice you've been pouring a huge amount of energy into a mental activity that isn't even necessary.

In that same essay I referred to before, Dogen then said, "To forget the self is to be illuminated by everything." It no longer feels like there's a central "I" sitting inside you forever cut off from everything else. You start to see your self — as in the self that you thought was yours and yours alone — in everyone and everything.

Then Dogen said, "When you're illuminated by everything, your own body and mind, as well as the bodies and minds of everything else all drop away." Your sense of self is no longer your main point of reference. It's still there. You can access it any time you please. It just no longer takes a place of central importance. It all drops away, and you notice that this isn't just you doing something. It's the entire universe becoming clear. Clear to whom? It no longer makes any difference.

Dogen ends his little mini-rant on the self by saying, "No trace of realization remains. And that no trace continues endlessly." You don't have a realization because the reference point called "you" is forgotten.

Of course, later on you can consciously recall this experience. But you'll also know that your memories of it aren't the same as the experience itself any more than your memory of a KISS concert is a KISS concert.

I guess all that sounded kind of weird.

Let me try putting it another way. Let's just stick with imagining ourselves as two selves. One self, let's call it Self number one, is all upset about his girlfriend breaking up with him. Meanwhile, Self number two sort of observes that upset and experiences it. Then maybe who we are really isn't Self number one but Self number two. And it's that Self number one that we can start to observe when we meditate.

Of course, this is all just metaphor. There aren't really two selves. But we can say that our personality is not our self. Our feelings are not our self. Our experiences are not our self. This can go on and on. So finally the Buddhists just give up and say there is no self. It doesn't mean all that other stuff doesn't exist. But the idea that all these things — all these "heaps" or "aggregates" as the ancient Buddhists call them — are one single integrated thing that is the real "me" starts to seem absurd. You might as well just give up the idea.

When people get into Buddhism they sometimes hear ideas about dissolving or even annihilating the ego, and they worry that they'll lose their sense of identity if they start meditating. But that's not what happens. I had those fears too. But then I looked at my teachers and noticed they both had very strong, very clear personalities. Meditation obviously had not turned them into bland Zen-bots with no discernible character or individuality.

Sadly, though, when I visit meditation centers I often run into people who seem to be trying their best to transform themselves into a caricature of what they think a Zen person ought to be, which is generally a vacant-eyed blob with no opinions and no emotions. But that's just another persona they're cultivating — another concept of self.

I feel like all of us are pieces of a big puzzle that is the universe. A puzzle piece has to be a certain size, shape, and color in order to properly complete the puzzle. If one of the pieces of the puzzle manages to transform itself into a perfectly round beige-colored featureless lump, then it can no longer do its job of completing the puzzle.

So rather than eliminating your personality or smoothing it into something you imagine to be a Zen personality, it's better to find out more clearly just what sort of puzzle piece you already are. That appears to be what my teachers did and what all the great masters of the past did too. They were all very clear individuals. Kodo Sawaki certainly was, and Dogen, and Ikkyu, a fourteenth-century Zen Buddhist monk who was such a wild character they still make cartoons about him in Japan. The list could go on indefinitely. But if you just take a quick look through the history of Zen, you'll find it's full of extremely colorful characters.

Terms like *dissolving* or *annihilating* the ego are misleading. I think I understand why they were used in the past. In some sense it does feel like the ego dissolves. But it doesn't dissolve like it got hit by a blast from Mr. Spock's phaser. Rather, it dissolves like an Alka-Seltzer in a glass of water. It's still there, but now that it's dissolved it can do its job better.

As for annihilation, I don't think the ego ever really gets annihilated. It'll always be there in one form or another. What gets annihilated is the belief that I am what I thought I was. That doesn't mean I become nothing. It just means that I no longer fixate on a particular image of myself.

Phew! You have no idea how much time it took to write this letter!

I really don't know if the concept of no-self makes any better sense to you now than it did when you started reading. I hope it does. I promise I'll write about something else next time.

Keep your pitchfork sharpened! You never know when you'll need it!

Brad

13. THE CENTER OF A UNIVERSE
WITH NO CENTER

DEAR MARKY,

Yesterday was Guy Fawkes Day. You know how in the song "Remember" by John Lennon he sings, "Remember the Fifth of November"? Well, that's Guy Fawkes Day. It celebrates the day, November 5, 1605, that a guy named Guy Fawkes was arrested for trying to blow up the House of Lords and King James I along with it. I only know this because someone told me and I took notes.

Last night the people who are hosting me here took me to the annual big bonfire in the city of Oldham, about half an hour's ride from Hebden Bridge. Rebecca, the woman hosting the Zen retreat at Hebden Bridge, has a friend named Dave who is a professional fire juggler. So I watched him juggle lit-up bowling pins and other crazy things.

The fairground where the bonfire was held was damp but cheerful. There was a helter-skelter, which, it turns out, is a big curvy kind of slide and not, as Charles Manson believed, a call for a worldwide race war. They sold curry and chips and mushy peas and sticky toffee pudding. I love British junk food.

The life of a low-rent traveling Zen teacher is full of weird things. The Dalai Lama may not sleep in squats in Berlin, but I bet he doesn't get to watch fire jugglers at a Guy Fawkes Day bonfire either.

I wanted to get back to the question of who or what I am. I would love to have talked with you about this when you were alive. Not to teach you from my great store of wisdom but to find out what you thought about such matters. You'd probably have been able to teach me a few things.

The Buddha is said to have refused to answer four questions: 1) Is the world eternal? 2) Is the world finite? 3) Is the self identical to the body? And 4) Do we continue to exist after death?

This is one of the things that makes Buddhism unique among the religions of the world. Other religions concern themselves mainly with these kinds of questions, while Buddhism rejects them.

The reason the Buddha rejected these questions is that he believed they did not lead to the end of suffering. He wasn't concerned with anything but how to overcome suffering right here and now.

Even so, I want to spend this letter pondering my own version of these four questions. But I'll pare it down to just two: What is the universe? and What am I?

One of the most interesting revelations I ever had from doing zazen is: I am not at all what I thought I was, and the world is not at all what I thought it was.

And when I say not at all, I mean: Not. At. All.

I'm not sure I can explain what I think I actually am or what the universe actually is. I'm not sure it's worthwhile explaining it, because I'm probably still mistaken. Scratch that! I am *definitely* still mistaken!

For me one good way to express the whole no-self thing that I wrote about in my previous letter is this: Every single idea I ever had about who and what I am turned out to be so utterly and absolutely mistaken that it's best to say I have no self at all.

Of course, since pretty much everyone else still believes in the fiction of self — both about me and about themselves — I still have to accommodate it in terms of how I talk and how I behave. In fact, the idea of self is so pervasive, I find myself slipping back into it constantly.

I mean, just look at how I had to phrase that in order for it to be proper English. *I* find *myself* slipping back into the idea that self is real. There's no other way to put it that doesn't sound goofy. And because I am saddled with a language that takes the existence of self as a given, I am bound to find the belief in self creeping back up on me.

But let's step back a few paces and try to define what we're talking about. I think that the basic ideas I had about who I was and what the world was before I started studying Buddhism were pretty much the standard view nearly everyone subscribes to. So let's look at those ideas first.

I figured I was a human on planet Earth. So what does that mean? In my case it meant that I was unique, an individual, distinct from all other individuals. I was one thing — a single and undivided unit. I had a time and place of origin. I would have a time and place of death. I thought that my mind was my own possession. It was my mind and nobody else's. I thought my past was real and that my memories of that past were reasonably accurate. I thought I knew myself. And I was certain beyond any shadow of doubt that other people were not me.

I wasn't sure about God or life after death or any of that stuff. But I knew for sure that my death was my death and no one else's, and that the outside world would carry on pretty much as usual after I died. I didn't necessarily believe I had a soul, but I was open to the idea that I might. I thought time was a real thing and that it was my enemy because it was actively trying to kill me.

I figured that the world I lived in was sort of like the Monopoly board that my little shoe or thimble or hat or whatever moved around on top of. It was the stage on which I played out my life, as Shakespeare put it. The universe was essentially inert and dead. It contained living things. But all of us living things were small-scale anomalies inhabiting a big, mostly dead universe. We were kind of alien to the thing we lived inside of.

Furthermore, I was an alien to humanity as a whole. I had friends and relatives, of course. But in general, I walked alone on my own path. My interactions with others were fleeting and ultimately meaningless. Even if those interactions might seem significant to me or to someone else at the time they happened, they really didn't have much bearing on anything, certainly not on the big, incomprehensible, and mostly lifeless universe.

Other people had no connection to me. Not really. Sure, maybe I could be friends with someone — like you, for example — or even fall in love. But that connection was just between us. It had no real significance beyond that.

Discovering that all this — and I mean all of it! — was completely wrong was a huge shock. This is why so-called enlightenment experiences that Buddhists occasionally talk about are always described in such outlandish terms. It's a big surprise to discover that everything you thought you knew was completely wrong.

But it's not as if this wrong view is suddenly overwritten and replaced by the correct view in a moment of great awakening. It's not as if I had a mystical experience in which I went from one unshakable view of things to another equally unshakable view of things. Establishing the correct view seems to be a much, much longer process.

Rather, all I really knew for sure was that I'd been completely wrong for pretty much my entire life. And, by extension, I discovered that the standard view of things that nearly everyone takes for granted was also utterly mistaken. Not just superficially wrong in spots, but wrong right down to its core.

Of course, this is also what crazy people think. There are actually psychiatric diagnoses for people who believe that the basic standard worldview I outlined above is wrong. Sometimes they'll even medicate you and counsel you until you start believing in the standard worldview again.

But I am fairly certain I am not crazy. I don't appear to myself to be crazy, and no one responds to me as if I were crazy.

I mean, I probably seem eccentric. An oddball. But no one has yet said they think I need to be medicated to get me back to the right way of thinking.

This is actually part of the Zen training in action. It's one of the reasons why we go very, very slowly in our practice. If you go too fast into this sort of thing, you *will* go crazy. Guaranteed! The only way to do it and keep any semblance of sanity is to take it extra slow.

I will grant you that the standard worldview appears to work. It appears to account for most things we encounter day to day. If I want some lunch, I can slice some bread, put some cheese and pickles between the bread slices, the way they do here in England, shove the whole thing into my mouth, and chew. Therefore, bread, cheese, and pickles are real, and I am real. My sandwich and I are not the same thing. When I eat a sandwich no one else tastes it but me.

Furthermore, logic works. The scientific method works. Dinosaurs really existed 70 million years ago, and they did not ride on Noah's Ark circa 4000 BC. The Earth is one planet in a galaxy full of planets and stars. It's not flat and it's not the center of everything.

I would be a fool to try to go against any of that.

And yet I know that the standard way of understanding the world we live in is deeply mistaken. Even if it works most of the time.

I was watching the movie *Event Horizon* on my laptop the other day back in that room in Berlin. I'm sure you must have seen it because, like me, you were a sucker for science fiction movies. I don't know how I failed to see that movie until now.

As you'll recall, it's about the world's first faster-than-light spaceship, the *Event Horizon*. The *Event Horizon* goes missing and suddenly reappears seven years later in orbit around Neptune. Sam Neil and Laurence Fishburne head up the crew of another spaceship that goes out to find out what the deal is.

Once they board the *Event Horizon*, weird, spooky shit starts happening and people start getting killed. Sam Neil comes up with a theory to explain what's going on, and he has a hard time getting Laurence Fishburne, who plays the captain of the rescue ship, to listen. But he's very insistent. As I watched this, it suddenly became clear to me why it's important to have the right theory about what's going on. And not just when you're in a spaceship being attacked by a mysterious extraterrestrial force.

We need to have a theory about what's going on, because the correct theory will help everybody react properly. In the case of this movie's plot, it can give them a chance to escape with their lives.

This is why having the right view of things is important in general too. The wrong view will cause you to act the wrong way. The right view will cause you to make the right decisions. It's not just some philosophical conundrum for eggheads to sit and ponder. It has a lot of practical implications.

I used to read spiritual books in the hopes that the authors knew the right way of looking at things, the right theory, and the right view and could tell me what it was. This was early on in my practice. So I already had an inkling that the standard view was mistaken. But I hadn't settled yet on Buddhism, so I was looking at a wide range of theories, many of which were pretty out there.

What I found in those books was mostly either pure bullshit or empty speculation. Some of them tried to argue for ideas based on ancient superstition. Others just seemed like the kinds of weird notions you get sometimes when you're stoned. The latter were more interesting than the former, but they still didn't help me very much.

But just for you, Marky, I thought maybe I'd try to speculate a little bit about what might actually be going on in this universe I've found myself in. This will be based on my personal experiences. Even so, I don't present the following as a deep truth that I've discovered and that I firmly believe. Instead, I offer it as informed speculation based on a long examination of my own mind in the quiet.

I don't think human beings really are discrete, individual units. I know we can operate as if we were. But I think that when we do, we can make serious mistakes. I think it might be better to conceive of ourselves as processes in a system. A wave is a process within the ocean. If you wanted to, you could name each wave, you could state the characteristics that differentiate it from other waves, or you could talk about the time of the wave's origin as its "birth" and the time when it hits the shore as its "death." You could carry on in this manner for a long time and start to think of waves as discrete, individual things. All this would be coherent, at least up to a point. But it wouldn't be a correct view of what waves really are.

It's harder to understand ourselves as processes within a larger system than it is to think of waves that way. We perceive ourselves as discrete units. I can even seemingly prove to myself that I am a discrete unit by, for example, stepping on someone else's toe and noticing that they feel pain and I do not.

Frankly, I think a lot of people spend much of their lives doing things like this to try to keep proving their eternal separation from everyone and everything else. Greed, anger, and hatred are all great ways to prove to yourself that you are eternally separate from everyone and everything else.

But I have come to believe it is a flaw in our perceptions that makes it seem that we are discrete units. My consciousness seems to be mine and mine alone. But that doesn't mean it actually is. I've seen that sense of separation break down a number of times and reveal something that seems more real and true. But I had to work hard to get to the point where that could happen.

Maybe this particular life right now, this Brad Warner life, is like a layer in an onion. The layer is complete unto itself. Once somebody peels that layer off and eats it in their salad, it's gone and it's not coming back. But it isn't the whole onion.

That's a lousy metaphor. But it's one among many lousy

metaphors I've come up with. I might try a few more as these letters continue.

Thing is, you can only talk about this by using metaphors. But maybe that isn't as big of a deal as we think, because you can only talk about *anything* by using metaphors. Even if I tell you something as mundane as "I took a poop this morning," the only way you understand that is by using my poop as a metaphor for your own experience of pooping.

There's a *Star Trek: The Next Generation* episode called "Darmok." It's season 5, episode 2, in case you get Netflix wherever you are. In that episode, the *Enterprise* encounters some aliens whose speech makes no sense. The universal translator they use to talk to aliens works just fine. But everything the aliens say comes out like, "Darmok and Jalad at Tanagra" or "Temba when the walls fell." It turns out these aliens use a language based on an elaborate mythology that everyone in their society knows. But if you don't know the mythology they're referring to, there's no way to understand the metaphors they're using.

The episode itself is actually a great metaphor for language in general. All language is metaphorical. Even mathematics is a metaphor for actual things. Science also operates by exchanging metaphors. More universally understood metaphors help communication work better. Once Captain Picard studies up on the aliens' mythology, he's able to understand them. But when it comes to the aspects of life I'm talking about right now, the pool of people who understand it is so small, there really isn't a good system of metaphors to communicate it. Not yet, anyhow.

As to why we don't see things just as they are, I really don't know. But when I say we don't see things properly, I'm including even our physical sense of sight, as well as our other senses. I think we literally cannot see things as they really are. The same goes for all our senses. And because of this, any explanation we come up with is bound to be wrong. So we can't figuratively see them correctly either. Maybe it's not what humans are built for — maybe we're not made to see everything exactly as it is.

Having said that, I don't think that means we're utterly incapable of getting at least some slightly better perspective. We just have to work at it.

When I think about you, Marky, I think that you died and you're not coming back. Yet I also strongly suspect that you're still with us too. That doesn't mean I believe you're a ghost or an angel now — or even a demon, although I keep joking like that when I sign these letters. I don't even believe you've been reincarnated.

I think that what you thought was your consciousness turned out not to be yours at all. I suspect that maybe, as you passed from this life, you might have caught a glimpse of that. Maybe right now you're trying to work out what you saw at that moment. But maybe you are no longer you at all.

God. It just sounds stupid when you type it out like that. Sorry!

Just before I left for Europe I met with my first Zen teacher, Tim, and he said he feels as if he is the center of a universe with no center. What's even weirder is that that makes perfect sense to me. That's how I feel too.

Each of us is the center of the universe. Like, literally. And yet none of us is the one true center. Even though, on the other hand, all of us are exactly the One True Center.

I saw a video in which Neil DeGrasse Tyson was talking about higher dimensions. In the middle of the video he casually put forth the idea that we ourselves might exist in more than just the four dimensions we are familiar with — the normal three, plus the dimension of time. We might, he said, simultaneously exist in dimensions that we cannot perceive.

He said this kind of fast and slid right into another topic. Which made me wonder. Did he think it was just a random speculation? Or did he think maybe his audience couldn't understand it? In any case, I thought it was an intriguing idea.

I'm not sure this is the one true and final scientific explanation for what I'm talking about. But I think that what I'm expressing here doesn't have to be about so-called spiritual realms that exist beyond our material world or any of that kind of stuff. I don't believe in the supernatural, although I do think there are aspects of the natural world that we do not yet comprehend. It would be incredibly arrogant to imagine we know it all...

Bleh! I just read this letter back and I feel like I made a huge mess of my attempt to explain my view of this stuff.

I think this is why the Zen tradition is to leave certain things unstated. It's not that we're trying to be all obscure and weird. It's just that every time you try to encompass it in words, it gets all goofy.

I think I'll go on to an easier topic next letter.

Stay hydrated!

Brad

14. INTUITION

DEAR MARKY,

In my last letter I mentioned John Lennon's song "Remember." That got me thinking about other songs from Lennon's solo albums, and I remembered one called "Intuition." Do you remember that one? It was kind of a filler album track from his *Mind Games* record. Honestly, it wasn't that great of a song. That whole album was a little lackluster. Like he was trying to remake the *Imagine* album but couldn't quite get it right.

The reason I bring it up, though, is that Nishijima Roshi used to use the word *intuition* all the time. It was his favorite way to translate the Buddhist term *prajña*. Most people translate *prajña* as "wisdom." But Nishijima didn't like that translation.

Sanskrit is a distant cousin of English, so there are some similarities. For example, the *pra* part of *prajña* is related to the prefix *pre* from English words like, well, *prefix*, for one. Or words like *prehistoric* or *predestination*. It means "before." The *jña* part is a shortened version of the word *jñana*, which means "knowledge." So *prajña* literally means "before knowledge" or "prior to knowing," if you like that better.

So Nishijima was right. The thing that comes prior to knowing is not wisdom, it's intuition. Ancient Buddhists held *prajña* in very high regard. They said it was the highest form of understanding.

How do we know what we know? Honestly, I don't know. But I can make some guesses. For example, I know your name because you told me. I also know most of what I know about your backstory because you told me or I heard it from other people, although some of it I know because I was there to witness it. I assume that most of what I know about you is reasonably correct because I don't have any serious doubts about my memory and, besides that, if I was wrong about anything significant, you would have told me when you were alive.

Of course, there may be parts of your story I just assumed but that we never discussed. I could be wrong about those parts. There may be things that we both remember wrong. Or you might have lied to me about some things. I don't think you did, but it's possible.

Knowledge is useful. If I know your name is Marky, then I know what name to yell if I want your attention. If I know you like Hüsker Dü, then I know whose album to buy you for your birthday. And so on.

But *prajña*, intuition, comes before knowledge. Shohaku Okumura, one of my favorite contemporary writers on Zen, says in his book *The Mountains and Waters Sutra*, "The Dharma Eye, or Buddha's wisdom [*prajña*], is not a certain way of using our brains. It is what's there when I let go of my thought. It sees both sides of reality." Dogen calls *prajña* "wisdom that knows at a glance."

This isn't a personal sort of wisdom or knowledge. It's based on interdependence, on the underlying unity of all things. Intuition comes when we relax our personal knowledge and allow the knowledge that comes from everything to filter into us.

Nishijima Roshi used to say that whenever we encounter a situation in which a decision must be made, we instantly know what to do. However, he said, we are also very clever — too clever, in fact. And our clever brains spring into action almost immediately after intuition appears and start muddying up the waters. Pretty soon we don't know what was intuition and what was a thought that came up right after intuition. We get confused. Even though we know what to do, we feel like we don't.

Initially I found that hard to accept. I did not trust myself to know what the right thing to do was in every moment. But that was not what Nishijima was suggesting. My personal self — that collection of specific desires and aversions that I mistakenly refer to as my "self" — really can't be trusted to know the right thing to do. It doesn't even know what's best for me, let alone for anything or anyone else.

Intuition is different. It's not *my* intuition. Intuition is more universal. It doesn't belong to anyone. It's hard to believe in such an idea. I know because I didn't believe in it when I first heard it. It was one of many things that Nishijima said that at first I thought were wacky.

I just realized that I've mentioned Nishijima a whole lot in these letters, but I never really told you much about him. Maybe I should pause here for a second and do that.

The man I knew as Gudo Nishijima Roshi was born Kazuo Nishijima in 1919. I first encountered him in 1994, which would have made him...hang on while I do the math...seventy-five years old. My first teacher, Tim McCarthy, was a white guy from Ohio who was just ten years older than me. We liked a lot of the same music — he often quoted Frank Zappa lyrics and was especially fond of the dirty ones — and we both loved dodgy science-fiction films and *The Three Stooges*. He was very easy to relate to.

Nishijima was totally different. He was old. His head was shaved. He wore black Buddhist robes. He was Japanese. He was, in fact, the very image of what you'd expect a Zen master to look like. Straight out of Central Casting, as they say in LA.

But that was just on the surface. Underneath all that, Nishijima was an iconoclast. Although he had been ordained and given dharma transmission by Rempo Niwa Roshi, the former head of the Soto-shu, Nishijima hated the Soto-shu.

Oops. I'd better explain what the Soto-shu is. They're basically the Soto Zen Buddhist Vatican. They're a lot smaller than the Vatican, of course, because there are far fewer Soto Zen Buddhists than there are Catholics. But they operate in pretty much the same way. They're an organization that arose around the time that Japanese institutions of all kinds were looking to the West to see how to model themselves. Although no one says this officially, it's pretty evident that the Soto-shu looked to the Vatican for their inspiration.

They're a central organizing body that certifies Zen priests, administers temples, and generally coordinates the activities of clerics and temples that are members of the organization. You don't have to be a member of the Soto-shu in order to be a Soto Zen Buddhist priest, but in Japan it's expected. The Soto-shu has far less influence outside Japan, though.

These days a few organizations in the United States and in Europe are trying to be their own versions of the Soto-shu. Some of them are having a bit of success. I find most of what comes out of these organizations pretty dubious myself and have no interest in joining any of them.

Nishijima used to call the Soto-shu "a guild of funeral directors." Because that's the main role of Soto Zen Buddhist priests in Japan these days. Japanese people are funny about religions. For the most part, they don't really believe in them the way we in the West do. So they'll go to the local Shinto priest for happy ceremonies like coming-of-age festivals and suchlike, they'll go to Christian churches for weddings because Western-style weddings are very popular in Japan, and when it comes to sad stuff like funerals, they go to the Buddhists.

Nishijima was a member of the Soto-shu, but he mostly ignored them. He was very dedicated to Dogen, the nominal founder of the Soto-shu. The Soto-shu didn't actually exist in Dogen's time; they just retroactively named him as their founder. As far as Nishijima was concerned, any ceremony or regulation that the Soto-shu invented after Dogen died was not really legitimate, so he just ignored it.

When I first started studying with Nishijima, I didn't like him very much. I went to his Zen classes mostly because the time and place they were held were convenient for me and I liked the fact that he taught in English and wasn't as obsessed with ceremonies and services as most Japanese Zen priests. On the other hand, he seemed pretty stodgy and conservative, which was a huge contrast with Tim. He could also be very opinionated. It seemed as if he thought he was the only one in the world who got Dogen's message right. I later found out that wasn't entirely true. But he did think there weren't a lot of other people who understood Dogen, certainly not within the Soto-shu, the self-proclaimed official keepers of Dogen's teachings.

I still remember the incident that first got me thinking differently about Nishijima. Japan in the 1990s was undergoing something very much like what happened when kids in the West first embraced punk rock in the late seventies and early eighties. It wasn't exactly the same stylistically, but it sprang from the same impulse to break away from the past and from tradition and forge a new and better way.

So you'd see lots of kids on the streets dressed in bizarre, outlandish costumes — multicolored hair, wild-colored outfits, weird makeup, and so on. When you were alive you must have seen photos of the kids congregating in Tokyo's Harajuku district with their crazy clothes.

The place we met for Nishijima's Zen classes was Tokyo University, which isn't too far from Harajuku. And we met there on Saturdays, which was the big day for kids to get decked out and go to Harajuku. On Nishijima's route from his home to the university, he passed right through that area every time he came to class.

One Saturday Nishijima started off his lecture saying, "As I was coming here today I saw a group of young people who were dressed very strangely." And I thought, Oh boy! Here it comes. We're gonna get a lecture about how decadent Japanese kids are these days and how they should go back to dressing like normal people.

But instead Nishijima said, "And I thought this is a very good thing. It shows that Japanese people are finally learning how to be themselves." That was the moment I started liking Nishijima Roshi. Maybe that was the moment he became my teacher.

I stuck with the old man for the rest of the time I lived in Japan, going to almost every lecture and retreat he held. I talked to him privately many times. Eventually, he asked me to be his successor. I didn't want to do it at first, but he kind of set it up so that I didn't have much choice. He asked me to do it as a personal favor to him, and I really couldn't say no without feeling like a complete dick.

So that's what Nishijima was like, and that's why intuition is important. I'm not sure if I really conveyed either of those things very well. But I think I've gone on long enough for one letter.

Don't do anything I wouldn't do down there!

Brad

15. THE NO-BULL EIGHTFOLD PATH

DEAR MARKY,

It's been a few days since I wrote you a letter. I hope you didn't miss me too bad. England was a bunch of fun, but I'm in Poland now. Yep. Behind the former Iron Curtain!

I was met at Kraków Airport by the folks who published the Polish edition of *Hardcore Zen*. They talked one of their employees into being the "Brad-sitter" while I'm here. Her name is Katarzyna, which is Catherine in Polish, but she said I can call her Kaja, which is pronounced "ka-yah." That's a lot easier.

We spent five hours in a first-class car on the train to some town whose name is spelled Wrocław but pronounced "Vrotz-law." The train car we were in had two toilets. The floor of one was covered in barf, and the light in the other one didn't work. I chose to use the dark one.

Now I'm at the home of a nice punk rock–ish Polish couple whose names I cannot spell. They have a cat whose name sounds like Bazilla, although they laughed like crazy when I said it that way. It's a nice place and things are finally quiet enough that I can write you another letter.

I figured maybe I was going too fast in my previous letter, and that if you were ever gonna get a picture of what Buddhism is I'd better concentrate on basics. I already mentioned one of those basics in passing, which was the Noble Eightfold Path that the Buddha supposedly said would lead the way out of suffering. As you may recall, the eight folds of the path are right view, right intention, right speech, right action, right livelihood, right effort, right mindfulness, and right concentration.

Another basic Buddhist thing is the Ten Precepts. These are don't kill, don't steal, don't misuse sex, don't lie, don't get high, don't speak of past mistakes, don't put people down, don't covet, don't get mad, and don't slander the Buddha, the Buddhist teachings, or the Buddhist community. The way you officially become a Buddhist in the Zen tradition is by taking a public vow to uphold those precepts. I'll explain more about that in a bit.

There must be a few thousand commentaries on what each of the eight folds and each of the precepts mean. I'll tell you what I think they mean and leave it to you to ask whatever dead Buddhist masters you meet in the afterlife to give you their takes on what they mean. I'm going to go through them kinda quick. There are whole books written about each one, but I don't want to do that.

Right view. To me this means knowing that you don't know. I mentioned why having the right view is important when I wrote about that movie *Event Horizon*. Ancient Buddhist texts about right view are very critical of people who get too wrapped up in trying to answer unanswerable questions. As I said before, the questions Buddhists regard as unanswerable are precisely the kinds of questions most other religions try to provide answers to, like the nature of the soul, the afterlife, God, the origin of the universe, and so on.

I think we'll never completely understand this world and how it works. We do know a few things, and often that knowledge is useful. That's fine. But it's better to take the view that our own understanding at any given moment is provisional. Just because you think you're right doesn't mean that you're right. You need to keep an open mind.

Right intention. This one really hangs some people up. Some spiritual communities these days have ceremonies in which they "set their intentions" for the new year instead of making resolutions. They seem to feel that good intentions are the most important thing ever, no matter where those intentions lead them.

But as my grandma always said, the road to hell is paved with good intentions. Actually, *my* grandma never said that. Maybe yours did. Lots of people's grandmas said that. And they were right. Sometimes you have the best of intentions and still make a mess of things.

Intentions are important. But it's more important to watch what happens when you do and say things. If you mean to do something good but it ends up hurting someone, it's not enough to just say, "I didn't mean it, that wasn't my intention!" You have to make up for what you did.

But when Buddhists in the olden days said "right intention" they were actually being much more specific. They didn't mean you had to have right intentions in general. They meant that you had to have a true intention to follow the Buddhist path. Sometimes this fold of the Eightfold Path is translated as "right resolve." You're supposed to resolve to keep on the Buddhist path, no matter what. For example, you're supposed to resolve never to hold ill will toward anyone and never to commit harm. That doesn't mean you never have a bad thought or never hurt someone. It just means you resolve to try not to.

Right speech. The Buddha apparently had six criteria for himself about what to say and when to say it:

1. If it wasn't factual, wasn't true, wasn't beneficial, wasn't endearing, and wasn't agreeable to others, he didn't say it.
2. If it *was* factual and true but not beneficial, not endearing, and not agreeable to others, he didn't say it.
3. If it was factual, true, and beneficial but not endearing and not agreeable to others, he didn't say it.

4. If it was not factual, not true, and not beneficial but it was endearing and agreeable to others, he didn't say it.

5. If it was factual and true, and it was also endearing and agreeable to others but not beneficial, he didn't say it.

6. If it was factual, true, beneficial, endearing, and agreeable to others he still had a sense of the proper time to say it because, according to the old scriptures, he had sympathy for living beings. ("Right Speech: Samma Vaca," Access to Insight, November 30, 2013.)

He also admonished his monks to avoid talking about politics, crime, war, clothes, food and drink, vehicles, heroes, who they were crushing on, their relatives, or what happens after you die and how the world was created. And no gossip. In short, everything that has ever been discussed on the internet.

The Buddha set the bar pretty high. In my own case, I think those six criteria for what to say are really useful. But I still sometimes talk about stuff like clothes and heroes and politics and so forth. Sometimes it's useful to make small talk. I think the Buddha's first band of monks were a special case, and maybe things have changed since then.

Right action. The items cited in the most ancient Buddhist texts under the heading of "right action" ended up being the first five precepts of the Ten Precepts, namely, don't kill, don't steal, don't misuse sex, don't lie, and don't get high. I'll get to those in a minute.

To me, right action just means don't be a jerk. In one of my books I paraphrased Dogen as saying, "Even if the whole world is nothing but a bunch of jerks doing all kinds of jerk-type things, there is still liberation in simply not being a jerk."

Right livelihood. Sometimes it seems like American Buddhists think there are only two acceptable jobs — yoga teacher and therapist. But that's just silly.

Pretty much any job you do can be done in the spirit of right livelihood, although in some jobs it's harder to do this than in others. Still, it's not like there are Buddha-approved jobs and Buddha-unapproved jobs. It's more a matter of how you do what you do for a living. Once I went to my teacher saying I thought I should quit my job at that monster movie company and be a full-time monk who ran a temple. He told me to stick with my job. He thought I could better serve the world by making monster movies than by running to a temple and pretending to be a monk.

Right effort. This mainly means making the proper amount of effort in Buddhist practice. The Buddha compared it to tuning a stringed instrument. Too much effort is like tuning the strings so tight that they snap. Too little effort is like not tightening them enough so that everything sounds awful and out of tune. He never said anything about getting the instruments *pretty close* to in tune, like we always did at punk-rock gigs.

So don't try too hard. But also don't let the idea of not trying too hard be an excuse to not try at all.

Right mindfulness. This is where mindfulness enters the conversation in Buddhism. It's one-eighth of the Eightfold Path. I'm sure you heard of mindfulness when you were alive. It's still the hottest thing going!

There's a funny story about this that I found on a website called Access to Insight, which is a nice compendium of early Buddhist teachings. The story they have up there goes like this:

The Buddha says, "Suppose, monks, that a large crowd of people comes thronging together, saying, 'The beauty queen! The beauty queen!' And suppose the beauty queen is highly accomplished at singing and dancing, so that an even greater crowd comes thronging, saying, 'The beauty queen is singing! The beauty queen is dancing!' Then a man comes along, desiring life and shrinking from death, desiring pleasure and abhorring pain. They say to him, 'Now, look here, mister. You must take this bowl filled to the brim with oil and carry it on your head in between the great crowd and the beauty queen. A man with a raised sword will follow right behind you, and wherever you spill even a drop of oil, right there will he cut off your head.' Now what do you think, monks: Will that man, not paying attention to the bowl of oil, let himself get distracted outside?" ("Right Mindfulness: Samma Sati," Access to Insight, November 5, 2013.)

Of course, the monks say that the guy will not let himself get distracted by the beauty queen. The Buddha then says that the bowl of oil stands for mindfulness. He says his monks have to concentrate on the here and now, no matter what distractions might appear.

One of the problems I see these days is folks trying to secularize Buddhism by removing the mindfulness part and presenting it as a thing in and of itself. Of course, being mindful is not a bad thing. But Buddhism is a fully formed system of which mindfulness is just one part. The other aspects of Buddhism aren't just arbitrary. They exist for a reason. Carving mindfulness out and trying to practice it without the other stuff might not work out so well.

I want to get through the rest of the folds, so I'll come back to that topic later.

Right concentration. In early Buddhist texts there are lots of details about what right concentration means. They use the word *jhana* to refer to special states of concentration.

You're supposed to start with the first *jhana*, which is "rapture and pleasure born of withdrawal accompanied by directed thought and evaluation." Then you go to *jhana* number two, which is "rapture and pleasure born of composure, unification of awareness free from directed thought and evaluation — internal assurance." After you get that, you go on to *jhana* three, which is "equanimous and mindful" and "the abandoning of pleasure and pain." Finally, *jhana* four is "equanimity and mindfulness, neither pleasure nor pain" and "concentration that leads to a pleasant abiding in the here and now." ("Right Concentration: Samma Samadhi," Access to Insight, November 30, 2013.)

Personally, I don't get all that. I don't see how anyone can judge what *jhana* they themselves are in, and I don't see how someone else could judge it from the outside either. So it seems a little silly to me even to worry about it.

The Zen folks basically just allow whatever state they're in to be exactly as it is without trying to determine if it's *jhana* number three or whatever. They don't even try to progress from one state of mind to another. This is because the idea of progress means evaluating things in terms of linear time. But the only real time is here and now. So comparing your state right now to your memory of a state from the past or to your imagination of a state you anticipate getting to in the future just takes you away from here and now.

That's the Eightfold Path in a nutshell. Now let's talk more about the Ten Buddhist Precepts.

There were originally hundreds of Buddhist precepts. When the Buddha first started his little band of merry meditators, there were no rules. But, as with all human communities, conflicts and troubles started right away. Every time there was a dispute, they brought it to Buddha's attention, and he told them what to do to resolve it.

The monks memorized these solutions and made them into a set of rules. When the Buddha was dying, he said that it was important to keep the major rules but that the minor ones could be ignored. Sadly, for his more pedantic followers, he never said which rules were major and which were minor. So some sects of Buddhism still keep all of them.

The Zen sect was one of several sects of Buddhism that tried to do what the Buddha had clearly implied they should, which is to think for themselves. Someone looked at all the rules and winnowed them down based on what the rules pertained to. They came up with ten major precepts.

I've been using the words *rule* and *precept* somewhat interchangeably here. But there is a difference. A rule is a rule. If you break it, you get penalized. The earliest versions of the Buddhist precepts were very specific and were treated much more like actual rules. Just like regular rules, monks could be punished for breaking them. The precepts as they've come down to us in the Zen sect aren't like that. They aren't so much rules but strong suggestions. They're so openended it's hard to really know if someone has broken them or not.

Actually, it's impossible to know if *someone else* has broken one of the Ten Grave Precepts, as they are known. I think it is possible to know if *you yourself* have broken one. I think it's useful to use the precepts to judge your own behavior. But I think it's a problem to try to judge others on their adherence to the precepts, because you never know exactly why someone else might have done whatever they did.

Don't kill. That one's pretty obvious. On the other hand, how far do you take this? Some Buddhists are vegetarians. Others are not. Neither of my teachers were, although they both endorsed my own vegetarianism as being a good thing. Still, even vegetarians end up killing things to stay alive. It's part of the nature of living things to consume other living things.

The early Buddhists had some rivals called the Jains, started by a guy named Mahavira. Those guys were so committed to the principle of doing no harm that some of them refused to eat anything except fruits and vegetables that had fallen from trees and vines, and they walked with a broom in their hands to sweep away any bugs they might step on and a mask over their mouths to avoid accidentally killing any bugs by breathing them in.

But even doing that, you still end up killing stuff. I think the best you can do is to try to minimize your amount of killing and try not to kill unless it's really unavoidable.

Don't steal. This is another obvious one. But what if you're poor and have to steal medicine for your sick child? It's a cliché, but there really are rare instances when stealing might be the more ethical option. Still, such instances are extraordinary and uncommon, so it's better just not to steal stuff.

Don't misuse sex. The early Buddhist monks and nuns were celibate. But when Buddhism started to become a thing nonmonastics did, they needed a more inclusive precept than straight-up abstinence. Originally, the rules said a nonmonastic Buddhist shouldn't have sex with anyone under the protection of their parents (what we'd call an underage person), married people, engaged people, or prisoners.

It's odd that prisoners made the short list. It'd be really hard to have sex with a prisoner. Probably the idea of conjugal visits didn't exist in those days. The other rules seem pretty straightforward to me.

You'll note that no forms of sexuality are specifically forbidden. Like, it doesn't say you can't have gay sex, unless of course it breaks one of the other rules. The only specific Buddhist prohibitions against homosexuality that I know of are directed at monks and nuns. It seems that some of the early monastics thought the rule of celibacy only applied to heterosexual sex. So the Buddha had to point out that boy-on-boy and girl-on-girl action were also prohibited for monks and nuns.

I wrote a whole book about this subject. This precept really seems to bug Western Buddhists a lot. But I think it's pretty simple. Just don't be a jerk when it comes to sex.

Don't lie. This is another easy one. The same sorts of caveats that apply to the precept about stealing also apply to this one. There may be times when not telling the truth is appropriate or necessary, such as when someone asks if their clothes make them look fat. Buddha's six criteria for right speech also apply here. Sometimes it's better to just say nothing at all if telling the truth isn't going to help anyone.

To me, a lie isn't simply distorting or concealing the truth. You lie when you tell someone something that's false in order to gain something for yourself at someone else's expense. This definition fits with the Buddhist idea that none of us is a discrete individual, that we are all intimately connected to each other. If you look at it that way, trying to gain something for yourself at someone else's expense makes no logical sense. So don't lie.

Don't get high. This is yet another one that bugs a lot of folks. There are a bunch of variations. Some versions say, "Don't live by selling liquor." Some people reinterpret that as meaning we shouldn't try to delude others. But that's covered by the previous precept about lying.

Noah Levine, author of the book *Dharma Punx* and founder of Against the Stream, a group that mixes Buddhism with the recovery gospel popularized by Akron's own Alcoholics Anonymous, thinks this precept ought to be taken literally. In actual practice, most Buddhists I've known — both in Europe and America, and in Japan — will sometimes do drugs and drink in moderation. Personally, I think Levine is right. Even so, I'm pretty much like most other Buddhists in that I'll have some smoke or some drink now and then but always in limited quantities.

Don't speak of past mistakes. The standard version of this one goes, "Don't discuss the faults of Buddhist practitioners." Some people like to make that more universal and say, "Don't discuss the faults of others."

Personally I like the version that says, "No speaking of past mistakes." I like it because it can apply to your own mistakes as well as those made by others. Don't talk about *anyone's* mistakes, even your own.

Obviously, there are times when you have to point out some-one's mistakes or acknowledge your own. That's fine. Point them out if you must, but don't dwell on them. Once a mistake has been acknowledged, the only sensible thing is to try to correct whatever went wrong and avoid making the same mistake again.

Don't put people down. The standard version of this is "Don't praise yourself and berate others." Which is just good advice, if you ask me. Nobody likes a braggart, and nobody likes being put down. So don't do that.

Don't covet. The standard version of this one goes, "Don't be-grudge the Buddhist teachings." These days folks like to make the precept more universal, and it's become more about being covetous of anything, not just the Buddhist teachings.

One of the main Buddhist virtues is generosity. You don't have to be stupidly generous. But it's good to give what you can to those who need it.

Don't get mad. This is another one people get hung up on. Normally it's phrased "Don't give way to anger."

I feel like you can divide anger into two phases. The first phase of anger comes on suddenly in response to a situation. It happens so fast there's not much you can do about it. Maybe something triggers you in some way. Maybe it's almost a physiological reaction to a sit-uation. In any case, it's hard to avoid.

The second phase of anger is when you take that initial burst and hold on to it. You make it into a part of your self-image; *I* am angry. *My* anger belongs to *me*. You hold grudges. You plot revenge. You hate. It can get ugly.

Letting go of anger can be hard. It's especially hard when you have every right to be angry. But even then, it's better to let it go. That doesn't mean you have to tolerate a bad situation or give in to it. You can still make things right. But do so without anger. Or, if you can't manage that, do so with as little anger as possible. Try to put your anger aside and get on with what needs to be done.

Don't slander the Buddha, the Buddhist teachings, or the Buddhist community. This one seems really specific. Like don't put down the religion.

It was probably meant that way originally. But I think we can take it a little more universally. Maybe we can substitute *truth* for *Buddhist teachings* and agree not to slander the truth, those who teach the truth, or those who practice the truth. That removes it from being about one specific religion or one specific type of community. At least, that's how I look at this one.

So there you go. That's basic Buddhist ethics. It's all pretty sensible stuff, if you ask me.

According to Dogen, being ethical was the real point of Buddhism. Being ethical was far more important to him than achieving enlightenment. He wrote a chapter in his masterwork whose title translates as something like the title of Spike Lee's fourth film, only stated in the negative. Instead of *Do the Right Thing*, Dogen says *Don't Do the Wrong Thing*.

According to Dogen, any given action can be right, wrong, or neutral. He says that there is ultimately no right or wrong and yet, he says, when we take action there is right and there is wrong. He was all about contradictions, our Dogen!

In my own lived experience, I can see that some things I do are right and some things I do are not right. So I try to do the right things and avoid doing the not-right ones. I think if enough people started making that simple idea their criterion for ethical behavior, we'd all have a lot less trouble.

Ta for now!

Brad

16. YOUR KARMA RAN OVER MY DOGMA

Dear Marky,

I've been traveling around Poland for the past several days. My gigs here have been a mixed bag.

On the way to Opole University, the car I was in got pulled over by the cops. The guy who was driving managed to get it sorted out. But it was a bit of a hair-raiser for me. I had no idea what I'd do if I ended up being questioned by the Polish police. Not that I'm doing anything illegal, but jeez.

Then when we arrived at the university, we found out the flyers hadn't been printed and no one knew I was coming. Nine people from the university's Buddhist group showed up, and that was the entire audience.

I did two other gigs in which fewer than ten people attended. But I also did some with respectable crowds. So far I've spoken at a new age bookstore, a normal bookstore, a Zen center, and a bar.

At one point, I was told we were going to go see Auschwitz. But then it rained real hard the day we were supposed to go and they told me it was closed.

Whenever I do a talk that's translated into a foreign language and then I do a Q&A session afterward, I wonder if the translation matched what I actually said. Kaja seems like a good translator. But the questions I get back are always full of oddities like, "Are you conscious in your dreams?" or "What about the ancient prophecies of the next Buddha?" People seem really interested in all that esoteric stuff.

Sam Harris, a famed neuroscientist with a popular podcast who is now styling himself as an expert in all things related to meditation, wants to save us all from that kind of stuff. He calls it "woo-woo" or just "woo" for short. He claims to have written the only book on meditation that's completely free of woo. I tried to read it once. Couldn't get through it. Not because of its lack of woo, but because to me, reading a book by Sam Harris about meditation must be similar to what it would be like for Sam Harris to read a book by me about neuroscience.

In any case, woo-woo is what Harris calls all unsubstantiated religious beliefs. He says, "If you believe a cookie is the body of Elvis Presley you're a crazy person" and "but if you believe a cracker is the body of Jesus Christ you're just a Catholic."

Lots of Westerners have turned to Buddhism to try to find a religion that's free from superstition, dogma, and belief in the supernatural. They're inspired by the Buddha's words in the *Anguttara Nikaya*, where he says, "Do not get carried away by superstition; believe in deeds, aspiring to results from your own deeds through your own effort in a rational way; [don't be] excited by wildly rumored superstition, talismans, omens, or lucky charms [Shut up, Buddha! That's one of my favorite cereals!]; do not aspire to results from praying for miracles."

Or they like Buddha's words from a speech he made to the people of the Kalama tribe: "Do not go upon what has been acquired by repeated hearing; nor upon tradition; nor upon rumor; nor upon what is in a scripture; nor upon surmise; nor upon an axiom; nor upon specious reasoning; nor upon a bias towards a notion that has been pondered over; nor upon another's seeming ability; nor upon the consideration, 'The monk is our teacher.' Kalamas, when you yourselves know: 'These things are bad; these things are blamable; these things are censured by the wise; undertaken and observed, these things lead to harm and ill,' abandon them."

When people believe in the supernatural, it generally means they believe in things that defy the law of cause and effect or in effects that don't match their causes. And, as I mentioned, Dogen said that Buddhism requires a deep belief in cause and effect.

Lots of Westerners, therefore, understandably expect Buddhism to be totally scientific and rational. But then they go to a Buddhist temple and hear all sorts of weird spells and incantations. They may encounter monks who hold beliefs in demons or in bodhisattvas with paranormal powers. Even in the Zen Buddhist tradition, probably the least woo of them all, sometimes you'll find prayers and spells and even the occasional references to heavenly realms or celestial beings, both good and evil. But the biggest bugaboo of them all, the one that seems to vex all of Buddhism, is the twin beliefs in karma and reincarnation.

Let's start with karma. If Moe pokes Curly in the eyeballs, Moe feels a mild wet sensation in his fingers and Curly feels a much stronger sensation in his eyeballs. Moe, in turn, feels nothing in his eyeballs and Curly feels nothing in his fingers.

A lot of people think that the theory of karma means that someday Curly will poke Moe in his eyes. Or maybe Larry will poke Moe in the eyes in the future as the karmic result of Moe's eye poke to Curly. Or perhaps one day Moe will get a nasty eye infection with no apparent cause, but this eye infection actually came about as the karmic result of Moe poking Curly in the eyes.

Dogen wrote about karma in an essay called "Karma in the Three Times." The "three times" are past, present, and future. In this essay Dogen says that sometimes one receives the effects of the causes one enacts immediately, sometimes the effects come after a little while, and sometimes the effects happen a very, very long time later.

So maybe Moe doesn't even get poked in the eye in this lifetime. There has been sufficient time since their deaths for each of them to have been reincarnated and to have settled the karmic score of Moe's many pokings of Curly's eyes during the 1930s and '40s.

The belief in this sort of karma is soothing to those of us who would like to believe there is justice in the universe. I, for one, would very much like to believe that good things will happen to people who do good things. I'd like to believe that people who do evil things will be punished.

And yet, as far as I know, you never did anything so bad that you deserved to get cancer. My mom never did anything so bad as to deserve the slow death she endured from a degenerative disease. Meanwhile, all kinds of assholes are getting away with all sorts of heinous shit and living it up in big mansions or getting elected to high political office. It's really hard to believe there's any kind of justice anywhere.

But reincarnation fixes this failure in the theory of karma to account for what we see happening all the time. Because even if you don't get your just deserts in this life, you'll get them in another one.

Putting it that way makes the whole thing sound like a made-up story intended to help us feel good about bad things. But I want to put that objection to the side for a bit because I think it's important to be clear about what Buddhists actually think reincarnation means. The Buddhist idea of reincarnation is not the same as the Hindu idea, which is more properly called transmigration, even though a lot of folks also refer to the Hindu belief as reincarnation.

The idea of transmigration goes something like this. Inside each of us lives a little piece of God called "atman." In chapter 2 of the Bhagavad Gita, the main holy book of most Hindus, verse 13 says, "As the Spirit [atman] of our mortal body wanders on in childhood and youth and old age, the Spirit wanders on to a new body; of this the sage has no doubts." Verse 17 of that chapter says, "Interwoven in his creation, the Spirit is beyond destruction. No one can bring to an end the Spirit which is everlasting." And verse 22 of the same chapter says, "As a man leaves an old garment and puts on one that is new, the Spirit leaves his mortal body and then puts on one that is new." (From the 1962 Penguin Classics translation by Juan Mascaró.)

Dogen said that people who imagine that transmigration is the Buddhist view are completely wrong. He also said, as I noted in a previous letter, "Firewood, after becoming ash, does not again become firewood. Similarly, human beings, after death, do not live again."

The Buddha denied the existence of the atman/Spirit. He said there was no such thing. However, even though he denied the idea of a soul that puts on new bodies the way we change T-shirts, the Buddha did not deny the idea of rebirth.

One of the earliest stories we have in which the historical Buddha talks about reincarnation takes place in a village called Nadika. I found it in a book called *Gotama Buddha: Volume Two* by Hajime Nakamura.

In that story, Buddha's cousin and longtime attendant Ananda asks Buddha what became of a monk named Salha, who was from Nadika, after he died. Then he asks the same things about a female monk from Nadika who'd died. Then he asks about a male lay follower of the Buddha from Nadika who'd died and a female lay follower, also from Nadika, who had died. In all he asks about the after-death fates of twelve different dead followers of the Buddha from Nadika. In one version of the story it says that ninety of Buddha's followers from Nadika had died.

It makes me wonder if there was some kind of plague going around the village or something. The sutra doesn't say. But the incident took place when Buddha was nearly eighty years old. So maybe these followers were also old folks.

In any case, the Buddha tells Ananda what happened to each of these people after they died. The ones who had realized the profound truths he taught entered nirvana, never to return to the world of the living. Others got pretty close and would have to live only one more life before entering nirvana.

For Buddhists, what gets reborn is not an eternal, unchanging soul. Rather than believing in a soul that migrates from body to body, Buddhists believe in an ever-changing collection of elements that hang together for a while but are not a single, indestructible unit. These are the skandhas or aggregates/heaps I mentioned in an earlier letter. Still, most Buddhists feel that this temporary arrangement hangs together for multiple lifetimes, maybe even millions of them. So in some ways, it's sort of like a soul passing from one body to the next.

My first Zen teacher liked to use an analogy about a candle to explain this belief. If you use one candle to light another candle and then immediately blow out the first candle, is the flame on the second candle the same flame or a different one? It's hard to say. In some sense, it's a new flame. But its existence depends on the previous flame. So, in another sense, it's the same flame.

According to the Buddhists, the causes and conditions that came together to become you probably stayed together even after the life they collectively lived as Marky Moon ended. Maybe by now they've become another person, or animal, or even celestial being or demon. I think you'd have liked to be a demon, Marky!

On the other hand, in an essay "Life and Death," which appears in volume four of the Nishijima/Cross translation of *Shobogenzo*, Dogen said, "In the time called 'life,' there is nothing besides life. In the time called 'death,' there is nothing besides death. Thus, when life comes it is just life, and when death comes it is just death; do not say, confronting them, that you will serve them, and do not wish for them."

So as far as most Zen Buddhists are concerned, maybe we reincarnate, and maybe we don't. Either way, it's far more important to live this life fully than it is to fret about what might come next.

Since I don't know exactly what I am, I am open to the possibility that something I might call "me" could have something it might call "experiences" after Brad Warner passes from this mortal plane or even before Brad Warner appeared. Given some of the stranger experiences I've had around my Zen practice, it seems reasonable to expect that this journey did not begin on that day in March when I popped out of my mom's womb and that it won't end the day I keel over. I've seen glimpses of something bigger than that, something that I am intimately connected with.

But, in the final analysis, I really don't know. So the best course of action, it seems to me, is to try to live this life as fully as possible at every moment. Because right now I know that I am alive.

As for karma, I also don't know. But I feel like it's true. Karma, when presented as something that happens to individual beings, seems an iffy proposition. But if you envision humanity as a single unit, then I think it makes sense to say that any disturbance created by one part of that unit affects the entire unit. And if it affects the entire unit, then it's going to affect the part of the unit that started the disturbance in the first place.

So when Moe pokes Curly in the eyes, the pain Curly feels will be Moe's pain as well, whether he notices it now or notices it much, much later.

And maybe what we call consciousness isn't a localized phenomenon that each of us possesses but a shared phenomenon we all partake of. In which case maybe the idea of reincarnation isn't so crazy after all.

But, like I said, you know by now whether reincarnation is true or not; however, either you can't tell me or you won't.

In any case, have a good afterlife or a great nonexistence. Whichever it is.

Brad

17. SOME KOANS YOU OUGHT TO KNOW

Marky,

I'm back in Germany again. I haven't written you for a few days, but you probably didn't even notice. In the meantime, I took a flight down to Munich. This tour was planned stupidly — by me. I'd like to have grouped all the German things together, but I couldn't. Ah, well.

I did a talk here last night, and now I'm on a long train ride to a retreat center in the wilds of Bavaria. The scenery outside is amazing. We're going along some river. I can't tell you which one it is, but it's gorgeous. Oh, my god. We just passed the city of Dachau.

I'm gonna be on this train for a while, so I thought I'd spend the time writing about one of the most popular yet least understood aspects of Zen: the koans. Even as someone who had no interest at all in Zen, you've probably heard a few of them. Koans are those weird unanswerable questions like, "What is the sound of one hand clapping?" or "What was the shape of your face before you were born?" or "Where the hell did I put my car keys this time?"

If you look up koans online or read old books about Zen, they'll sometimes tell you that the koans are illogical stories meant to get you out of your habitual way of thinking by presenting unsolvable riddles.

I completely disagree. Koans are not riddles, even though some of them sound like it. They're brief stories intended to teach some of the weird ways Zen folks have of looking at things.

This letter won't be a comprehensive scholarly survey of the koans. It's my own personal collection of koans that I like and that I thought you might enjoy too. I've tried to organize them a little bit, but not much. So they're more or less in random order, except when they aren't.

I went through the three major koan collections — *The Gateless Gate*, *The Blue Cliff Record*, and Dogen's *Shinji Shobogenzo* — and picked out the koans that had the most meaning for me.

I've put these koans in my own words for a few reasons. First, the koans were originally in Chinese, so unless you acquired the ability to read ancient Chinese after you died, you'll never read the original versions. Second, most of the koans exist in multiple variations. The ancient masters apparently didn't worry too much about getting the wording exactly right. Like I said, they are not riddles or word games in which the precise wording is vital. The final reason is practical. Since I might use these in a book someday, I didn't want to get complaints from other translators for stealing their versions. In most cases, I'm telling you the koans the way I remember them.

I heard most of these during my early years of studying Zen with Tim McCarthy. Many of them kept cropping up again and again. Sometimes I'd meet them in various writings about Zen. Others just kind of popped into my mind on a regular basis, usually when I was doing something completely unrelated to Zen — which, for me even now, is most of the time. You know, like when I was walking down the street, or folding laundry, or filing papers at work or something, these would just sometimes come to mind.

I've written little commentaries for each of them. But I don't claim much for these commentaries. They're just my personal observations. You shouldn't regard them as any kind of definitive statement about these stories. Maybe you shouldn't even read the commentaries at all. It might be better to just have your own experience of the stories. Anyway, here goes nothin'!

A monk asked Zen Master Joshu, "Does even a dog have Buddha nature?"

Joshu said, "Yes!"

The monk said, "If it has Buddha nature, why is it a dog?"

Joshu said, "It knows how things are and does what needs doing."

Another monk asked Joshu, "Does even a dog have Buddha nature?"

Joshu said, "No!"

The monk said, "Why? I heard all things have Buddha nature!"

Joshu said, "Because our viewpoint is produced by our experiences in the past."

(*Shinji Shobogenzo*, case 1:14;
this is a longer version of *Gateless Gate*, case 1)

In order to understand this koan, you have to be in on a joke that gets lost in translation. In the Chinese dialect in which this koan was composed, the word for *yes* is pronounced "u" as in "Ooh, aah! Look at the fireworks!" The word for *no* is pronounced "wu." When you shout these words, you sound like a dog barking.

The main point of the story is that yes and no — to have and to have not — are human concepts. They're useful in lots of cases. But the real world exists as it is beyond any sort of conceptual framework we use to understand and navigate our way through it.

Buddha nature is one name that we Zennies use for the underlying oneness of all things. So everything has — or is — Buddha nature. Even dogs or pigs or politicians.

When Joshu was asked about whether a dog has Buddha nature,

he responded by barking like a dog. He was trying to say that a dog is exactly what it is, regardless of whether or not we define it as having Buddha nature. He answered the question in contradictory ways to further emphasize this point.

> Show me the shape of your original face before your parents were born!
>
> (*Gateless Gate*, case 23)

There's a backstory to this koan.

In the early days of the Zen lineage, so the legend goes, the actual begging bowl and robe once used by the Buddha were passed down from teacher to student. No one knows if that's really true, but even today a symbolic bowl and robe are handed over in the ceremony in which you officially become a Buddhist teacher. The ones I got came from a shop called Nakano Hou-ei Ten (Nakano Buddhist Accoutrements) in Tokyo's Ueno district.

Anyway, according to the stories, a famous master named Hui-Neng received the Buddha's robe and bowl in secret because this other guy named Ming was jealous of him and thought he deserved them. We do not know if Ming was merciless like Emperor Ming from Planet Mongo in *Flash Gordon* or not.

In any case, Hui-Neng left the temple in the middle of the night, but Ming chased after him. When Ming caught up with Hui-Neng, Hui-Neng said, "Dude, if you want this stuff so bad, take it. They're just symbols anyway."

The story goes that Ming tried to pick up the robe and bowl, but they were too heavy for him to lift. He said to Hui-Neng, "I didn't come for the stuff. I came for the teachings. Please teach me."

Hui-Neng said, "When you don't think of good or bad, what is your original face, the one you had before your parents were born?"

On hearing this, Ming was enlightened. He said, "What is the deepest teaching?"

Hui-Neng said, "There's no secret. When you realize your original face, the secret is yours."

Ming was like, "Right on. Now I'm like a person drinking water who knows whether the water is hot or cold."

So that's the backstory.

It's very common for Zen teachers in the Rinzai sect to ask their students to show them their original face. The Soto sect also has a lot of stuff about one's original face.

On the one hand, conventionally speaking, you had no face before your parents were born. On the other, if you believe in reincarnation, maybe you did. But even then, there would be no way for you to show it to anyone. So it's an impossible question.

Or is it? If the present moment is eternal, then there is no real difference between your face right now and your face in the distant past.

Anyhow, if anyone ever asked me to show them my original face, I think I'd just roll my eyes. What a stupid Zen cliché! You expect me to take you seriously?

A monk asked Joshu, "What was Bodhidharma's intention when he came to China?"

Joshu said, "The oak tree in the front garden!"

(*Gateless Gate*, case 37; *Shinji Shobogenzo*, case 2:19)

I mentioned Bodhidharma in an earlier letter. He's the guy who brought Buddhism to China. He supposedly sat in a cave alone, meditating for nine years. His commitment to meditation makes him very attractive to the Zen school.

Nobody really knows Bodhidharma's actual story. Some even doubt he existed at all, while others think he's a composite character created from the stories of a number of similar monks who brought Buddhism into China.

One could say that Bodhidharma started a movement, since Zen

Buddhism became huge in China. But that was much later. Apparently, Bodhidharma himself was just happy to meditate in his little cave all alone. Unfortunately for him, word got out and curiosity seekers started pestering him to teach them how to meditate. After much persuading, he eventually accepted four students, three men and one woman. Those four students had students of their own, and thus a movement was born. Or so the stories say.

Bodhidharma didn't come to China with the intention of starting a cultural movement. He just wanted to find a quiet place to meditate.

When Joshu answered with a seeming non sequitur about an oak tree, he was indicating a phenomenon of nature — a tree — that just does what it does without any intention. It might provide shade, or branches that can be used for kindling. But it doesn't intend to do that. It just behaves according to its nature. As did Bodhidharma.

A monk asked Master Seigen Gyoshi, "What was Bodhidharma's intention when he came to China?"

Seigen Gyoshi said, "He just acted as he was."

The monk said, "I don't get that. Can you explain it another way?"

Seigen Gyoshi said, "Come over here."

The monk approached him.

Seigen Gyoshi said, "Remember this clearly."

(*Shinji Shobogenzo*, case 1:10)

This one is an easier version of the same thing. When Seigen says, "Come over here" and the monk responds, the monk is doing what comes naturally without any specific intention. Seigen is trying to give the monk a concrete example of how Bodhidharma behaved.

A monk asked Zen Master Joshu, "When everything returns to the One, where does the One return to?"

Joshu answered, "When I was living in a place called Sei, I made a cotton robe. It weighed six pounds, one ounce."

(*Blue Cliff Record*, case 45)

When I first started writing about Zen on the internet, I used to get emails from people who wanted to out-Zen me. This was before you could have a comments section in a blog, so they had to write me directly rather than getting the thrill of demonstrating their coolness to other readers. Anyhow, someone sent me the first part of this koan in an email with the question, "What say you?" after the monk's question.

He was apparently attempting to engage in what they call "dharma combat." This is where monks try to out-Zen each other by tossing weird questions like this back and forth. Unfortunately, you can't really do this effectively by email. It has to be spontaneous and face-to-face for it to work. I mean, come on. I could've just looked up the answer and sent it back to him!

I don't remember exactly what I said. But the best answer is more or less a variation of Joshu's answer. Instead of trying to answer this impossible question with a load of speculation disguised as wisdom, Joshu just states a fact. There is no way to answer this question without speculating, so Joshu's answer is as good as you can possibly get.

A monk is running away from a tiger. He jumps off a cliff. On the way down, he grabs a branch. He looks down and sees another tiger at the bottom, looking up at him hungrily. The first tiger is still up there trying to get him from the top. A white mouse and a black mouse are circling the branch, eating it. It's gonna break pretty soon. Just then he notices some berries hanging from the branch. He picks a couple and eats them. They taste delicious.

(*Collection of Stone and Sand*, case 18)

This one doesn't appear in the major koan collections. So it probably doesn't qualify as a koan in the strictest sense. It's more of an old Zen-inspired story.

The reason I'm including it is that I remember hearing it from my first teacher, Tim, very early on in my study. Tim had to explain the painfully obvious metaphor to me, so I'll explain it here. You can skip the next bit if you're smarter than I was and have already figured it out.

The tiger at the top of the cliff represents birth, while the tiger at the bottom represents death. The white and black mice represent time, the days and the nights of our lives passing by at a furious pace, eating away at our lives, ensuring that, at some point, we're definitely gonna get eaten by the tiger at the bottom of the cliff and there's nothing we can do to prevent it.

Eating the berries represents the most sensible way to deal with the situation. Which is, enjoy what there is to enjoy while you can. It's not necessary to spend all your time obsessing about the two tigers, which is what — metaphorically — a lot of the kinds of people who get into this Zen stuff tend to do way too much.

Whenever someone asked Zen Master Gutei about Zen, he just held up one finger. The master had a young attendant. After a while, whenever someone asked the attendant about Zen, he too held up a finger. Master Gutei heard about this and called his attendant to him. When the attendant arrived, Master Gutei asked about Zen. The attendant held up a finger. The Master whipped out a sharp knife he had hidden in his robe and lopped that finger right off! The attendant was screaming and crying. Just then the master called the attendant's name. The boy looked up. Master Gutei held up one finger. The boy was instantly enlightened. When Master Gutei was on his deathbed he said, "Ever since I attained one-finger Zen, I used it all my life and I could never exhaust it." Then he died.

(*Gateless Gate*, case 3; *Blue Cliff Record*,
case 19; *Shinji Shobogenzo*, 3:46)

This story is found in all the major koan collections. It's considered important in every Zen lineage.

When I first heard this story and the one that follows about the cat getting cut in half (Oops! Spoiler alert!), I wondered if these were supposed to be taken literally. If so, then Zen sounds really sadistic! Actually, a lot of people do take these stories literally and for that reason reject the whole Zen thing out of hand.

I've known a lot of Zen teachers in my time, and I can't imagine any Zen teacher ever slicing off someone's finger or cutting a cat in half even hundreds of years ago. I don't think there's any good reason to take these stories literally. My guess is that what really happened was far less dramatic. Like maybe Gutei twisted his student's finger and maybe Nansen, in the story that follows, actually just took the cat home for himself. But, like fish stories, the tales just kept getting bigger and bigger as they were retold. Or maybe the stories were always just pure metaphor and never actually happened at all. In any case, I don't believe Gutei ever really cut off a guy's finger or that Nansen ever really cut a cat in half.

The metaphor in this one is pretty obvious. Gutei had a unique understanding of Zen and expressed it in a way that suited him. The monk didn't really understand what his teacher said, but he pretended he did by imitating him. When he cut off the monk's finger, Gutei made it impossible for the monk to imitate him. Then he showed the monk his finger again and the monk finally got it for himself.

I know how Gutei feels! Ever since I started writing these punk-influenced Zen books, I've seen loads of people trying to imitate what I do. They usually come across as obnoxious assholes.

Maybe I do too. But these folks are always mean-spirited and caustic in ways that, I swear to God, I never am.

In any case, this is a really common thing. Zen students often imitate their teachers without really understanding them. But the whole point of the practice is to become truly yourself, not to become like a tribute band to your teacher.

Zen master Nansen came across two of his monks arguing about which one owned a cat (in some versions they're arguing about whether or not the cat has Buddha nature). Master Nansen grabbed the cat by the scruff of its neck with one hand and grabbed a knife with the other. He said, "Unless one of you can say something true, I'll cut this cat in half!" The monks couldn't answer. So the master sliced the cat in half. Later that evening the monk Joshu returned from town (Joshu appears in lots of these stories). Nansen told him about the incident with the cat. Joshu took off his sandals, put them on top of his head, and walked out. Master Nansen said, "If you'd been there you could have saved the cat!"

(*Gateless Gate*, case 14; *Blue Cliff Record*, case 63/64; *Shinji Shobogenzo*, 2:81)

As I said, I do not believe any actual cats were harmed in the creation of this koan.

On the other hand, Gudo Nishijima, my ordaining teacher, seemed to believe that Nansen really did kill the cat. He explained this koan by saying, "Nansen violated the precept not to kill in order to teach something to the monks. Such behavior was completely wrong, because to observe the precepts is the most important matter for a Buddhist monk.... Walking out with his sandals on his head was Joshu's way of demonstrating this contradiction at the heart of Nansen's teachings."

With all due respect to my late teacher, I don't read it that way at all. I think it's a metaphor about the inability of anyone to ever say exactly the right thing. It's like when someone close to you experiences the death of a friend or parent. What do you say? You can get paralyzed trying to come up with exactly the right thing. And lots of us do. We're so afraid of doing the wrong thing that we do nothing at all.

Joshu just *did something*. He may not have given the most eloquent response. The fact that it was such a bad response is precisely the point! He responded. All those monks had to do to save the cat was to respond somehow. But they didn't. They seemed to be waiting for their teacher to tell them what to think. The cat being killed represents how they killed Buddhism by being too hung up on getting it exactly right to just do something.

> Everybody knows that Bodhidharma had a beard. But in the eye of enlightenment, Bodhidharma has no beard. Why not?
>
> (*Gateless Gate*, case 4)

Every depiction of Bodhidharma shows him with a big, bushy red beard. So this koan is like someone saying, I dunno, something like, "Michael Jackson never wore one sequined glove."

The idea is that who Bodhidharma really was — or who any of us really are — is beyond his physical characteristics or even his individual personality. Like all of us, Bodhidharma was an expression of the universe. What he was — and what you are — has no specific set of characteristics. We're all just pimples on the butt of the Absolute.

> A monk came to Master Joshu's monastery (the same Joshu we saw as a monk earlier) and asked for his teachings. Master Joshu said, "Have you had breakfast yet?" The monk

said he had. Master Joshu said, "Wash out your bowl." The
monk was instantly enlightened.

(*Gateless Gate*, case 7; *Shinji Shobogenzo*, 1:67)

This one is pretty easy. One of the main points of Zen is that it's
not about extraordinary accomplishments and towering insights.
It's about discovering that ordinary, mundane experiences, like eating breakfast and washing your dishes, are really incredible, even
miraculous. Think of how the universe has come together in just the
right way to produce you sitting on your toilet reading this letter, for
example. Wait a minute. Do they even have toilets in the afterlife?
Anyway, any infinitesimal change in any one of a zillion things that
went on in the past, and no one would be reading this at all. So *this*
is a miracle!

> Whenever Zen Master Fuke — which is pronounced "foo-
> kay," not "fook" — went into town he'd ring a bell and say,
> "If a clear mind comes, let it come. If a cloudy mind comes,
> let it come."
>   Master Rinzai told a monk to grab Fuke and ask him,
> "What if neither a clear mind nor a cloudy mind comes?"
>   Fuke said, "Tomorrow there's gonna be a big feast at
> the temple."
>   After Rinzai heard what Fuke had said, he said, "I
> thought Fuke was no ordinary monk!"
>
> (*Shinji Shobogenzo*, 1:22)

This koan is like a lot of the others I've included in this letter. Fuke
is held up as an example of someone who allows life to be just as
it is. He's not upset at himself when his mind is unclear, but he's
not particularly proud when it's clear since he knows clarity comes
and goes.
     Rinzai wants to know if Fuke really means this or if he's just

pretending, like the monk who imitated Gutei's one-finger Zen without really understanding it. When Fuke refuses to take the bait of the unanswerable philosophical question the monk puts to him, Rinzai affirms that Fuke is the real deal.

> Master Shakkyo asked Master Seido, "Do you know how to grasp empty space?"
>
> Master Seido said, "Sure!" and grabbed at the air.
>
> Master Shakkyo said, "That's not how you grasp empty space."
>
> Seido said, "Well, how do you do it, then?"
>
> Shakkyo grabbed Seido's nose and twisted it, like Moe always did to Larry and Curly.
>
> Seido said, "That was rude of you. But now I get it. Thanks!"
>
> Shakkyo said, "You should grasp space directly like this."
>
> (*Shinji Shobogenzo*, 3:49)

I love the *Three Stooges*–like aspect of this koan. Maybe Moe was a Zen master and Larry and Curly were monks. At least that's how I always think of them.

This one gets into the idea from the Heart Sutra that form is emptiness, and emptiness is form. Seido didn't really grab empty space. The space he grabbed at was full of air and dust particles and all kinds of stuff. Science now says that even deep space is not a pure vacuum. There are hydrogen particles and other things floating around out there. And space itself can be curved or bent, so who can say there is ever any actual emptiness anywhere?

If form is emptiness, then Seido's nose is emptiness too. Maybe the whole idea of emptiness is empty. Maybe all the nihilists are totally wrong.

Oops. Looks like I'll have to write you a letter about emptiness sometime.

> Master Ba was walking with Hyakujo, who was then his student. Some ducks flew by. Master Ba asked Hyakujo, "What's that?"
>
> Hyakujo said, "Ducks!"
>
> Master Ba said, "Where'd they go?"
>
> Hyakujo said, "They flew away."
>
> Master Ba twisted Hyakujo's nose. Hyakujo said, "Wah!"
>
> Master Ba said, "I thought they flew away."
>
> (*Blue Cliff Record*, case 53; *Shinji Shobogenzo*, 2:82)

This is another *Three Stooges* one, so of course I like it. I once saw an interview in which Moe demonstrated how he could make it look like he was twisting Larry's nose when he really wasn't. It's good to know he didn't actually hurt Larry.

There's a very nice little interview with Shunryu Suzuki, the founder of the San Francisco Zen Center, that you can find online. In it he talks about the blue jays at Tassajara monastery. Those blue jays are a pretty color, but they have a shrill cry that can get really irritating to hear all the time. And when you're at Tassajara in the summer, you hear them constantly.

Suzuki says, "You may say the bird is singing over there. But when we hear the bird, the bird is 'me' already. Actually, I'm not listening to the bird. The bird is here. I am singing with the bird. Peep-peep-peep. If you're reading something and you think, 'There's a blue jay over there. Its voice is not so good.' When you think in that way it's noise. But if you are not disturbed by the blue jay, the blue jay will come right into your heart. And the blue jay will be reading."

That's kinda the same thing this koan is saying. There is no division between the ducks flying overhead and the two monks on the ground watching them. You probably think I'm being metaphorical here, but I'm not. I mean this very literally.

A monk asked Master Tozan, "When heat and cold come, how do we avoid them?"

Tozan answered, "Go to a place that's neither hot nor cold."

The monk said, "What kind of place is neither hot nor cold?"

Tozan said, "When it's cold, let the cold kill you. When it's hot, let the heat kill you."

(*Blue Cliff Record*, case 43; *Shinji Shobogenzo*, 3:25)

I always think of this one whenever I'm in a place that's too hot or too cold. You're not supposed to literally let the heat or cold kill you. Rather, you drop the idea of you as something apart from the circumstances you encounter. You are a part of whatever situation you find yourself in.

An example of letting the heat or cold kill you would be responding in a sensible way to the temperature, like turning on a fan when it's hot or putting on a coat when it's cold. You stop fighting your circumstances and just do what needs doing.

Someone asked Zen Master Tozan, "What is Buddha?"

Tozan said, "Three pounds of flax!"

(*Gateless Gate*, case 18; *Shinji Shobogenzo*, 2:72)

I hate this koan. I hate it because it's one of those things people quote all the time, thinking they know what it means. I'm not even sure exactly what flax is! Some kind of grain, I guess. Oh, shoot! I just looked it up! It's a blue-flowered plant whose seeds are cultivated for making linen, though they can also be eaten and pressed for oil. Gosh.

Anyway, people love this one because it sounds all Oriental and stuff. It's really just saying that the Buddha is more than the specific

person who lived and died a long time ago in India. The Buddha
is even more than the teachings of Buddhism. The Real Buddha is
everyone and everything. Just like Elvis in that old Mojo Nixon song.

A monk asked Master Ummon, "What is Buddha?"
Master Ummon said, "A dried-up shit-stick!"

(*Gateless Gate*, case 21)

This one is basically the same as the previous one, only a grosser
version. I was just having a look at the book *Zen Buddhism: Selected
Writings of D. T. Suzuki*, published in 1956. In that book they changed
the stick to a "dried-out dirt-stick." I guess they didn't think readers
were ready for the real wording in 1956.

And, just FYI, in the days before toilet paper, one of the ways to
clean off your butt was to use a lacquered stick to sort of dig the stuff
out of there. In Dogen's *Shobogenzo* there's a chapter on the proper
way for a monk to use the toilet. I paraphrased that chapter in my
book *Don't Be a Jerk*. It also includes instructions on what to do with
shit-sticks when they got too dirty. They cleaned and reused them as
often as they could — ugh! But once they got too crusty and dried
out, they were thrown away. That's the image the koan is playing
with. So even that crusty gross old poop-stick is a manifestation of
the Buddha.

A monk asked Baso, "What is Buddha?"
Baso said, "Mind here and now is Buddha."

(*Gateless Gate*, case 30; *Shinji Shobogenzo*, 3:79)

"Mind here and now is Buddha" was a common saying among Zen
Buddhists for a very long time. Dogen wrote an essay with that as
the title. In that essay he criticizes the idea that there is something
that we can call "mind" or some special state we can call "mindfulness" and that this something or this state is the real goal of Buddhist
practice.

Rather, he emphasizes the "here and now" aspect of the statement. Here and now is a manifestation of the Absolute, or a manifestation of Buddha. This goes for whatever and wherever here and now happens to be right here and right now. When Fuke says if a clear mind comes, let it come, if a cloudy mind comes, let it come, he's expressing this same attitude.

> A monk asked Baso, "What is Buddha?"
> Baso said, "Not the mind, not the Buddha."
>
> (*Gateless Gate*, case 33)

Oh Baso! Didn't you just say... Aw, never mind. Zen guys are always contradicting themselves.

The point of this koan is kind of like Dogen's point in his essay about the previous one. Whatever you think Buddha is, or whatever you think mind is, those are just concepts. They aren't the real things themselves. So, yes, on the one hand, mind here and now is Buddha. But be careful that you don't take that statement to mean that what you *think of* as mind is Buddha, or even that what you *think of* as Buddha is actually Buddha.

> Master Nansen said, "Mind is not the Buddha. Wisdom is not the Way."
>
> (*Gateless Gate*, case 34)

Here we go again. This is an expansion on the previous two koans we looked at. The koan assumes the listener already knows that traditionally mind is the Buddha and wisdom is the Way. It's like if a respected Catholic priest said God is not the father, Jesus is not the son. You'd have to wonder what the hell would make him say such a thing.

Again, the lesson is that what you think of as mind is not actually mind, nor is what you think of as wisdom necessarily wisdom.

Tokusan visited his master, Ryutan, to ask him some questions. After a while it got pretty late and Master Ryutan said it was time for Tokusan to go back to his room. Tokusan went out but came right back in saying, "It's really dark out there!" Master Ryutan lit a wax-paper candle and handed it to Tokusan. Just as Tokusan was about to take the candle, Master Ryutan blew it out.

At that moment Tokusan got enlightened and made a deep bow. Ryutan said, "What truth did you see?"

Tokusan said, "From now on, I'll never doubt what the old Zen masters said, that mind is the Buddha."

(*Gateless Gate*, case 28)

I first heard this story a long, long time ago, and it has always stuck with me. I'm not exactly sure what it means.

Superficially, it seems to be a riff on Buddha's last words to his students as he was dying: "Be a lamp unto yourselves." Don't look to some outside source for the truth — even if that source is Buddha — but to yourself. But look honestly. Don't just regard your own opinions as true. Question yourself deeply and see if what you *think* is true actually *is* true.

I put it after those last few koans because now we're back to the idea that mind *is* Buddha. We saw this idea first appear a few koans earlier and then saw it refuted.

We can assume that Tokusan has already absorbed the lessons of the previous koans and is using the word *mind* here as a way of expressing the inexpressible. He's also learned the lesson of some of the koans we looked at previously that you gotta say *something*. So he used a pretty clichéd phrase that he was confident his teacher would understand when he said it right then and there.

Joshu asked Nansen, "What is the Buddha's Way?"
Nansen said, "Ordinary life is the Way."

Joshu said, "Then do we need to try to get it, or what?"

Nansen said, "If you try to get it, it runs away."

Joshu said, "If we don't at least try, how can we know it's the Way?"

Nansen said, "The Way isn't about knowing or not-knowing. To know is to nurse delusions. Not to know is to be senseless. When you realize the Way beyond doubts, your mind is as big and boundless and wide open as the sky. Why argue about it?"

Upon hearing this, Joshu got enlightened.

(*Gateless Gate*, case 19)

Here again we are told that ordinary life is the Way. Yadda-yadda-yadda. Tell me something I don't know!

Joshu, quite sensibly, asks if we need to do anything special to realize this. I mean, if our ordinary life is the Buddhist Way, what do we need a Buddhist Way for? This was basically Dogen's question, the one that drove his quest to seek the true source of Buddhism by taking a dangerous sea trip to China in a rickety boat of the type that often sank halfway through the journey.

Nansen tells Joshu that if he sought ordinary life, it would run away. Which is kind of like saying, "Don't think about a pink elephant." If you try to be ordinary, you'll fail because trying to be ordinary is not ordinary.

Joshu is understandably still mystified about what he's supposed to do. So Nansen tells him that it's not about knowing or not-knowing. It's about being wide open and boundless, as you already are.

Master Reimoku said to Master Sekito, "If you can say one thing I agree with, I'll stay. If not, I'll leave."

Sekito didn't say anything.

Reimoku turned and started walking out, swinging his sleeves as a gesture of pride.

Sekito yelled at him, "Hey, monk!"
Reimoku turned his head.
Sekito said, "From birth to death it's just like this!"
Reimoku got enlightened.

(*Shinji Shobogenzo*, 3:100)

This is yet another one that goes way back for me. I don't know when
I first heard it, but I know I heard it from Tim McCarthy because I
can still hear his voice saying chirpily, "From birth to death it's just
like this!"

Sekito figured he'd bested old master Reimoku with his request.
But Reimoku made him understand that his intellect and his ego were
not the real him. He did this by simply calling to him and thereby
getting him to pay a little bit of attention to reality for just a couple of
seconds. Then he pointed out that everything was exactly like that.

One time Master Tokuzan said after a lecture, "I don't want
to have any discussion tonight. If anyone asks a question,
I'll hit him with my stick."

A monk stepped up and prostrated himself before the
master.

The master hit him.

The monk said, "Ow! I didn't even ask a question.
Why'd you hit me?"

The master said, "Where are you from?"

The monk said, "I'm from Korea."

The master said, "I shoulda smacked you thirty times
before you even got off the boat!"

(*Shinji Shobogenzo*, 1:31)

The monk is probably bowing as if to say that he respects the master's wishes. But the master hits him anyway. The monk doesn't

understand why he just got hit, so he asks. The master responds by asking him where he's from.

Sometimes Zennies take getting asked where they come from as some sort of a koan. Like, oooooh! Where *am* I from? So they'll try to come up with some fancy-pants Zen answer. It's actually a little risky to ask people you encounter in Zen places where they're from. Seriously. Sometimes I have to be like, "Hey. Settle down. I just meant, where did you grow up?"

But rather than trying to be all Zen and stuff, our monk gives an honest, no-nonsense response. The master likes this and affirms him by saying he should have hit him — that is, been his teacher — even earlier.

Another way of looking at the last line is that even just seeking out a teacher in the first place by making a long journey from Korea is a kind of question. The monk left his home because he thought the truth was to be found somewhere else. In this case, you could read the teacher as admonishing him for trying to find the truth anywhere but in the here and now.

I guess those interpretations contradict each other. But I think a lot of times you can find contradictory meanings in these stories and, even though the interpretations are different, they're both still true and still useful.

> A couple of monks were watching a flag and arguing over whether it was the wind moving or the flag moving. Master Hui-Neng, the Sixth Patriarch of Zen, heard them and said, "It's not the wind moving or the flag moving, it's your minds that are moving!"
>
> (*Gateless Gate*, case 29)

Dogen liked this one and referenced it a lot. One chapter in which it's mentioned is called "Inmo," but in my book, *It Came from Beyond Zen*, I called it "It Came from Beyond Zen."

We're back to the idea that the mind is not separate from reality. The mind does not perceive reality by standing away from it and being a separate thing. Rather, it is part of the reality that it perceives, as are the perceptions themselves. The witness to reality *is* the reality it witnesses. In this story, Hui-Neng is trying to call direct attention to this.

The wind, the flag, the movement, and even the monks and Hui-Neng himself exist not *in* the mind but *as* the mind.

There's a philosophical idea out there called "solipsism." It's the notion that the only thing that exists is your mind. Everything else is an illusion. This koan might seem to be indicating this idea. But it's not.

To a solipsist, the only mind that exists is his or her individual mind. To a Buddhist, mind is everywhere and includes everything. It's infinitely larger than any individual's singular mental experience.

> Zen Master Goso said, "It's like a cow going through a latticed window. The head, the horns, and all four legs get through, but the tail gets stuck. Why's that?"
>
> (*Gateless Gate*, case 38)

I once asked Nishijima Roshi about this one at one of our many talks in his little office. I said I felt just like that cow in the story. He just said something like, "There is no cow!" and redirected me to talk about what was really going on in my life.

I've always thought of this one as a metaphor for the way we seem to have great awakening experiences and yet still end up right where we started. It can feel like you've made some kind of major breakthrough, but there's still something holding you back. And that something is holding you back so hard it's like the whole damned cow has managed to get through the tiny little window, but now the tail is stuck. And not just stuck like it got caught on something, but stuck so hard it's like it'll never get through.

Bodhidharma was in his cave doing zazen. Taiso Eka (a.k.a. Huike) who would later become the Second Patriarch of Chinese Zen, came up behind him and said, "Please, master, ease my mind!"

Bodhidharma said, "Bring your mind here, and I'll ease it for you."

Taiso Eka said, "I've looked all over the place for my mind, but I can't find it anywhere."

Bodhidharma said, "There! I set your mind at ease!"

(*Gateless Gate*, case 41)

This is a really popular one. It's so easy to understand, I don't think I even need to explain it. I've included it in the list because, if you've never heard it, it's one you ought to be familiar with.

According to the legend, Huike was Bodhidharma's first Chinese student. He really, really wanted to know what Bodhidharma could teach him about zazen. But Bodhidharma just left him out in the snow in front of his cave and ignored him. The story has it that, in order to prove his sincerity, Huike cut off his arm and presented it to Bodhidharma as proof that he was serious.

That just sounds psycho to me. If I were in Bodhidharma's place I'd have wanted nothing to do with Huike.

Tim thought that this was yet another Zen "fish story." He figured that Huike had lost an arm somehow — maybe he got attacked on his way to Bodhidharma or maybe he had an accident — and that his lack of an arm got incorporated into a legend to show how determined he was to practice Zen. That sounds a lot more legit to me. Maybe he showed up at Bodhidharma's place saying something more like, "See! I even lost an arm on my way here, but I still came! Now will you let me in?" Or maybe after Bodhidharma wouldn't let him in something happened to his arm and Bodhidharma figured he was partly to blame so he let Huike in.

There once lived an old woman in a hut at the foot of Mount Tai, on top of which stood a Zen temple. Every time a monk asked her how to get to the temple on top of the mountain she'd say, "Straight ahead." After the monk started going she'd laugh and say, "Tsk! Another monk walking up the hill!"

Master Joshu heard about this and decided to test her himself. So he went to the old woman and asked her how to get to the temple. The same thing happened. As Joshu walked off she laughed and said, "Tsk! Another monk walking up the hill!"

When he got back to the temple Joshu told his monks, "I have tested and defeated the old woman for you!"

(*Shinji Shobogenzo*, 2:33)

I remember hearing this koan from Tim McCarthy when I was just a little sprout. God, I must have been annoying to him. Maybe that's why he told me this one. I was another damned monk walking up the hill in the direction he pointed me in. Like a trusting teenage idiot.

I'm a writer of Zen books these days and some people think I'm wise. I don't think I'm all that wise. And you didn't. But they do. God bless them.

In a way, those poor folks who think I'm wise are like one of those monks and I'm the little old lady in the hut. They ask me for directions by buying the book and I, through the words in the book, point them up the hill. Maybe I see them walking out of a shop with a copy of my book under their arm and I shake my head and go, "Tsk! Another truth seeker, buying my book!"

It's not that I feel contempt for them. It's not that I'm trying to trick them — or you. I worked really hard on those books and on these letters too. I do not take my job lightly! I am trying to give you and anyone else who reads my stuff the very best spiritual advice I possibly can.

My reaction to people who buy my books does not come from contempt or from thinking someone's a dummy for reading my stuff. On the contrary, I know I've given them the best advice I can. But I also know that if they try to follow *my* way they'll just get lost. They have to use what I tell them to help them discover *their own* path. If they try to imitate me, they're just like Gutei's assistant raising his finger without understanding what it means.

I'm glad people buy my books! I hope they'll buy all of them. It helps me pay the rent, plus I think they're genuinely good books, if I do say so myself. At the same time, if anyone were to slavishly follow what I say, they'd never get anywhere.

That's one of the ways I look at the old lady in the story. She's not trying to fool anyone. She's just acknowledging the absurdity of the situation and the fact that everyone has to start out by listening to someone else.

The other thing the old lady is saying to the monks is that the truth is right here, wherever you are. Why go up that hill to find it at a temple when it's right here? Joshu defeats her by following her directions. In doing so he's acknowledging that, while the truth *is* right here wherever you are, you still need some kind of discipline to be able to harmonize with it.

Getting back to the example of me and you and my readers and this book, no one needs my books. You don't need *any* book! And yet just as books like *Zen Mind, Beginners Mind* and *Shobogenzo* were really helpful to me, I hope my books will be helpful to whoever reads them. The truth is right here where you are before you read a word of any book. And yet sometimes a decent book can be a support for your own real efforts.

So those are my favorite koans. I hope you liked some of them.

TTYL!

Brad

18. EMPTINESS

Dear Marky,

I made it to that retreat center I mentioned in my last letter. It's called Benediktushof and it's a little ways outside a city called Würzburg. It's a stately old Benedictine monastery surrounded by miles of rolling hills and lush forests. About thirty people from all parts of Germany have gathered here to sit and stare at the walls with me for the next five days.

Since mentioning emptiness in my last letter to you, I've been thinking a lot about it. Just before I headed off to this retreat center, I was in a German shop that specialized in science-fiction stuff — books, comics, DVDs, toys, and so on. There I found a special German double-disc-edition DVD of my personal favorite Godzilla movie, the one that used to be known in the US as *Monster Zero* or sometimes *Godzilla vs. Monster Zero*. The currently available DVD edition in the US is entitled *Invasion of Astro Monster* for reasons that are far too nerdy to go into here.

The German double DVD version has a bunch of extras available only in Germany, and I'm a geek so I bought it. The movie was originally called *Kaiju Daisenso*, which translates to "The Great Monster War." When it was first released in Germany it was retitled *Befehl aus dem Dunkel*, or "Command from the Darkness."

The German title actually comes from a novel by Hans Dominik, who was sort of a German Jules Verne or H. G. Wells type, a guy who wrote science fiction in the late nineteenth and early twentieth centuries well before science fiction became a big thing. Apparently the German film company that had the rights to distribute *Monster Zero* had also paid for the option to make a film based on Dominik's novel. Rather than actually making that film, they just slapped the novel's title on a Godzilla movie that they imported from Japan.

Anyway, I like that title. It's very evocative. The first person I asked mistakenly translated it as "Message from the Darkness," which is even better. A message, a communication, from that which is unknown, perhaps even unknowable.

In Zen we often talk about emptiness. But we could use other words. St. John of the Cross wrote about what he called "unknowing," which is in many ways analogous to the Zen idea of emptiness. Lately I've been talking about silence rather than emptiness. That word works better for me. We could refer to the same idea by calling it darkness, in which case much of Zen Buddhist philosophy is a message from the darkness. When we talk about emptiness in the Zen sense, we're trying to indicate the area of life, the universe, and everything that we cannot express in words.

There's a recent scientific theory that emptiness gave rise to the universe of form. The idea of the big bang has been widely accepted for decades now, but nobody can explain where that tiny little ball of stuff that exploded into the universe as we know it came from. Now some theoretical physicists are saying that maybe emptiness itself gave rise to the whole phenomenal universe. Lawrence Krauss wrote a book about this called *A Universe from Nothing*.

These physicists need only a little more coaxing to make the leap that the Buddhists made a thousand years ago, that what we know as form didn't just derive from emptiness. It *is* emptiness. One of the manifestations of absolute nothing is this world, is you and me.

Silence, or emptiness, is the most powerful thing there can be.

Nothing can ever harm it because it is nothing. Nothing can escape it. Silence underlies everything. Silence is the basis of all sound. It's there even in the loudest place there is. Emptiness is the basis of all form. Emptiness is what allows form to be form. Form is what allows emptiness to be emptiness.

Darkness, or silence, or emptiness is the unimaginable. It's beyond our ability to comprehend. In a transcribed talk that can be found in a book called *Embracing Emptiness*, Kobun Chino Roshi talked about what he called "holy silence." He said, "Holy silence is the space where your psyche can be totally free, without hindrance. It is like clean air with no dust. Mind is captured by matter but when matter is not there, the mind recovers its nature, which is time and space itself. It is not just the concept of space, but actual space, actual time, without ignorance."

The silence that many of us fear is the basis of ourselves and of everyone and everything else there ever was, will be, could be, or isn't. It is the ground of all being and nonbeing. There is no reason to fear complete nonexistence. Complete nonexistence is what you are made from.

Form is emptiness. Emptiness is form.

This is a message from the darkness that is me to the darkness that is you. It's a message from that part of ourselves that is darkness, that is silence, that is the unknown and unknowable.

But rather than being a message from aliens contacting us from the darkness of outer space and asking us to lend them Godzilla — which is what happens in the movie *Monster Zero* — it is ourselves telling ourselves that there is nothing to fear, nothing to run from, nothing to cling to, nothing to fight for or against. That which terrifies us more than anything else is just ourselves. Our infinite and nonexistent selves.

We are all silence. We are all nothing. We are, all of us, the ground of all being and nonbeing.

And if that's so, what sense does it make for one aspect of nothing to fight with another aspect of nothing over how much nothing each aspect possesses? Especially when we all possess nothing, which is the same as saying we all possess everything.

As you can tell, I have been doing far too much staring at walls over the past few weeks. It makes loony ideas like this start to make sense. And not just make sense. It starts to make them the only ideas that make sense. The conventional way of looking at things starts to seem like a kind of sustained madness.

Another way to understand the Buddhist concept of emptiness is, I think, a little simpler. We cannot understand the final truth of things, since all our concepts are just approximations of reality — even the really detailed scientific concepts. Given that, maybe it's good to relax a little in our attempts at understanding things and instead understand everything as emptiness.

This doesn't mean everything is an insubstantial void. It just means our ideas about things are all fundamentally mistaken and therefore fundamentally empty.

Huh. That didn't take as long to explain as I thought it would! I wish I could get letters back from you to see if I'm making any sense here. But since I can't, I'll just have to keep pressing on.

Don't forget to wash behind your ears!

Brad

19. ARE DRUGS THE GATEWAY TO ZEN?

Dear Marky,

Today I'm starting a retreat at a place in Switzerland called Felsentor. It means "rock arch," as in an arch made out of rock. I got a ride from Benediktushof to Munich, where I stayed for a day. Then I took a train to Lucerne, Switzerland. Then I got on a boat crossing Lake Lucerne. The boat ride took about an hour through some of the most breathtaking countryside I'd ever seen. You shoulda been there!

Felsentor is way up on a mountain on an island. Or at least I think this is an island. The boat landed at a little village, and I was taken on a tram that went up and up and up. Then we got out at a little station in what looked like the middle of nowhere. I dragged my luggage along a winding dirt path until we went through the actual rock arch for which this place is named. Somehow someone built a really cool Zen temple behind that.

I wanted to write something to you about drugs and Zen. This seems especially appropriate to write about while I'm here at Felsentor. You see, Felsentor was established by a student of my first teacher's teacher, Kobun Chino. That student is named Vanja Palmers. These days Vanja is a great believer in the idea of mixing hallucinogens like LSD and magic mushrooms with Zen practice. I completely reject that idea. Vanja is off somewhere else while my retreat is going on, so I guess I won't get to debate him on it.

As you'll recall, I was in Hamburg when I heard that you died. Then I traveled to the Netherlands to do a bunch of talks and retreats. There was a little something I left out of those early letters. In the Netherlands marijuana is kind of like beer is in the States. It's legal, just like it is now in lots of places in the US, including California, where I live. But it's been legal in the Netherlands for quite a bit longer, so over there it's not some weird drug that only hippies and hipsters use. The so-called coffee shops where they smoke it are populated by all kinds of people. You'll see a few hippies, sure, a bunch of hipsters too. They're everywhere. But you'll also see middle-aged guys who look like they might work in construction sitting around sharing some smokes; you'll see groups of housewives chatting over a joint. It's just normal.

When I arrived in the Netherlands not long after you died, I started hitting the coffee shops. The last time I saw you, you shared your medical marijuana with me as we sat on your couch making small talk and watching stupid movies. After you died, I wanted to get high again and maybe in some weird way connect with you. Or something. All I knew for sure was that I was sad and I hoped the weed would make me less sad.

Mind you, I was *not* smoking before my Zen lectures or at the retreats, or even when I was writing you letters. Those times and places are far too sacred to risk being mentally altered. But on that tour of the Netherlands, after my job was finished, after the lectures were over or the retreats had ended, I'd go out to the coffee shops and get as high as I could. This is not good Zen practice. I'm not proud of it, but that's what I did.

Unfortunately for me, this just made me sad *and* high rather than merely sad. I gave obliviating my sadness through drugs a chance, but it didn't work.

Even so, lots of people in my world think that certain drugs can do more than just alleviate their suffering. They think drugs can enhance spiritual practice. LSD, mescaline, psilocybin, DMT, MDMA, and even cannabis are touted for their spiritual benefits. This idea was first propagated in the sixties. It went away for a while — as well it should have. The drug explosion of the sixties didn't exactly lead to a more enlightened age in the seventies and eighties. And it became evident to anyone with any sense that psychedelic drugs were not going to lead to anything like that. But, astonishingly, that ridiculous and fully disproven idea has made a huge comeback in the past few years.

People get mad when I say it's not right for drugs to be promoted as Buddhism. When you question the notion that drugs can be a part of a healthy spiritual practice just like Trix cereal is a part of a healthy breakfast, some folks take it as a personal insult. Like when you tell a Clash fan you think the Ramones were better. Which they were. But it's okay with me when those folks get mad. Sometimes you have to make people mad.

When a recent spate of articles espousing drug use as dharma practice appeared in popular online Buddhist magazines, I felt that they required a strong rebuke from someone with the proper credentials to say, "No, it isn't." I knew no one else was going to step up. So I fired up my laptop at a coffeehouse somewhere in Germany — meaning a regular coffeehouse that sells coffee, not a weed bar like they have in the Netherlands — and shot off some comments.

I was mean and ornery. I frothed at the mouth. I called people bad names. I said they were charlatans. It was ugly. But I felt like it had to be done. The precepts say you shouldn't criticize other Buddhists and that you should be kind. But sometimes other Buddhists need to be criticized, and sometimes the kindest thing you can do in a situation is not always the nicest or friendliest thing.

Before I go any further here, I want to say that I'm actually in favor of the scientific and medical research being done these days on psychedelic drugs. I am glad the restrictions on those studies are being lifted. I have personally benefited from that. As you might recall, I am prone to severe headaches. A doctor in Germany who comes to a lot of my retreats prescribed a drug for me called rizatriptan. It's the only thing I've tried that actually helps my worst headaches, and I've tried nearly everything.

Rizatriptan is derived from the same ergot fungus that makes LSD. Those headaches used to cause me to lock myself in my room at the Clubhouse moaning in the dark for half a day. Maybe you'll remember that. In a roundabout way, research into psychedelic drugs has made it possible for me to manage my headaches.

There are other uses being looked at for these drugs — in psychiatry, end-of-life care, and so on. I think that's great. What I do not think is great is when these kinds of drugs are promoted *as being compatible with Buddhist practice*. It really irks me when I see the big Buddhist magazines getting into the act.

A lot of people look to Buddhist magazines for guidance and support. Then these magazines tell them things like, "For some Buddhists, experiences of selflessness induced by hallucinogens are tools for practice" or "Ayahuasca can accelerate a type of spiritual growth that we need on the planet right now." Or they quote others who say things like, "We know that psychedelics are a valid doorway to dharma practice" and "When I took psychedelics, I actually experienced what before was only a philosophical concept."

These glowing endorsements of drug use have an effect. I know they do, because they had an effect on me.

When I was in my teens, I started wondering hard about the nature of reality. It was urgent to me because I had just found out that a devastating genetic disorder ran in my family. At sixteen I learned that I could be rendered fully incapacitated by this illness by the time I reached my thirties. I had my midlife crisis early.

I wanted answers, and I wanted them quick. I didn't know how much time I had left. Luckily, there was already a body of leftover literature from the druggy heyday of the sixties waiting for me at discount prices at every used bookstore in town. I especially dug *Be Here Now*, the tale of how Harvard psychology professor Richard Alpert teamed up with his friend Timothy Leary to explore their inner worlds by using LSD, mescaline, and other substances. Alpert later changed his name to Ram Dass and became a celebrated guru to the stars. I also read *The Center of the Cyclone*, in which neuroscientist John Lilly researched the innermost core of his being with various kinds of hallucinogens. In fact, I read everything I could get my hot little hands on about psychedelic spirituality — issues of *High Times* magazine, books by Carlos Castaneda, whatever. I devoured them all.

Then I started asking around about where I could get my hands on some acid.

I eventually found some. I bought it from an aging hippie who kept the blotter stored in his freezer on top of a layer of frost as ancient as the Antarctic in his filthy, roach-infested kitchen. I popped the tab in my mouth and let him drive me home, sitting in the bed of his rusty pick-up truck as it sped along Interstate 76.

The drug didn't kick in until we reached my place. That's when I became convinced that all my teeth had disappeared. Pretty soon I was seeing pretty colors everywhere and watching trails form behind my arm when I waved it in front of me. It was pretty far-out, man!

But I didn't take LSD to try to relive the sixties. I took it in the spirit of consciousness exploration and self-discovery. I took it because I thought it would open the doors of perception and free my mind to experience true reality.

Only it didn't. The best I can say for LSD is that it confirmed for me that there were radically different ways of perceiving. I had suspected that before, but after taking acid, I knew for certain. But then I made the mistake of thinking LSD could show me more.

So I took it three more times. My final acid trip was a waking nightmare of epic proportions. I lost the concept of time. I remember trying to tell myself that I'd be sober in a couple of hours. But the idea of hours meant absolutely nothing to me. I honestly did not know if two hours was a short time or if it was eternity. I tried to close my eyes for some kind of relief. But the insides of my eyelids were flashing at me like neon signs. I spent the entire trip in a state of concentrated terror that felt like it would literally never end.

That was more than thirty years ago, and I can still return to the horror I felt on that endless night. I don't even like writing about it now.

I wrote about that monumentally bad trip in my first book, *Hardcore Zen*, and a lot of people got the impression that I gave up on acid just because of that one bad experience. On the contrary, if I'd thought there was something there worth exploring, I could have put the bad trip behind me and soldiered on. I was damned serious about the meaning of life and prepared to take some hard knocks on the road to discovering it, if that's how things had to be. But it was clear that what LSD offered was not what I was interested in. Once I had the experience of seeing things in a radically different way and knowing that it was possible to do so, the lessons I could learn from LSD were finished.

Sure, my experiences with LSD did give me some eye-opening moments. But there was also a whole lot of confusion. My senses got all screwed up. At one point I was convinced that secret messages were appearing in my bedroom rug, but they kept changing before I could read them. I put on Jimi Hendrix's *Electric Ladyland* album, and I thought the music was emanating from gigantic celestial mirrors in outer space. Stuff like that.

Earlier on my current tour, I met a guy in Stockholm who was a real enthusiast for DMT, which a Netflix documentary calls "the spirit molecule." As we walked along a brick road past fairy-tale fountains and giggling blond kids on little bicycles, he regaled me with stories about how, when you take DMT you see aliens and can even talk to them.

Now, you might expect me to have dismissed this as stupid druggy talk, but I did not.

To me it seems entirely plausible that there are intelligent non-human creatures elsewhere in the universe. I am, in fact, very interested in that possibility. Furthermore, it also seems entirely plausible to me that advanced aliens could be capable of communicating mind-to-mind with humans. Why not?

And I will even grant the possibility that maybe some kind of drug could facilitate such communication. I've read a few Philip K. Dick novels, after all. Seriously, though. I mean it. I do not rule out the possibility that a drug could make it possible for humans to talk to aliens.

There's a lot we don't understand about human biology. We know nothing of the ways advanced intelligent nonhuman creatures who evolved on other worlds may communicate. Furthermore, if I really believed there was any chance people could communicate with aliens by taking a drug, I'd be on that in a second. Are you kidding? Talking to aliens? Count me in!

But then I had to step back. 'Cuz I asked that guy what the aliens told him. His reply was an embarrassing stream of goofy Deepak Chopra–level spiritual gobbledygook. So I have to ask myself, if people are really out there taking drugs and talking to aliens, why do these aliens always seem to just talk in dopey new age clichés? Why, if advanced alien species are so keen on communicating with humanity, do they never say anything you couldn't find in some hippie magazine? If they're so far beyond us, why are they so dumb?

Furthermore, if drugs were the way "in" to a world of greater empathy and deeper understanding, why did the Age of Aquarius end up producing so many burnouts and spawn the horror of those awful Woodstock revivals twenty years later? Why didn't the Ecstasy craze of the nineties lead to a new era of empathy in the twenty-first century?

I discovered zazen not too long after my bad acid trip. My teacher told me that it was the kind of practice that doesn't show its effects for a very long time. This didn't make me happy. But by using

LSD I'd seen what happens when you try to jump into this stuff too fast, and I knew that was never going to work. So I was stuck with the slow lane.

There's a popular cliché that says drugs are like taking a helicopter to the top of a mountain rather than climbing it. You get the same breathtaking view as someone who has climbed the mountain, they say. But they're wrong. It's not the same view. Not at all.

Let's say you meet a veteran mountaineer, the kind of guy you find a lot of here in Switzerland. Let's say he's got more than a quarter century of climbing experience, and he's written books on mountain climbing and routinely instructs others in the art of climbing. And let's imagine what would happen if you tried to convince this guy that people who take helicopters to the tops of mountains get everything that mountain climbers get, and get it a whole lot easier.

To the mountain climber, the guy in the helicopter is just a thrill seeker who thinks the goal is simply to reach the top of the mountain and that climbing is an inefficient way to accomplish this goal. He just doesn't get it. At all.

The helicopter guy misses out on the amazing sights on the way up. He doesn't know the thrill of mastering the mountain through his own efforts. He doesn't know the hardships and dangers involved in making the climb. And he'll never know the awesome wonder of descending down the mountain back into familiar territory. All he's done is given some money to a person who owns a helicopter. When there are no helicopters around, the poor guy is helplessly grounded.

Enjoying the pretty view at the top is just one small part of the experience. It may not even be the best part. To a mountain climber, every view from every point on the mountain is significant and wonderful.

Meditation involves every single moment of life. "Peak experiences" can be fun. But they no more define what life is about than so-called mundane experiences. In fact, life is mostly about mundane experiences. When you start thinking that only your most thrilling experiences are significant, you have already lost the most precious thing in life: the ability to fully immerse yourself in every experience. The idea that psychedelic drugs can somehow enhance Buddhist practice makes no sense to me at all. How is my real experience of life in the present moment enhanced by messing with the chemistry of my brain?

For having this attitude, I've been labeled a "fundamentalist" and a "puritan." But look, I'll be honest. If I believed there was any possibility of better understanding the fundamental nature of reality by ingesting some substance that would open wide the doors of perception and allow me a glimpse of the Godhead, I'd ditch Buddhism in a second and go get me some of the "good stuff."

I'm not so attached to the idea of being a Buddhist that I'd pass over a faster way if I thought there was one. If I really thought I could get the benefits of decades of Buddhist practice in mere hours, as I've seen some people claim, you'd better believe I'd be into that. If it were a choice between being a good Buddhist or getting a deeper glimpse into the nature of reality through some other method that was incompatible with Buddhism — like using drugs — then I'd definitely look into it.

But I've done them both myself, and I can see the difference. It boggles my mind that some people cannot seem to make that distinction. It's like cookies and soap. If you can't tell the difference, there's something wrong with you.

Remember that one of the most fundamental Buddhist precepts is "don't get high." This is foundational stuff, not something that was added centuries later. People who say Buddhism is compatible with psychedelics literally do not know the first thing about Buddhism.

Then there's all this talk these days about "consciousness hacking." What does that even mean? I'm not interested in trying to tailor my consciousness to fit some idea I have about how it ought to be. What do I know about how it ought to be? I'm more interested in what it actually is.

That's because mundane life, just exactly as it is, with no en-hancements or hacks at all, is incredible. How is this supposedly "ordinary world" I find myself living in even possible? There isn't anything even remotely like planet Earth for at least 25 trillion miles. That's the distance to Proxima Centauri, the nearest star. And it's probably not even that close! Maybe there is nothing even remotely like this astonishing place anywhere else in the cosmos.

The life I am living right here and right now, "mundane" as it often seems, is an inconceivable, improbable, unfathomable, deeply wondrous and mysterious thing. I have no interest at all in trying to make my experience of it any murkier than it already is.

Besides all that, as a Buddhist teacher, I have a responsibility to the people who look to me to tell them what Buddhism is about. I don't know who is out there listening to my stuff, but I do know that for a lot of people, sobriety is a very fragile thing. They're look-ing for any excuse at all to get back into drugs. I can't say anything positive about drug use and still maintain a clear conscience. Maybe some people can — with their weakly worded caveats about being responsible and having guidance. But I can't.

And when lots of supposed Buddhists start rambling incoher-ently about how drugs can be a doorway to deeper practice or can accelerate spiritual growth, I feel like there are people out there who need someone with some authority to tell the truth; they need some-one to say clearly and unambiguously that that is a lie.

Tricycle, the Buddhist magazine, not the thing you rode around on as a kid, published an article recently about the new trend of using psychedelics as part of Buddhist practice. The article is largely about a woman named Spring Washam, a teacher at Spirit Rock, a fancy-schmancy meditation center in California.

According to the article, Washam says she sees a "recurring pat-tern at American dharma centers of students expressing dissatisfac-tion with their practice." They feel like they've plateaued. She says, "They go to retreat after retreat after retreat, get more blessings by more rinpoches [teachers], and they're like, 'I'm not fundamentally feeling like I'm changing anymore.'" This is why they're open to doing drugs as part of their spiritual journey. (Gabriel Lefferts, "Psychedelics' Buddhist Revival," July 27, 2018.)

To me this is like saying reality is not enough. The infinite universe, extending forever both outward to the endless depths of space and inward to the boundless depths of the soul, the real world, a mystery of mysteries, this profoundly weird place we live in, this profoundly unfathomable thing we are, *this* is not enough? I just can't get behind that idea.

It's a little like what Dogen says about the Great Miracle as opposed to "small-stuff" miracles in his essay "Mystic Powers." In this essay he talks about stories of supposed miracles performed by Buddhist masters of the past. He doesn't deny the possibility that these things actually happened. But he says that they're just "small-stuff" miracles and are only possible within the Great Miracle that is existence itself.

To me the insights one might get through drugs are small-stuff insights at best. Maybe, in some very rare cases, they have some positive effect for a little while, at least until the high wears off. But I'm not looking for such shallow insights. I am interested in what I can discover about what the druggies often deride as the mundane and humdrum world of everyday life. That to me is the Great Miracle.

Why would I want to zip off to Proxima Centauri in the imaginary spaceship of the mind when Proxima Centauri is no more extraordinary than planet Earth? When my little "Proxima Centauri" is, in fact, just all the stupid movies I've seen about aliens recombined and regurgitated under the influence of a drug?

The fact that I exist as an "ordinary human being" is, in fact, not ordinary at all. This mind and this body, just as they are, without being altered in any way, are rare and extraordinary things.

That is what I am interested in exploring — mundane, boring, ordinary, unaltered reality.

Even if psychedelic drugs might provide some minor flashes of real insight, they also scramble up your brain, making it nigh unto impossible for you to process those insights. Maybe you'll meet Jesus for a couple of seconds, or even some aliens. But do you really want to be high as a kite when that happens?

In any case, drugs suck as a spiritual method. You made good use of medical marijuana, which got me to change my mind that it was just an excuse for stoners to get wasted legally — even though it totally also is that. And yeah, maybe some people get a tiny bit of insight while high. But ultimately I'm more interested in what this world is than what the world of drugs might be.

Stay high, Marky!

Brad

20. HE WASN'T BREATHING

Dear Marky,

I want to backtrack a bit and tell you a story about another dead guy that came up when I was at Benediktushof. Maybe you can relate.

Every day at Benediktushof I did what I normally do at retreats. I offered what they call dokusan. It's a private consultation with the teacher of the retreat.

When I lead retreats, I typically offer dokusan to everyone who comes as long as there's enough time. The Benediktushof retreats are nice because there's always plenty of time for everyone. At shorter retreats, I sometimes have to put a time limit on these meetings. But at Benediktushof, everyone can have as much time as they please.

Sometime in the middle of the retreat, a tall guy named Franz showed up for his turn. His last name was Kummer. That means "sorrow" in German. He told me that his wife's last name was Trost, which means "consolation." Together they have a little company that harvests and sells honey. It's called Kummer und Trost, literally sorrow and consolation.

When Franz came in for his turn, I could tell just by looking that he had something on his mind, but he took a long time to get it out.

After talking around whatever he really wanted to say for a while, he pulled a fifty-euro bill out of his wallet and set it on the floor between us. I should mention here that when we do dokusan, both parties sit on cushions on the floor. He said he'd give me the fifty euros if I'd listen to a story he wanted to tell me. I said he didn't need to give me any money, that I'd listen to the story anyway. But he left the money where it was because he said it was important to him.

He started off by telling me that he had a friend who was an undertaker. One day all of his undertaker friend's usual assistants were either busy or drunk and he had an undertaking job he needed to take care of. He called Franz and asked if he would be willing to help out. It seems a guy had died in his home — not Franz's friend's home, the dead guy's own home. Franz's friend needed to go out there, collect the body, and bring it to the funeral parlor. Franz said he'd help out, not really knowing what he was getting himself into. He'd never done anything like that before.

When Franz and his friend arrived at the dead guy's home, they found a bunch of his friends sort of milling around outside. There were also a couple of big dogs that Franz told me looked like the kind who would normally go after or at least bark at strangers. But they were also milling around, hanging their heads sadly.

Franz and his undertaker friend went inside and saw the dead guy sitting in an easy chair. He wasn't old, Franz said. Probably under forty. He was a big guy, though, over six feet tall and maybe weighing more than two hundred pounds. Franz said this in metric, by the way, two meters and more than a hundred kilos. The dead guy must have had cancer, Franz thought, because all his hair was gone. He also smelled pretty bad because he'd pooped all over himself when he died, like most of us will when our time comes. I guess you know all about that part, eh?

Anyway, with great effort Franz and his undertaker friend managed to get the guy out of his chair and into a body bag, and then they carried him to a gurney waiting outside. They drove him back to the funeral home and got down to the business of getting him ready to be buried. They cleaned him up, taking care to treat him with as much dignity as possible. They then dressed him as his friends requested, in his favorite T-shirt, a black one with a skull and crossbones on it.

While doing this, Franz said, he became aware that the dead man was in the room with them. Not just in body, but in mind as well. Franz said he could feel that the guy had no problems except one. Franz paused, waiting for me to take the bait. So I asked what the dead man's problem was. Franz said, "He wasn't breathing."

Franz told me he could feel very distinctly that the guy was perplexed as to why he was no longer breathing. Everything else was fine, as far as the dead man was concerned. He just wasn't breathing anymore, and that didn't make any sense to him.

After the job was done, Franz's friend handed him a fifty-euro bill, the very same bill that was now sitting on the floor between me and Franz. Franz said he had carried that bill around in his wallet ever since that day. For months he felt like he just couldn't spend that money. Nothing he had come across since then seemed profound enough to spend it on. But now he wanted to give it to me.

Usually, I'd have refused to take money at a dokusan; it seems weird. But Franz clearly wanted to give it to me, and to say no would not have been right.

I took the money, not knowing quite what to do with it. I felt the same kind of responsibility Franz had. A little while later, Franz came back to me and asked if I would donate it to your funeral expenses. So I PayPal'd fifty euros to the person who was collecting money for your funeral.

Like you, the guy that Franz had to prepare for his funeral had had his time here on Earth, and now things had changed. No matter how well we live, time catches up with everyone. Which brings up the question: What is time?

One of the very first koans I encountered was not one of the standard ones you find in books. It was something my first teacher, Tim, heard from a teacher of his. Tim's teacher snapped his fingers and said, "Before you heard that sound, where was it? After you heard it, where did it go?"

About a decade and a half after I heard that koan, I got it. I was working for Tsuburaya Productions and was at what's called a *sha'in ryoko*. They usually translate that as "company trip," which is technically correct. But Japanese-style company trips are their own beast. For one thing, no one outside the company is allowed. No spouses, no kids, no emotional-support animals, just employees of the company. They take you to an exotic place for the weekend and arrange lots of group activities during the days and lots of drinking parties during the evenings.

I don't like to drink, so at all these affairs I'd end up being the only sober guy in a room full of drunk people. At one company trip I was hanging out with this woman named Mayu Umezaki. She worked in the sales department, and we'd talk sometimes at work.

For reasons I can't remember, I was trying to tell her about Zen. But since she didn't speak English I was trying to explain it in Japanese. She was drunk and my Japanese was always iffy. It was understandable to people like Mayu, who actually made an effort to listen to me, but it was far from standard Japanese.

I remembered that koan and told it to her in badly pronounced, mutated, but basically understandable Japanese. As I was saying the koan, I suddenly got the answer. So I said to her, "I just figured it out! Do you want to know the answer?"

She said, "Okay." She probably thought I was insane by that point. Even if I'd translated the koan perfectly, it's still a weird question. But she was game to hear my answer.

So I poked her in the shoulder.

That was the answer! That was the moment when I understood what time was.

At that moment I did not doubt my answer at all. Nor do I doubt it now. But when I told Nishijima Roshi the story I just told you, he said, "That's a good answer. Another answer would be before you snapped your fingers there was no sound, then there was a sound, then after that there was no sound again."

That was the moment when I understood what explanations of time were. In my previous letter I told you about an acid trip in which I lost my understanding of time. I was plunged into the eternal present and I panicked. I panicked because I wasn't ready for it yet. This is what those kinds of drugs often do. You might get a revelation of something true, but because you haven't done the necessary work to get to that revelation, you aren't able to make much of it.

This doesn't always result in panic. In fact, the exact opposite very often happens. You might instead get super excited and happy at what you assume to be a wonderful accomplishment you've just achieved. I think you're better off with panic than that kind of excitement. At least panic could lead you to do the work you need to do. When you get super excited, you tend to assume you no longer need to work.

Anyhow, by the time of that company trip, I'd done a lot more work and I was ready to be plunged into the eternal present. In the eternal present, poking someone in the arm is real action right now. The question in the koan is not irrelevant, though. The koan question is real, and it's meaningful. There are two ways to go with the answer. One is to do something real like poking someone in the arm. And the other is to give a totally obvious — *well, duh!* — type of answer like Nishijima Roshi did.

Any other sort of answer is just brain farts.

Dogen wrote an essay called "Uji." He took a normal word that usually means something like "sometimes." But the characters used to spell that word out mean "being" and "time." He used this as a way of explaining how being and time are never separate.

We tell time by comparing the relative motion of things. We used to do this by looking at the movements of the sun and the stars and then comparing them to other things like average rainfall or temperature. Now we measure it by creating clocks that track the decay of atoms and we compare these to how mad our girlfriend gets about how late we are. But in any case, time is movement and change. If everything in the entire universe froze solid and never moved or changed, you couldn't say time was passing. Time doesn't exist outside of the beings who experience it.

I am time, and you are time. I won't even say you *were* time. You *are* time, even though you're not experiencing time the way I am, I assume. What you are is time. The action you take is time happening to time.

A friend of mine named Lauren Crane, who is a dude in spite of his first name, once said, "Be here now is often presented as a choice, as if there is some way you can *not* be here now. It should be presented as a realization, a caution. You are not in the past or future. You can only be in the now. You're stuck in the now."

The past is experienced in the present as memory. The future is experienced at the present as anticipation. It's not incorrect to say that I have a past and I will have a future. But past and future are cut off and only this moment is real. It is always now.

Being only exists in this now, in this exact moment.

You can plan for the future. It's a sensible thing to do. But you do your planning for the future right now. When your plans come to fruition — or fail to — the time when they do so will also be now.

Your past too was also now. It was now when we sat outside the Clubhouse watching that lightning storm; it was now when you drummed for my band in high school.

Now shoots through all of time.

It was now because we were there. Now that we're not in those places, now looks different. But it's still now, and it will always be now.

But it's also really late and I have to get up early tomorrow. So for now, I'll sign off.

Sleep tight!

Brad

21. WHAT IS ZEN AND WHAT IS JUST ASIAN CULTURE

MARKY,

The retreat at Felsentor went all right. I got to see the grave of my first teacher's teacher, Kobun Chino. Kobun died near Felsentor when he apparently tried to save his young daughter, who was drowning in a lake. No one really knows exactly what happened because no one else was around. They just found them both drowned in the lake. Maybe if you see them wherever you are, you can ask.

I'll be heading to Portugal tomorrow to be the keynote speaker at something called the Worldwide Critical Buddhist Conference. They're putting me up in a hotel for a few days. I rarely stay in hotels on these tours because I can't afford them. So that should be interesting.

While I was at Felsentor I started thinking about something I meant to address a long while back. Felsentor is built just like a Japanese Zen temple. It's so Japanese, I almost felt as if I were back in Japan at one of Nishijima Roshi's retreats at Tokei-in Temple in Shizuoka. I've also done a lot of retreats at places that were not Asian looking at all, like Benetiktushof, for example, which was originally a Catholic monastery. This got me thinking about something I often get asked about, which is how to differentiate between what is really Zen practice and philosophy and what is just Japanese culture.

Remember back in that very first letter I wrote to you where I was talking about how I didn't want to talk to anyone about (fucking) Zen? I said that because a few days earlier I'd given a talk at a Zen place in Münster — you know, like Herman and Lily and Grandpa. It was those Münsters in Münster I was thinking of when I wrote that.

When I arrived in Münster I was sick. I've been sick on and off throughout this tour. The worst part was when I got the spinal tap. The Münster trip was a bit before that. Being sick was, I think, mostly a response to how sad I was about you dying. By the time I arrived in Münster, I'd heard you'd slipped into a coma and weren't expected to come out of it. Not that I blame you for my being sick. I was just really down about the whole matter of you being back in America dying and me not being able to do anything about it.

Anyway, in Münster I ran into this guy I'd met the previous time I was there who really wanted me to talk at the Zen place he attended. I was totally *not* up for it. It wasn't one of my scheduled stops. But I had told the guy in an email about a week before I arrived in Münster that I'd do it, and I didn't want to let him down. So I said to him, "Look. I feel like crap right now. I'll go to this thing, but just promise me it'll be easy."

He was all like, "Okay, don't worry! It'll be easy!"

Well, it turned out it was a long ride on two buses over there, which was not what I needed just then. But I made it to the place. It was up a flight of stairs in a big room above a pastry shop. It seemed like maybe it had been built as an office.

They'd gone totally Japanese inside their little temple. They had sliding shoji screens made of rice paper and black lacquered wood. They had calligraphy on the walls. They had those little tables that are so low to the ground you have to sit on cushions on the floor rather than on chairs, just like in Japan. In short, the place was more Japanese than most places I've been to in Japan, and that's not an exaggeration. In some aspects it was more Japanese than even Felsentor.

One of the ways it was super-duper Japanese was that this group had all the Japanese Zen rituals down pat, almost like it was cosplay. You know, "costume play," like you see at an anime convention, where people dress up like the characters from their favorite Japanese cartoons. These German Münsters were very serious about being Japanese Münsters. They were Frankensteins, but they wanted to be Godzillas.

After a forty-minute period of zazen followed by a little ceremony — perfectly performed — I was sitting there at that little table with snot oozing out of my nose, running off every few minutes to use the toilet because whatever I had was affecting my guts too, to do a Q&A session that I didn't know I was expected to do. Nobody seemed to notice. They were totally focused on the Zen of it all, you see.

They weren't bad people or anything. They were just really into their hobby. Like *really* into it. For them the question of the difference between Zen and Japanese culture seemed not to matter. But for other people it really does. Some people even consider Zen Buddhism as practiced by anyone outside Asia a form of cultural appropriation.

One day some guy on Facebook had this to say about me: "Please, white American dude, tell me again what Buddhism is. He knows white Buddhism, he's cultural appropriation [I'd fix the guy's grammar here, but I'm not sure what he meant], he makes money off defining a culture that does not belong to him — which he tried due to his many failed business ventures and bands — and I have no problem with his identifying as Buddhist but with any white American defining Buddhism when that culture doesn't belong to them."

That wasn't the first time I'd heard people saying that something they call "white Buddhism" is an example of something they call "cultural appropriation." And it's not the first time I have been accused of being part of this terrible thing.

I'm not sure what "cultural appropriation" really means. Every culture adopts things from other cultures they come into contact with. Every supposedly "pure" culture is mostly a conglomeration of things that culture has appropriated from other cultures. There are no more pure cultures than there are pure races.

Now, I know it's a dick move to, say, put on a Native American feathered headdress and run around going "Ugh!" and "How!" Or to wear a kimono and a set of plastic buck teeth and go, "Me so horny!" Exploiting another culture for crass commercial gain is also a rotten thing to do.

So let's accept that something that can legitimately be called "cultural appropriation" can exist. Then is "white Buddhism" cultural appropriation?

If you ask that, then you have to ask some other questions. Is Japanese Buddhism cultural appropriation? Is Chinese Buddhism cultural appropriation? Are Tibetan Buddhism, Thai Buddhism, or Sri Lankan Buddhism cultural appropriation?

Buddhism did not originate in any of these cultures. So any form of Buddhism you find in those places has been appropriated.

The historical Buddha was a member of the Shakya people, and there is some debate as to whether the Shakya homeland was in what we now designate as India or what we now designate as Nepal. So perhaps you could even ask if Indian Buddhism is cultural appropriation.

Right from the start, Buddhism was a missionary religion. I know, I know. I've already said that Buddhism is not a religion. But I will admit that in some ways it is a religion and in some ways it's not. In the sense that it has always had something we might call "missionaries," Buddhism is a religion.

The historical Buddha decided to teach what he had discovered to other people. He made no distinctions between caste, race, culture, or gender. He believed that any human being could become just as enlightened as he had. He did not regard his philosophy as belonging to his culture, nor did he think that anyone from outside that culture who put his philosophy into practice was stealing it from his people. He regarded all humans as "his people."

After the Buddha died, the people he had taught his understanding to went even further in spreading the practice and philosophy. There were Buddhist missionaries teaching white people in Europe about Buddhism well before Christian missionaries got there. They didn't have a lot of success, but it wasn't for lack of effort.

In the Middle Ages, the Catholic Church even designated the Buddha a saint when they were trying to incorporate a small cult of "white Buddhists" in Eastern Europe. These folks had a religion based on a guy they called Josaphat. In an effort to win them over, the Catholic Church designated Josaphat a saint. Only it turns out that the legends of Saint Josaphat were derived from stories of the Buddha. Josaphat was a corruption of the word *bodhisattva*. Later on, the Catholic Church realized its mistake and decanonized Josaphat.

Every culture that appropriated Buddhism has changed it in significant ways. This includes the Asian cultures that appropriated Buddhism from other Asian cultures.

I think one of the best things to happen to Buddhism in recent years is that it has been studied and practiced by people of many different races and cultures. This has transformed Buddhism in the West from something exotic and "other" into something much more real and practical. This is precisely what the historical Buddha and his original followers clearly wanted. If you want to read more about this, I'd recommend *The Making of Buddhist Modernism* by David L. McMahan. That is, if you can read things wherever you are these days, Marky.

"White Buddhism," to use the dopey designation my Facebook friend gave it, is a latecomer to the Buddhist party. But if any Buddhism can be called "cultural appropriation," then literally *all* of what we now call Buddhism has to be called cultural appropriation. In which case calling it cultural appropriation is completely meaningless.

Sorry for the rant. I wanted to talk about how to separate what is truly Buddhist from things that are just matters of Japanese culture, or matters of Thai culture, if you're coming from that tradition, or Tibetan, Chinese, or Korean culture, and so on. It's a valid question.

It's a tricky thing to do. Just look at Christianity. Most scholars of Christianity will tell you that much of what we think of as Christianity these days has its roots in Greek philosophy rather than in the teachings of a first-century Palestinian Jew. Christmas and Easter actually originated as pagan celebrations of the winter solstice and the coming of spring. How much of Christianity is truly Christian, and how much of it is just matters of European culture? Can you neatly separate them?

People have tried. But what you usually end up with is something weird. I'd say that maybe Christianity wasn't really Christianity until it had passed through a number of different cultures and picked up a lot of influences from them.

I feel like you might as well give up on ever finding a version of any religion that's completely untainted by any elements of the culture it formed in or the cultures it was exposed to. Even if you could do that, how could you help but see it through the lens of the culture you were brought up in?

But okay. Even given all that, I think we actually can still ask about how much of what is practiced at Zen temples both here and in Japan is truly Zen and how much is just Japanese culture.

My personal approach to the matter of what is Japanese culture and what is Zen is to try to avoid extremes. I feel like you need to be careful if you're going to try to separate what is truly Zen from what is merely Japanese. You don't want to accidentally throw the baby out with the bathwater. Unfortunately, some folks leave the baby in the bathtub and never even try to let it out. Which is probably not so good for the baby.

To continue that metaphor, I think it's better to take the baby out of the bathwater but maybe not be in such a hurry to dry it off completely just yet. I know, it's a weird metaphor. But I think it's not such a bad way to think of it.

If you're not sure which aspects are Japanese and which aspects are Zen, maybe try a bit of both mixed together and see how it works. Don't be in a hurry to reject the cultural stuff before you understand what it means.

I think that the best approach is to keep the aspects of Zen practice that have worked in the past and have lasted a long time. This goes even for aspects we may not immediately like or even understand.

For example, chanting sutras in languages you don't understand is one aspect of Buddhism that's lasted a long time and crossed many cultures. Often when non-Japanese people hear the traditional-style chanting of the Heart Sutra, for instance, they assume they're hearing Japanese. Not so. It's actually a mishmash. Some of it is Chinese, and some of it is Sanskrit transliterated into Chinese. Then the whole thing is pronounced in a style invented by the Japanese for pronouncing Chinese words. I would bet that there isn't a single person on Earth who hears the version of the Heart Sutra they chant in Japan and understands what it's saying as if it's in their native language. Yet Japanese Buddhists have been chanting it that way for ages. Maybe there's a reason.

In this particular case, I think there's a good compromise. Chant the Heart Sutra in your native language some of the time, and chant it in the traditional style other times. That way, when you hear the old-fashioned version, you have some idea what it's saying while still benefiting from the special sound of the traditional chant.

Posture is another area in which the tradition is useful. I know a lot of places where they say you can meditate in any posture you feel comfortable in. I've tried that, and as I wrote earlier, in my experience it just is not true. I think it's better if you can get as close as possible to the traditional posture for zazen, even if you can't quite manage it exactly. This mostly involves finding ways to arrange your legs such that you can maintain an upright, unsupported spine if you happen to be one of the many who cannot manage to get your legs into the lotus or half-lotus posture.

Decor is another area where you can look to tradition. Zen temples don't need to be full of tatami mats, shoji screens, and ancient calligraphy. But an uncluttered, minimalist environment in muted colors works best. It doesn't necessarily have to look all Japanese-y, but it should follow something like the established style for best results.

For clothing, you don't need to shave your head and dress in black robes. But loose-fitting clothes in muted colors help make individual meditators more comfy and make the overall environment more suitable for practice.

Along these same lines, one thing lots of American Zen people enjoy wringing their hands about is inclusivity. The demographic at Zen centers in America tends to skew mostly white. We don't want anyone to feel like they can't do Zen practice because of silly, superficial things like race, gender, sexual orientation, and so on.

However, one of the problems when it comes to Zen and inclusivity is that Zen is not a very warm, welcoming, and inclusive sort of practice for anyone. It never has been. In fact, it has always been quite the opposite.

The stereotype of how one entered a Zen monastery in Asia in the past was that you first gave up everything you owned except for a begging bowl and a set of robes. Then you climbed up to the top of some foreboding mountain, dodging bears and mountain lions and yetis. When you got to the monastery, you pounded on the door and begged to be let inside before you froze to death or got eaten.

Eventually one of the monks might take a look at you and tell you to get lost.

If you were very determined and stayed on the front porch for several days in spite of starving and getting rained and snowed on and having to fend off predators and bugs, they might take pity on you and let you inside. Even then, you'd hardly be treated like an honored guest. You'd have to prove your usefulness to the community by doing the crummiest grunt work that no one else wanted to do. Maybe in a few years you'd graduate to a higher status, but only if you worked really hard at it.

Inclusivity? Ha! Good luck with that!

Despite this harsh attitude, Zen monasteries were also traditionally known as places that would not reject you just because of your ethnicity or social status. Men and women usually trained separately, but apart from that everyone mixed together.

In fact, in the rigorously stratified caste system of ancient Japan, you could essentially erase your lowborn status by becoming a monk and thereby stand outside that system entirely. Still, you had to prove you were serious about the practice and that you were prepared to do whatever it took to keep the monastery running.

The fact that you could change your social status by becoming a monk was such a big deal societally that laws were enacted to prevent people from pretending to be Buddhist monks. There was a time when you could face the death penalty for eating meat while dressed as a monk, for example.

America in the twenty-first century is very different from ancient Japan. Compared to ancient Japan, our Zen monasteries are positively cuddly. Furthermore, we Americans have a strong national ideal of including everybody and making sure no one feels left out. And yet this is often at odds with the traditional Zen way of being rigorous and uncompromising.

One thing I learned about Americans and our notions of inclusivity and tolerance while I was living in Japan is that we Americans are generally seen as being extremely demanding and entitled. To Japanese people, we all seem to have some special need and we all insist that this special need be accommodated by every person or institution we encounter. We will talk endlessly about our special needs and we expect to receive lots of "oh, you poor, poor thing"– type responses as folks go about trying to make us feel comfortable and included.

In Japan they don't do that. But it's not because they demand that everyone conform. This is one of the biggest misconceptions about Japanese society, if you ask me. It's not that Japanese culture demands conformity for its own sake. It's more that individuals in Japan understand that their society has a limited capacity for meeting everybody's specific needs. Asking for special treatment of any kind can make you seem like a spoiled prima donna.

As a vegetarian living in Japan, for example, I quickly found out I couldn't rely on anyone else to meet my dietary demands or even feel very sympathetic to them. This was the food that was available. If I didn't want to eat it, that was my problem, not the problem of the person who made the food. Japan, being a small isolated island nation with limited resources, has developed a culture that values being satisfied with whatever is available.

I feel that an important part of what Buddhism is supposed to teach us is a sense of how to stop making demands on the world to accommodate what we want. This is central to the very purpose of Buddhism. It's about reaching beyond our individual wants and desires to find something deeper and more truthful. It's about being happy with what you have to be happy with.

All societies are set up to accommodate the majority. That's not because society is mean and bigoted. It's because for most of human history we've been damned lucky just to get whatever we can get. We couldn't accommodate everyone's individual wants, so we built things to accommodate what was seen as the average person, and then we let those who weren't average figure out how to make that stuff work for them. Yes, bigotry exists. But it's a separate matter.

A typical American Zen Buddhist center can be thought of as a very small and often impoverished microsociety. They're usually barely able to cater to the needs of the most average types of individuals who might show up.

Even if a Zen center could accommodate all the various special needs that its American members are inclined to demand, I don't think they should. It worries me to see lots of American Zen folks so distressed about inclusivity that they forget what the purpose of our training really is.

Zen training is intended to free us from the demands we make on the world to be kind, comfortable, accommodating, and unfailingly harmless. It is intended to remove us from our comfort zones and present challenges. It is supposed to be uncomfortable.

The intention of the practice is to get rid of the props we use to make life easier and learn to still be relaxed and content, even under trying circumstances. Our usual American demands to be seen and heard as individuals or as representatives of some group identity are inappropriate in a Zen setting.

For fifteen years of my life I was a racial minority and an immigrant. I don't claim that my experience as a white foreign guy in Kenya and in Japan were exactly equivalent to the experiences of minorities in America. Obviously not! Still, I do know very well what it's like to be the odd one out in a culture that is decidedly not your own. Everything smells weird and tastes funny and everyone stares at you. You can't be anonymous, no matter how hard you try. When you walk into a subway car, all of a sudden you're hearing conversations about the influx of foreign people into the country, conversations they think you can't understand. Your hair is strange. Your manners are wrong. Nobody can pronounce your name. I am not insensitive to the way many people in a cultural majority fail to see how minorities can feel excluded, even when such exclusion isn't intentional.

We would like our Zen centers to be places where anyone can feel just as included as anyone else. But in order for Zen to be Zen, it can never feel totally welcoming or totally accommodating to anyone. I hope we can take steps to remove any unnecessary barriers to inclusion. And yet I hope that doesn't come about by trying to change Zen into something that's too accommodating, thereby losing its value.

It's going to take some time before there are American Zen centers in which black folks or Latinos or other nonwhite ethnicities make up the majority. But I am sure that one of these days we will start to see places like that. It took more than two thousand years for white folks to get into Zen. If it takes two hundred years for it to catch on with nonwhite folks, that will be a tenth of how long it took for white folks to get into it. And I don't think it will take as long as two hundred years! In any case, we've only had Zen centers in the USA for about fifty years. I think we need to have a bit more patience.

I gotta go get packed for Portugal. So I'll write you when I get there.

Brad

22. CRAZY WISDOM IS USUALLY MORE CRAZY THAN WISE

MARKY,

I am writing to you today from a really weird place. And I don't mean that I'm psychologically "in a weird place," although that also happens to be true. The physical space I'm in is deeply weird.

I think I'm in an actual cult compound.

I suppose I ought to backtrack a bit. Earlier this year I was invited to speak at something called the Worldwide Critical Buddhist Conference. The guy who invited me was a professor of comparative religions at Middlesex University in London. He told me that it was an annual gathering of folks interested in nonmonastic Buddhism. He said they would put me up in a hotel in Portugal for the five days of the conference and allow me to attend all its activities in exchange for my delivering a single hour-long talk. I looked the thing up on the web. It sounded legit, and it fit into my tour schedule, so I said, "Cool. I'll do it."

It turns out that the folks who sponsored that Worldwide Critical Buddhist Conference are based here in Amadora, Portugal. Their leader is a Belgian guy who is considered a high-level Buddhist master in the Taiwanese Great Mountain Buddhist tradition. He's got those weird eyes I always associate with religious cult leaders, kind of glassy and hypnotic. He's in charge of the place I'm staying at right now. They actually did get me a hotel for the first few days as promised, but for the past couple I've been in his compound.

A few days ago, I gave my talk at 9:00 AM at the start of the conference to a small audience that consisted mainly of Taiwanese guys in suits — most of whom slept through it. The only people who stayed awake for my talk were a group of students from Middlesex University.

After a few days of other lectures by other people — some of which I wanted to sleep through — they took us back to the hotel. After that, though, we all checked out of the hotel and they took us on a bus out to this place on a mountain a few hours' drive outside the city. The bus was rocking like crazy as we went up the windy road. We were so close to the edge, I kept thinking we'd plunge into a ravine. But we made it.

This place is huge! The guy who showed us around said it was built to accommodate five thousand people. There is a six-foot-tall gold framed photo of the Belgian master on one of the altars in the main room. The room is the size of a midsize concert venue, the kind of place a band like the Ramones might have played in the mid- to late eighties when they were starting to draw slightly bigger crowds. There were TV monitors all over the place, presumably so that folks in the back of the room would have a better view of the master while he was onstage.

It's obvious that loads of people live in this compound. There are huts all over the place, and I see a lot of toys and strollers around. So there are families too. Somehow that makes it feel even more like a cult.

There are a bunch of Buddhist scholars from all over the world here who were part of the conference. I've been talking to some of the Japanese scholars in Japanese so the folks who run the place can't understand us. One youngish Japanese scholar told me he thinks this group is just like Aum Shinrikyo, the people who in the nineties tried to jump-start the apocalypse by putting the poison gas developed by the Nazis on the Tokyo subway system. Twelve people died, and more than a thousand were seriously injured.

I hope they're not quite that bad. But, dang! I'd better start checking these events out better before I say yes to them. I got a free trip to Portugal out of it, but I hope I don't also die here.

Somehow it seems like this might be a good time to write to you about some of the crazier aspects of Buddhism. One of the weirder aspects of Buddhism you probably would have been interested in when you were alive is called "crazy wisdom." It's a phrase often used by Buddhist cult leaders to justify their breaches of standard Buddhist ethics.

Crazy wisdom is the idea that sometimes wise people act crazy and maybe even seem to be unethical. The term comes out of the Tibetan Buddhist tradition, but you see a lot of folks in the Zen tradition acting kind of crazy too. The most famous of these is Ikkyu, the legendary Zen Buddhist monk who got drunk and hung out with prostitutes a lot.

One of the foremost contemporary examples of so-called crazy wisdom was a Tibetan guy named Chögyam Trungpa Rinpoche. When Trungpa was just eighteen months old he was recognized as the reincarnation of a high Tibetan lama. He escaped Tibet's Chinese rulers when he was twenty years old, fleeing through the icy mountains on foot with a group of three hundred, only thirteen of whom made it across the border to India. He went to England and started the first Tibetan Buddhist center in the Western world.

Later on Trungpa founded Naropa Institute in Colorado, the first Buddhist university in the West. He also set up the Shambhala Foundation, a huge organization for spreading Buddhist teachings. Trungpa's influence extends far and wide. I keep running into organizations and people who have associations with him.

Chögyam Trungpa also allegedly screwed dozens of his students and then allegedly drank himself to death at age forty-eight. I mean, it's for sure that he died when he was forty-eight and that he drank a lot. However, some folks dispute the connection. His widow said, "Although he had many of the classic health problems that develop from heavy drinking, it was in fact more likely the diabetes and high blood pressure that led to abnormal blood sugar levels and then the cardiac arrest." On the other hand, his doctor said, "He had chronic liver disease related to his alcohol intake over many years." So there you go. I wasn't there, so I can't say what he died from.

I never met Trungpa myself. But I knew a guy who worked for him as an instructor at Naropa Institute. He used to tell me wild stories about Trungpa's excesses. One time, this guy said, Trungpa told him that demons were going to fly in through this guy's window at night and tear him to bits. Apparently the demons were going to take revenge for some offense this guy had committed against Trungpa. The demons never showed up.

A different guy I once talked to told me how he'd watched Trungpa down two forty-ouncers of malt liquor during a public dharma talk at a Zen center. Then there's the story I've heard from about half a dozen people about the time Trungpa forced a couple to participate in an orgy by ordering his uniformed guards to strip them naked against their will.

I'm not saying all these things really happened, because I don't know for sure. I'm just telling you about the kind of talk that's out there when people in the Buddhist community tell their stories of Trungpa.

And yet for all his alleged scandalous activities, Chögyam Trungpa is still revered by many people as one of the great Buddhist masters, decades after his death. Others ask questions. Was he merely a madman who conned thousands into thinking he was a wise master? Or was his crazy wisdom really more wise than crazy after all?

I've never been quite sure just what to make of Trungpa. His book *Cutting through Spiritual Materialism* is still one of my favorites on the subject of pursuing the dharma authentically. Yet, by many accounts, he was a drunk and a sex fiend. Even some of his greatest admirers say that.

He never tried to hide any of this, though. Perhaps that's what made it work. At the very same time as Richard Baker Roshi, head of the San Francisco Zen'Center, was getting flayed alive for having an extramarital affair, Trungpa was allegedly out there screwing dozens of his followers and nobody was too worried, as far as I can tell. The difference may be that Richard Baker kept his affair — or affairs; some say there was more than one — hidden until he was caught, while Trungpa was completely blatant about what he did.

So maybe sex isn't the real problem. Maybe the real problem is spiritual teachers who present themselves as one thing and then act completely contrary to that image. Whatever else you might say about him, Chögyam Trungpa did what he did out in the open for everyone to see. That way, nobody went into Trungpa's organization imagining him to be holy and pure then became deeply disappointed when it turned out he wasn't. If you were gonna study with Chögyam Trungpa, you had to accept the fact that he was a boozy womanizer right from the outset, *ahem*, allegedly.

Then there's the story of Ösel Tendzin. Tendzin was the man Trungpa appointed as his successor. It has been alleged that Tendzin liked to get it on just as much as his teacher. The problem was, it is alleged, that after Tendzin was diagnosed with HIV he continued having unprotected sex for perhaps as long as three years without informing any of his many partners of his condition.

Stephen Butterfield, a former student, said, "In response to close questioning by students, he [Tendzin] first swore us to secrecy and then said that Trungpa had requested him to be tested for HIV in the early 1980s and told him to keep quiet about the positive result. Tendzin had asked Trungpa what he should do if students wanted to have sex with him, and Trungpa's reply was that as long as he did his Vajrayana purification practices, it did not matter, because they would not get the disease."

"Tendzin's answer, in short, was that he had obeyed the guru," says Butterfield.

Gosh.

My sincere question here is this: Can a teacher be a lousy or at least questionable human being and still be a source of truth and wisdom?

As I said earlier, I really like the one book of Trungpa's that I read. There is definitely wisdom to be had there. In his book *Sex and the Spiritual Teacher*, Scott Edelstein points out that according to Buddhist philosophy, nobody ever remains exactly the same person throughout their entire life. In fact, what we are at any given time is as much a product of the environment we find ourselves in as it is any intrinsic personhood within us.

Therefore, it's understandable that somebody could be wise at one moment and a jerk at another. Lots of people are like that. Why should Buddhist teachers be different?

This doesn't excuse unethical behavior at all. But it helps explain how, for example, Chögyam Trungpa could write an amazing book about Buddhist practice in spite of his alleged drinking and partying and his allegedly questionable sexual activities.

Still, it's better to be consistent. Furthermore, I think it is even better to be ethical.

I don't condone the kind of unethical behavior I'm talking about here at all. I don't support it. I don't think anyone else should support that kind of behavior. If someone hears rumors that a teacher is doing unethical stuff, I think they ought to look into that. They should find out if the allegations are true, and if they are true, take whatever steps they can to rectify the situation. I tell folks all the time that if their "master" is doing weird stuff to them or to other students, they should speak out about it. It is not okay.

In recent years we've seen a lot of scandals within Buddhist communities. The late Eido Shimano, a Zen teacher in New York, was accused of sexually abusing his students, as was the late Joshu

Sasaki, a Zen teacher in California. A whole bunch of other Buddhist teachers have also been accused of various sorts of abuses. Not all the allegations are at the same level of badness, but these accusations do add up and create an image in people's minds about Buddhism.

Some in the mainstream media have suggested that maybe there is something fundamentally wrong with Buddhism that leads to the abuses they've reported on. But they probably have never heard of the Noble Eightfold Path or the precepts. Most journalists are pretty sloppy about such stuff. Or if they do know about them, they probably figure all us Buddhist teachers just ignore them. We do not.

I would suggest that the problem does not have to do with Buddhism but rather with large religious institutions in general and the effect that fame and power can have on a person — including the fame and power that come from being a spiritual leader.

All the major Buddhist scandals I am aware of took place in large institutions. All those institutions grew at a very rapid pace. Comparable incidents have happened in Hindu, Christian, and Islamic institutions that were similarly large and grew at a similarly accelerated pace. The Hare Krishna movement, a Hindu-based group, is a good example. Early on in their history, they pushed for rapid growth and ended up empowering a whole lot of people as teachers who shouldn't have been teachers at all. They did this, it seems, because they felt their movement needed to get as big as possible as quickly as possible. It was a disaster, leading to allegations of sexual abuse, criminal activity, and even murder.

There was a trend in the early days of Buddhism in the West of organizations pushing for rapid growth. In *Shoes Outside the Door*, Michael Downing's book on the scandals at San Francisco Zen Center (SFZC) in the early eighties, we see how SFZC experienced rapid growth in the previous decade under the leadership of Richard Baker. Meanwhile, Buddhist groups like Shambhala, the Zen Center of Los Angeles, Rinzai-ji, and others also grew explosively.

As documented in *Shoes Outside the Door*, several people asked

SFZC's leader, Richard Baker, the same question: "Does it have to be so big?" Baker consistently ignored those who advised him to break the organization down into smaller, independent units.

But it's a very good question. Do Buddhist institutions really need to be so big? Do they need to grow so fast?

It's not hard to see why it seems advantageous for a Buddhist group to get really big really fast. Without a gigantic donor base for SFZC to draw from, for example, there wouldn't have been enough money and people power for huge projects like the Tassajara and Green Gulch monastic communities. There wouldn't have been enough money and people power for transforming their temple in the city into the gorgeous place it is today. The same is true of many other similar Buddhist organizations, like the one I'm staying in right now.

All over Europe and the Americas we find spectacular cathedrals and magnificent churches. I stopped in Cologne, Germany, on this trip and right outside the train station is a magnificent church that dwarfs a lot of American football stadiums. In Asia there are Buddhist temples of similar scale and grandeur. Why shouldn't we Buddhists have some of these marvelous practice spaces in the West as well?

But again, I have to wonder if any of the institutions that administer such admittedly beautiful spaces are really as beautiful as the spaces they administer. Or is it intrinsic to the game of running such a ginormous space that there are power plays and their attendant scandals? Is it even possible for an organization through which millions of dollars and thousands of people are flowing to remain untainted by the power, greed, envy, and other such passions that come along with handling that treacherous stuff?

I think a lot of the leaders of what end up becoming big sanghas get it into their heads that they are so very enlightened that they can handle this dangerous stuff. They seem genuinely surprised and confused when that turns out to have been a mistake.

In my own experience, I've found that it's not so much that Zen practice gives me superpowers that enable me to deal effectively with things like greed, anger, and delusion. Rather, the practice has enabled me to see more clearly when I am about to get into a situation where such things are likely to arise. Then it's up to me to decide . if I want to enter that situation.

I may feel like I am strong enough in my practice to deal with it, but then I have to step back and wonder if that feeling is also a delusion. I wonder if maybe it's my ego seeing a chance to enhance itself by saying, "Don't worry. Just a little bit of greed can't hurt. Come on. When are you gonna have an opportunity like this again?"

When I see myself having those kinds of internal conversations, I know it's probably best to walk away from whatever temptation is in front of me, even if it hurts to do so, and even if I have doubts about giving up whatever the thing in question might be. And I also often fail and end up taking the wrong action even while knowing I'm doing so.

In my experience of running a tiny Zen center in Los Angeles, I think I can understand some of the unfortunate things that so often happen in larger groups. For example, I now see why large institutions so often fail to hold rogue teachers accountable.

Once an organization of any size is established, that organization can start to take on a mind of its own. There are times when every individual member of an organization might be opposed to some action. Yet if enough of those individuals think that the action would be beneficial to the organization, they'll accept it as a necessary evil. You end up in situations where *no one* wants to do the thing in question, and yet *everyone* goes along with it anyway for what they believe will be the good of the organization.

Another factor is that Buddhists in America and Europe are keenly aware that they are seen as a fringe religion. They're aware that the general populace doesn't know much about Buddhism and is inclined to be suspicious of it. When a teacher within such a marginalized religion starts behaving badly, there's a strong tendency to want to bury that information so that the religion as a whole doesn't get tarnished by it. It's seen as a danger to Buddhism itself to let these things be known. This is a legitimate fear. As I've said, since the scandals I just mentioned broke there has been a lot of speculation that Buddhism itself is to blame.

This leads Buddhist institutions with bad teachers to try to deal with such things internally and to do so quietly. For example, if you kick a rogue teacher out of the group, there's a danger that teacher might spill the beans. After all, what have they got to lose once they've been stripped of the benefits the institution provides? So the institution tries to keep the scandal quiet and keep the person who caused the scandal quiet as well. And, like all of us, those involved in the cover-up hope the problem will somehow go away or take care of itself.

The larger the institution, the more at stake there is. A small group might be able to get rid of a bad teacher without too much being lost. There's usually not much money involved, and few people who will be hurt. Plus, in general a scandal within a small organization isn't very interesting to the media or the outside world.

A larger institution has much more to lose. A scandal in a big institution based on a fringe religion looks much juicier to folks with a twenty-four-hour news cycle to feed. Furthermore, large institutions are often the main financial support for many people within them. If a big institution goes down as the result of a scandal, it can be truly devastating to the livelihoods of everyone involved. So, again, there is more incentive to try to keep the truth buried.

And what is it all really for?

I'm not sure Buddhist practice really requires elaborate and ostentatious temples, fancy retreat centers in lovely locales, and vast communities. Do those things really help us practice? Sure, they might attract greater numbers of people. But are those people coming for the right reasons?

I'm not certain there are any actual benefits to really big sanghas in terms of what Buddhism is really all about. I know the desire for making huge Buddhist groups goes way back historically. But I'm not sure it was ever a very good idea.

I feel like whatever growth Buddhism experiences in terms of popularity among the wider human community has to happen at its own pace. We can't force it. We are better off being sincere and diligent in our own practice and letting other people come to it naturally, through seeing the truth of it. If we try to do anything more than that, we are doing a tremendous disservice to the practice, and it will always end up doing harm.

Sorry for the rant, Marky. This stuff is definitely on my mind as I sit here inside this compound wondering if I'll ever be allowed to leave.

Josh Baran, a former Zen teacher and author of *The Tao of Now* is one of those who thinks Buddhism itself is to blame. In a conversation I had with him on Facebook he said, "It may be the myth of the fully enlightened master/sage combined with the narrative of skillful means and crazy wisdom, and throw in demand for absolute obedience — produces a particular kind of abuse potential." I agree that this is the root of some of the problems.

But I don't think any of this stuff belongs in Buddhism. The idea of a fully enlightened master who must be obeyed as well as notions about crazy wisdom do exist in lots of contemporary Buddhist institutions. But such ideas are not fundamental to Buddhism itself. In fact, if you ask me, they shouldn't exist in Buddhist institutions of any kind. None of it. Ever. Let me go through Mr. Baran's points one by one and explain why they are not what I would call "Buddhism."

The myth of the fully enlightened master. This myth comes from the standard narrative of Gautama Buddha's life in which he sits under a tree and meditates and after a while — poof! — he's a fully enlightened master forever and ever, amen. From then on he's no longer plain old Siddhartha but is now the Buddha, the World Honored One.

But this myth came about only after Gautama Buddha himself was dead and gone and could no longer challenge it. Like every other great person who dies — John Lennon, Mother Teresa, JFK, Kurt Cobain, the list is endless — Gautama Buddha was mythologized after his death into something much more fantastic and unreal than he had been in life.

While he was alive, however, Gautama told of being visited by Mara, the evil Satan-like tempter in Buddhist mythology. His saying he was "tempted by Mara" is like a contemporary person saying "the devil made me do it." While some folks believe in a supernatural entity who actually makes them do bad things, most people use the phrase metaphorically. I think the Buddha did too.

What he was saying was that even after his so-called enlightenment, he was still dealing with the living karma of his preenlightenment years. Even the original and arguably greatest Fully Enlightened Master of our lineage was not the kind of "fully enlightened master" the myth makers want us to believe our contemporary masters are.

The narrative of skillful means and crazy wisdom. The idea of skillful means originates in the Lotus Sutra, in which the Buddha does whatever it takes to bring about realization in his followers even if, on the surface, it seems to be deceptive. Of course such a narrative is ripe for abuse. So is the idea of crazy wisdom, which can be used as a cover for plain old unwise craziness. The original intention of this narrative was to convey the idea that wisdom doesn't always look the way we think it ought to. This is true and important. But neither of these notions means that Buddhist wisdom always has to look crazy or that so-called skillful means must always be some sort of trickery.

The demand for absolute obedience. This is absolutely not part of Buddhism. No decent Buddhist teacher has ever demanded absolute obedience. It's antithetical to Buddhism, which stresses the necessity of questioning everything, including the supposedly enlightened pronouncements of one's own teacher. One charlatan Zen master, whom I will not dignify by naming, claimed that students need to "come under the teacher" like a cup under a faucet in order to receive his wisdom. It turns out a few of his students had indeed *come under him* — or at least faked it. Later on they said it wasn't very spiritual at all.

To say that the student must obey the teacher no matter what is to demonstrate that one has absolutely no clue what Buddhism is about. Submission must never be part of Buddhist practice. If a teacher demands a student be submissive to him, that teacher should not be trusted.

A student must be able to respect their teacher. But this has to go both ways. No one should respect a teacher who does not respect their students as well.

The other factor I think is crucial to point out in all this is that whether they meant to or not — and they probably didn't — these scandalized teachers taught us American Buddhists something very valuable. They taught us that we should never blindly obey religious authority figures even if they are Buddhist masters. Clearly we needed this lesson or none of these scandals would ever — indeed none of them *could* ever — have happened.

Remember that in these cases we're not talking about an Adolf Hitler–type figure with the might of the SS to enforce his will. Most of these so-called masters were just little men in fancy robes. The only thing they ever had that they could use to compel anyone to obey them were their students' desire to obey the arbitrary whims of a religious authority figure, their students' desire to be dominated. And it worked like magic — on some people who should have known better, who, I would argue, often did know better and chose to ignore what they knew.

To me, this is the key point. We all have within us a desire to be dominated. I think this comes from childhood when we had some kind of protector figure in our lives — parents, guardians, teachers — who took care of the difficult stuff for us. Some of us had good protectors, and others of us had lousy ones. Most of us had protectors who did the right thing sometimes and the wrong thing other times.

But no matter what kind of protector we had, lots of things were much easier when someone else dealt with them. I think we all have a secret desire to return to that state. We'd like to have someone take care of us, watch over us, deal with all the difficult things like paying taxes and getting groceries.

When some guru or Zen master seems to offer that, it can be really tempting. But it never works. It always goes sour. I think it's really crucial to acknowledge that we want this but also to be aware that we can never really have it.

Again, sorry for ranting. If I get out of here, I'll write you some more.

Brad

23. ESCAPE FROM THE COMPOUND

MARKY,

I made it out alive! Hooray!

Apparently the guy who invited me to the Worldwide Critical Buddhist Conference had to have a big talk with the higher-ups because he had criticized their leader. They suspended him from attending any events at the compound in Portugal for a year. Good for him! Personally, I think he should walk away from the organization entirely. Sadly, I don't think he will.

This morning I participated in a guided meditation with the group at the compound. We don't do guided meditation in Zen. Nobody talks while you sit. Well, occasionally they do this thing called *kusen*, in which the leader of the group will say a few words at the very beginning. My teacher really hated that tradition, though. He thought it was a total corruption of Zen practice to have any talking during zazen.

I always find guided meditation annoying. I don't like being told what to think about when I sit. I prefer to get into the pure experience of just sitting. It's not that I think guided meditation is evil or anything — I just find it distracting and unnecessary.

All the students went back to England yesterday, so they weren't around last night or this morning. I was pretty much on my own.

Nobody really interacted with me at the compound. Which was fine as far as I was concerned. I got the impression they were very insular and not really good with strangers.

Now I'm on a plane bound for the USA. As I mentioned earlier, some folks in Ohio wanted to have a memorial service for you, and they asked me to do a Buddhist thing to kick off the proceedings. I've been emailing back and forth with some of them, and I have a plan worked out. It'll be nice and respectful but also fun, I hope. I'll let you know how it goes.

Sometimes I wonder what people will say about me after I'm dead. I have a certain degree of fame, and so I'm aware that my death will probably affect people that I don't even know. That's a strange thing to think about.

I think I mentioned that my friend Pirooz Kalayeh made a documentary about me. Did you ever see it? It was finished not long before you started getting sick. Anyhow, in the film one of Pirooz's interview subjects muses that "Brad Warner probably won't be appreciated until after he dies." Or words to that effect.

I wonder if that's true. I'm certainly not one of the more popular teachers on the current circuit of hip spiritual masters. Lots of other people attract far larger audiences than I do. I earn enough money from my work that I can afford a one-bedroom apartment in Los Angeles without having to do a day job. That's pretty sweet, if you ask me. On the other hand, there are people doing basically the same kind of thing I do who are positively raking it in. We're talking like multiple mansions in exotic locales and all sorts of stuff. You can get legitimately rich doing the spiritual master thing. I'm not getting rich, but it can be done.

I've never been all that interested in being wealthy, though. Don't get me wrong. It's not that I can't imagine enjoying life in a big house up in the Hollywood Hills with a swimming pool overlooking the city. A couple of times I stayed with Moby in his place up there. It turns out that Moby and I once shared a stage together in Akron, Ohio, when Zero Defex opened for his hardcore band the Vatican Commandos in the early '8os. Moby was briefly interested in Zen, but he ended up falling into the hands of the Transcendental Meditation people and then he stopped answering my emails. I was sad about that because I had started to think of him as a friend. I never paid much attention to his music, so I wasn't being a fanboy when we hung out, although I was pretty impressed with his collection of synthesizers and drum machines.

Anyway, his house is sweet! It just goes on and on and on. I'm sure it cost a fortune, but then again, he has a fortune. It wouldn't be bad to live in a place like that. But you have to be either really ambitious or really lucky to get that kind of money, and I am neither.

One of the things Zen Buddhists sometimes chant during rituals is this old poem called the Loving Kindness Sutra. One of the lines is "Let one not take upon oneself the burden of riches." When I hung out with Moby, I could see that wealth was a burden. He talked about how it was hard for a rich person to know who his friends really were because everybody wants something from you.

Even the slight degree of fame I have can be annoying. I'm not recognized on the street that often, though it does happen sometimes. But when I walk into a Zen center or someplace like that, I get a lot of people staring at me and sometimes even demanding my time as if I owe it to them because they bought my books. I can just imagine how bad that would be if I had to deal with it every day. No, thanks!

When Buddhist teachers caution us not to seek wealth and fame, it's not that they want us to be all austere and poor and stuff, as if poverty were in itself some kind of virtue. It's because they know that fame and money are a trap. It looks very glittery and exciting from the outside. But it's a kind of poison, really. It makes it very hard to live a balanced life with a realistic outlook.

It would've been neat if your band Zen Sex Butchers had become famous. Or if my band Zero Defex had scored a hit song on college radio. Things would have been different for us. But would they have been better? That's hard to say.

All I know is I get to live this life I'm living now. Which overall is pretty good. One of these days, I'll be as dead as you are. So will Moby. So will everyone else. I guess none of us gets to hear what people say about us after we die. Or if we do, we don't remember it in our next incarnation. I suppose if we end up in heaven or hell we might get to hear those things and even remember them. I kinda doubt it, though.

While I've been writing these letters pretty much for my own sake, as I've been writing, I've been thinking of you. I've tried to stick to just the things I'd actually say if I were sure you'd really be able to read them. It's been weird. I've learned a few things in the process. I'm glad I did it.

For now, though, I think I should try to get a little sleep.

Catch you later!

Brad

24. THE WHOLE SHEBANG

DEAR MARKY,

I'm back in Los Angeles now, but not for long. The memorial service for you is in a couple of days. I'll be on another airplane tomorrow, this time bound for exotic and exciting Akron, Ohio, rather than some lousy European destination.

All through my European tour, when I haven't been writing to you, I've been working on rewriting some of Dogen's greatest hits. I did two books of Dogen rewrites, and one of these days I may do another. So every so often I plug away at one of his writings. There's one in particular I've been hammering away at that I feel might be especially relevant to this string of letters I've been writing you.

It was originally called "Zenki." That's pronounced "Zen-key," by the way. The *zen* part is not the same *zen* as in Zen Buddhism. Japanese has tons of words that sound the same but have different meanings, much more than English does. This *zen* means "all."

The *ki* part is funny. It most commonly appears in the word *kikai*, which means "machine." By itself it means "function." My teacher Gudo Nishijima, who translated this essay with his student Mike Cross, called it "All Functions," which is a really boring title. Kaz Tanahashi, who worked on translating Dogen with Ed Brown, came up with an only slightly less boring title, "Undivided Activity."

Masao Abe, who worked with Norman Waddell, called it "Total Dynamic Working." Underwhelming, if you ask me.

Much better is the title that Kosen Nishiyama, who worked with John Stevens, came up with, "The Total Activity of Life and Death." But my all-time favorite is the one my first teacher, Tim McCarthy, bestowed upon it (and that I stole): "The Whole Shebang."

It's an essay about life and death. It was written as a prepared speech for a daimyo, which was kind of like a samurai lord. So it wasn't written for monks or people with a deep knowledge of Buddhism. It was written for folks who had a lot of stuff on their minds other than sitting around meditating all day.

I figured maybe you'd be into seeing something this Dogen dude I'm so into wrote. Here it is below. I'll explain it afterward.

THE WHOLE SHEBANG

The Great Truth, when you totally and completely get it, is breaking free and is enlightenment. By "breaking free" I mean that life breaks free of life and death breaks free of death.

So there is breaking free of life-and-death and there is entering into life-and-death. And both of these are examples of completely getting the Great Truth. There is also throwing away life-and-death and making use of life-and-death. And both of these are also examples of completely getting the Great Truth.

Enlightenment is life. And life is enlightenment.

At the time of enlightenment, there is nothing but the total enlightenment of life, and there is nothing but the total enlightenment of death.

This pivotal moment right now causes life to be life, and causes death to be death. This very moment right now, which is the pivotal state of enlightenment itself, isn't necessarily big but isn't necessarily small either. It's not the entire universe, nor is it just one place. It doesn't last a long time, nor does it vanish quickly.

Life in this very moment right now is the pivotal state of enlightenment. The pivotal state of enlightenment is this very moment of life right now. Life isn't something that comes, nor is life something that goes away. Life isn't the experience of the present moment, and life isn't the realization of that experience.

Thus, life is the whole shebang. And death is the whole shebang.

There are a bajillion realities inside you. Among these there is life, and there is death. Just quietly think about it for a bit. Are your own present life and the bajillion realities within it part of life itself or not part of life itself? There isn't a single instant or a single real occurrence that isn't part of life itself. There's not a doggone thing or even so much as one state of mind that is not part of life itself.

Life is kind of like a guy on a boat. On this boat, I unfurl the sail, I steer with the rudder, I use the pole to shove off. But at the same time, the boat carries me, and there is no me beyond the boat. Because I'm sailing on it, the boat becomes a boat.

Let's closely study this mysterious moment right here and now. In this mysterious moment, there's nothing but the world of the boat. The sky, the water, and the shore have all become the time of the boat. Which is totally not like times when I'm not on the boat.

So life is what I make it, and I am what life makes me. While I'm sailing on the boat, my body, my mind, and everything that surrounds me are the whole shebang of the boat. The entire Earth and all the universe are the whole shebang of the boat. What I'm trying to say is that life itself is I myself, and I myself is life itself.

An old-timey Zen dude once said, "Life is the whole shebang. Death is the whole shebang."

We should really look into these words. Here's what they mean to me: When he says "Life is the whole shebang" it means that there's no beginning or end to life. Life is the entire Earth and the whole universe. Even so, this doesn't interfere with life being the whole shebang, and it doesn't interfere with death being the whole shebang either.

When he says, "Death is the whole shebang," to me that means that death is also the entire Earth and the whole universe. Even so, that doesn't stop life from being the whole shebang, and it doesn't stop death from being the whole shebang either.

Life doesn't get in the way of death, and death doesn't get in the way of life.

The entire Earth and the whole universe are right there in life, and they're also right there in death.

But it's not like the entire Earth is one thing and the whole universe is another. And it's not like the whole shebang operates as life sometimes and as death at others. It's not one undivided thing, and yet it's not separate things either. It's not identical, but it's also not different.

So the many real things we experience in life are the whole shebang. And the many real things we experience in death are the whole shebang. Furthermore, even states that are beyond life and death are the whole shebang too. Within the whole shebang, there is life and there is death.

The whole shebang of life and death is like a guy extending his arm. Or it's like a guy reaching back in the middle of the night to adjust a pillow. This is real mystical power and total enlightenment. Such things can only happen where there is limitless mystical power and lots of divine light.

In the very moment of enlightenment, the whole shebang of life and death becomes completely clear. We might feel like before enlightenment there was no enlightenment. We feel that way because we ourselves are a manifestation of enlightenment.

And yet the time before enlightenment was the previous manifestation of the whole shebang. And even though there was a previous manifestation of the whole shebang, that doesn't get in the way of the current manifestation of the whole shebang.

Every moment is the whole shebang. Even this one! Because this is so, our different ways of understanding are different fragments of enlightenment vying to be realized.

This talk was presented at the castle of Lord Yoshishige on December 17, 1242.

Here are a few notes about the essay.

I sorta secularized Dogen's opening statement. What he actually says instead of "the Great Truth" is more like "the Great Way of the Buddhas." People these days might take that as an endorsement of one religion — Buddhism — over others. In Dogen's time it wouldn't have been taken that way, so I changed it. Sue me.

I also worried myself silly over the phrase *breaking free*. My teacher Gudo Nishijima and his student Mike Cross used the word *liberation*. Tanahashi and Brown as well as Abe and Waddell translated it as *emancipation*. The word Dogen used is a weird compound of the character for penetrating or clarifying something and the character for dropping away. It means understanding something so thoroughly that you don't even need to think about it anymore. In that sense *breaking free* seemed to work.

In the fifth paragraph of my version there's a line where that weird word *ki*, which, you'll recall, means "functioning," comes up for the first time. I borrowed from Nishijima and Cross and translated it as "pivotal moment." I thought about making that sentence read, "This whole shebang causes life to be life and death to be death." That would have matched the title I gave the piece, but it didn't seem to reflect what the original says in this spot.

Where I have Dogen say, "Life isn't the experience of the present moment, and life isn't the realization of that experience," he's actually making an untranslatable pun. The word Dogen uses that often gets translated as "enlightenment" or "realization" is 現成,

which is pronounced "genjo." The pun he makes would read sort
of like, "Life isn't *enlight* and life isn't *enment*" — but in a way that
actually makes some sense. Dogen separates the two characters in
genjo and says something like, "Life is not *gen*, and life is not *jo*." *Gen*
means roughly "the experience of present moment," and *jo* means
"to become." I couldn't make a pun like Dogen did, so I just tried
my best to get at what I think the pun meant to those who heard it
back in 1242.

Where I have Dogen say, "Thus, life is the whole shebang. And
death is the whole shebang," he's using that weird phrase he uses
in the title of the piece that means something like "all functions,"
"undivided activity," or "total dynamic working" rather than "whole
shebang."

When I have Dogen saying, "There are a bajillion realities
inside you," what he actually says rather than "bajillion realities" is
more like "innumerable dharmas" (無量の法 pronounced "muryou
no hou"). In this case the word *dharmas* is hard to translate. Originally the word *dharma* meant the teachings of the Buddha. But it
later came to mean something much wider, like reality. Tanahashi
and Brown translate that line as "Know that there are innumerable
beings inside yourself." I get why they'd put it that way, but it sounds
kind of creepy to me, like some weird horror movie or a description
of multiple personality disorder.

A couple of sentences later, where I have Dogen using the phrase
life itself, he actually just says *life*. I thought it needed a bit of extra
emphasis here to make it clear he was talking about life as a holistic
thing rather than as one person's individual life. Although Dogen
would probably say that one person's individual life *is* "life itself" in
that holistic sense.

Then I have Dogen say, "Let's closely study this mysterious
moment right here and now." What I've paraphrased as "this mysterious moment right here and now" is Dogen using a favorite word of
his, the word *inmo*. This is a Chinese word meaning something like

"it" or "what," depending on the context. It's the kind of word you use for a thing you can't name.

In Dogen's view, everything in the universe is something you can't really name. I mean, you *can* name things. It's just that the name is never a full description, just like the name Marky doesn't really describe all that you once were. Dogen is emphasizing that this exact moment here and now is something weird and mysterious.

The stuff that comes after this, the stuff about the boat, is really about how we become ourselves. What we truly are is actually something much, much bigger than the small thing we imagine we are. And yet at the moment when I am Brad and when you were Marky, that's all there is or all there was. Everything that surrounds us is part of who we are, even though we don't notice it. In a sense, our universal nature doesn't matter during the moments when we fail to notice it. Our universal nature is identical to the small, personal self we think we are. At that moment, that's how our universal nature manifests itself.

Then after this, Dogen quotes an old-timey Zen master as saying, "Life is the whole shebang. Death is the whole shebang." The old-timey Zen master is actually named Yuanwu Kequin, which the Japanese pronounce as "Engo Kokugon" (the Japanese pronounce Chinese characters their own way). He lived from the year 1063 until 1135.

He's actually responding to a koan I wrote to you about earlier. Remember that story about the monk and his teacher going to visit a house where someone had died and the monk taps the coffin and goes, "Alive or dead?" The line about life and death being the whole shebang is from Engo's commentary on that koan.

Engo said something like,

How is it possible to climb up the silver mountain and the iron wall? Tonight I will place a flower on the golden brocade [which is sort of like saying "gild the lily," meaning add something unnecessary to a thing that's already complete]. I will open wide the barrier and discuss this koan. Life is the manifestation of the total function [i.e., the whole shebang]. Death is the manifestation of the total function. Again and again the teacher repeats, "I won't say, I won't say." Within this place, there is neither back nor front [meaning no duality]. We must accept it right here and now without being separated even by the width of one thread. Life and death fill the boundless empty space. Each and every bit and piece is the exposed red heart without separation or preference.

The part right after the quotation from Engo is a real mind-blower, if you ask me. Dogen says that life and death are both the whole shebang. Which is to say, in some sense, that life and death are not two different things. People who are alive always worry about life after death. Well, maybe death is present in life, and life is present in death. At least that's what it sounds like Dogen is saying here. Maybe if I want to know what death is like, I should take a look at my life right now.

Mel Weitsman, a teacher at Berkeley Zen Center, commented on this part of the essay in a talk he gave at the Chapel Hill Zen Center in 2008. If you have the internet where you are, it's on the Chapel Hill Zen Center's website and it's titled "Sojun Mel Weitsman Roshi on Dogen's Zenki." He said, "Dogen said that since the great Way of buddhas is beyond all dualities, including the basic duality of birth and death. From manifestation's point of view, each thing, including death, is life's total realization. And from death's point of view, each thing including manifestation is death's total realization. It is also called...the eternal now."

After blowing our minds with that one, Dogen starts going into some of that weird Zen-y stuff about things being not identical and yet not different, and so forth. Sometimes this gets turned into one of those awful Zen clichés. I know this one wanna-be Zen master who likes to go around saying, "Not one, but not two!" as if he's super cosmically aware. People give him confused looks when he says shit like that, and he hopes they'll assume he's really deep. Ugh!

All Dogen is doing here is emphasizing what he just said about the differences we make between things. Separation and undividedness are just concepts. Identity and difference are just concepts. We use those concepts to navigate through life, but life itself is beyond such concepts. You can't even say it's undivided!

I really love the line I rendered as "The whole shebang of life and death is like a guy extending his arm." Dogen says that just stretching out your arm is a manifestation of enlightenment. Every damn thing is a manifestation of enlightenment!

Our very existence itself is enlightenment. That's one of Dogen's main messages. Anything we do is the activity of the entire universe doing exactly what it needs to do at that moment. I know it's hard to believe this sometimes. But I think Dogen is right. It took the creation and continued existence of the whole universe just to put me in a room typing this out. Everything that ever happened in the past four billion years — or however long it was — led to this very moment. We should try not to forget that.

The thing about reaching for a pillow is a line Dogen also uses in an essay he wrote about compassion. He says that real compassionate action is like reaching back to adjust a pillow during the night. I take that to mean that compassionate action is just doing what needs to be done without even any conscious awareness of who is doing the thing and who that thing is being done for. We always worry a lot about why we do things, but maybe that's just the brain farting around. Maybe we just do what we do and that's all there really is to it.

Then Dogen says, "The time before enlightenment was the previous manifestation of the whole shebang. And even though there was a previous manifestation of the whole shebang, that doesn't get in the way of the current manifestation of the whole shebang."

So maybe we don't feel particularly enlightened right now, but that doesn't mean enlightenment is absent at this moment and that it might appear later. Whatever we do and wherever we are, that itself is the whole shebang. So wherever you are, Marky, is the whole shebang. And me typing this at my kitchen table with my neighbor's cat rubbing all over me because he wants attention is the whole shebang as well.

So there ya go! That's how I write when I write about Dogen. I hope it was at least entertaining. I gotta go pack up my robes for your memorial service. See ya there!

Ta-ta for now!

Brad

25. MARKY'S MEMORIAL

MARKY,

You should have been at your memorial service. You would have liked it!

As I think I said a few letters ago, a couple of your friends asked if I'd do some kind of a Zen priest thing at your memorial, and I was honored to do so.

They held it at a place called the Phantom Alley in Wadsworth, Ohio. It's a combination bowling alley, bar, and event space. As the name implies, the decor had a ghostly theme. Their motto is "It's scary how fun it is!" It wasn't far from where you lived when we were in high school, same end of town. I'm sure you would have enjoyed the fact that your memorial was held in a place like that. It was a perfect punk-rock funeral parlor.

A whole bunch of your friends and former bandmates showed up. Lots of people from the old punk-rock scene, many of whom I hadn't seen in a very long time, were there. Some members of your family also showed up. I'd never met any of them before.

I wore my black Buddhist robes with the yellow sash-like *o-kesa* on top. The *o-kesa* is a stand-in for the Buddha's original robes, which were said to have been passed down by his successors from generation to generation in India until they finally fell apart. The one

I have was sewn by a small family-run company, in Tokyo's Ueno district, that makes Buddhist robes professionally. It's traditional to sew your own *o-kesa*, but that tradition has largely disappeared in Japan. These days most Western Buddhist teachers have gone back to sewing their own. Luckily I was ordained in Japan since I'm sure if I'd sewn my own it would have come out a big ol' mess.

These were my fancy robes, Marky. Just in case that matters to you. I have three sets of Buddhist robes. I purchased my first set for my dharma transmission ceremony. Not really knowing what I was getting into, I just ordered the standard Soto-shu version in nylon instead of silk to save a bit of money. They still cost around $400. A few years later, after I'd realized those robes were beastly hot, I ordered another set of "summer robes," which were supposed to be lighter and cooler, but in reality were pretty much the same. There went another $400.

Finally, my friend Marc Rosenbush, director of the film *Zen Noir*, sold me one of the robes he'd commissioned for his movie. He wanted only $50. How could I refuse? Those robes are my favorite. They're made of cotton rather than nylon, so they're a lot cooler to wear. Plus, they're Rinzai-style robes, which means they lack the ornamental, and highly impractical, giant sleeves of a Soto-style robe.

But I'd been wearing those movie robes for about a year since they had their last cleaning. They had ridden around in my suitcase for my entire trip to Europe too. So their condition was less than ideal. I therefore decided to wear my fancy set, the first ones that I bought all those years ago, which I hadn't taken out of the closet in years. It seemed more fitting to wear the really good ones for the memorial service for you, Marky. So don't say I never did anything for you.

I recruited my friends Nina and Steve to be my assistants at the service. Nina had sat with me a bunch of times when I was living back in Akron briefly a few years ago, and Steve was a longtime Zen practitioner who knew more about standard Zen services than I did.

I decided to keep things as simple as I could. I printed out some copies of the Heart Sutra and the poem "Enmei Jukku Kannon Gyo" and passed them around to everyone there. Some of your friends and I put together a little altar with pictures of you and things you loved.

We improvised the altar by finding an old wooden desk in one of Phantom Alley's back rooms. It looked a lot nicer than the folding card table we initially thought we'd have to use. We placed a photo of you inside a *butsudan*, a cabinet-like thingy that usually houses photos of deceased relatives in Japanese homes. Folks from the Nichiren Buddhist sect — the guys who chant "nam myoho renge kyo" — also use them to enshrine copies of the Lotus Sutra. The one Steve kindly provided was one of theirs, a lightweight plastic model rather than the usual wooden kind. It looked nice, though. I bought the same kind of *butsudan* to house pictures of my mom at my dad's house after she died.

We placed some of your favorite food items on the altar, like one does at a Japanese memorial service. In this case we had a bottle of blueberry kombucha, a lollipop — I remember you sucked on them when you were trying to quit smoking — and some Death Mints candies in a coffin-shaped tin. In Japan I've seen such diverse items as bottles of sake and packs of cigarettes on altars, so this wasn't as weird as you might think.

Under the altar, your best friend, Jim — former guitarist for the Zen Sex Butchers — placed a copy of the Knack's debut album *Get the Knack*. Apparently one time Jim confessed to you that he liked the Knack. After his admitting to the cardinal punk-rock sin of enjoying the band who gave the world the horror of "My Sharonna," every time Jim had a birthday, or on any other occasion where presents were given, you went out to a thrift shop and bought a copy of their debut album, *Get the Knack*, to give him. Sometimes you'd buy four or five of them since they were always so cheap. Jim ended up with a couple dozen copies of that record. You even gave him a copy on eight-track tape one time. Jim had that eight-track autographed by the band during one of their reunion shows in the early nineties, he told me.

We put the other standard items on the altar: candles, flowers, a holder for the incense offerings. Then we performed the ceremony. We chanted the Heart Sutra and the poem "Enmei Jukku Kannon Gyo," which, as you may recall from my letter about Zen ceremonies, is an homage to the spirit of compassion in the form of the bodhisattva Kwan Yin (a.k.a. Kannon, a.k.a. Avalokiteshvara). Steve read a dedication verse.

The dedication verse goes, "In Buddha's diamond realm the sun of wisdom shines without ceasing. The sweet sound of Dharma soothes every troubled spirit like a fountain of cooling water. With full awareness we have chanted the Dharani (poem) of Great Compassion. May the Buddha with infinite beneficence illuminate this endless field dedicating the merit of this chanting to..." Then you say the name of the person being memorialized.

Rather than simply dedicating the service to your usual name, I canvassed your friends for all your various nicknames and listed them all. The best one, Luke Hammerhead — an inside joke about an embarrassing incident at a gig in Youngstown that I won't remind you of — got a good laugh from the crowd. I always think it's important to get at least one laugh at a funeral or memorial service.

The chant concludes, "May he, together with all beings, realize the end of suffering and the complete unfolding of Buddha's Way."

When the service was done, friends and family members gave short eulogies. I was especially moved by your mom telling the story of how you had approached her when you decided to change your name from the one she'd given you. She said you had her listen to Television's *Marquee Moon* album all the way through so she'd understand your choice. Our mutual friend Dave Materna read a poem he'd composed for the occasion. Your sister Cheryl said a few words. It was good.

After that we all chowed down on the potluck food people had brought. I loaded up on too much chips and hummus. Lots of people came up to tell me how moving it had been. I had been really stressed out about the whole thing, but it came off very nicely.

I suppose funeral services would be an example of the kind of "woo-woo" that Sam Harris and folks like him fret about. After all, there's an invocation of the Bodhisattva of Compassion, someone they'd likely label as a fictional character based on old superstitions. There's also all that stuff in the dedication about the Buddha's diamond realm and how the sound of the dharma soothes troubled spirits, and so forth.

I have to admit it all does sound pretty "woo-woo," even to me. As far as I know, you were an atheist. I'm sure you didn't believe in an afterlife. I wonder if you do now. I'm not saying that sarcastically, by the way. I'm not saying that like some sort of smug dude who knows there's an afterlife and therefore knows you believe in it now. I really, honestly do wonder.

I would guess that most of your friends feel the same way about religion and about life after death. It seems like your family was like mine, nominally some kind of Protestant Christians, but not really that into it. You never expressed any interest in the spiritual stuff I was into. And yet the memorial service felt like it was the right thing to do. All of us who were your friends and relatives wanted to do something to commemorate your life, and in that spirit, I think everyone accepted this, even if it might have seemed a little weird. But then again, you always liked weird stuff. So, in yet another way, it felt appropriate.

This just underscores my feelings about the whole woo-woo argument. Sometimes some of that woo-woo stuff just feels like the right thing to do. It's only when people get too hung up on taking it super literally that it becomes a problem.

I'm well aware that people taking woo-woo stuff far too literally is the root of a lot of human suffering. Yet I'm not so sure that trashing all the woo-woo stuff is how you solve that problem. I'm not sure it helps to try to make people who find value in the woo-woo stuff feel like idiots. I feel like a better solution is the one Buddhists have used for centuries. You keep some of the woo-woo stuff, but you also take care to never take it very seriously.

Anyway, I hope you will forgive me for being so woo-woo at your memorial service.

I left the memorial feeling some sense of what I guess people call closure. I wasn't with you when you died. But the memorial made it feel like it had really happened and that I could now move on.

I still miss you sometimes. Every once in a while I come across something I know you'd have enjoyed or thought was funny and, for just a second, I think about sharing it with you. Hell, this whole series of letters is part of that! I have to remind myself that I can't really share stuff with you anymore. At least not in the way I used to. And I'll never get another goofy email from you with a link to some weird video again. And when I remember that, for a few moments I feel sad that you're not around.

As Dogen said, we don't say that life becomes death just as we don't say that spring becomes summer. Life is life and death is death. At the time of being alive there's nothing but life. At the time of dying there's nothing but death. I guess you know that.

Anyway...

I hope these letters didn't just bore the crap out of you, Marky. I went on a lot longer than I ever planned to. But maybe I needed to get it out of my system. I feel better now. So at least that's something.

If you ever feel like replying, you know where to find me.

Peace, brother.

Your friend,

Brad

AFTERWORD

Hi, readers!

I have to fess up here about a few things.

The tour of Europe I described in this book is actually a mash-up of events from several different tours I've made of Europe. My European treks started with an invitation to Finland in 2009 to promote the Finnish edition of my book *Hardcore Zen*. Since I was going to be in Europe, I tacked some other events in different European countries onto that trip. Since then, I've done speaking and retreat-leading tours around Europe every year. They're always an adventure! Sometimes they're a good adventure, and sometimes they're less good.

The tour I ended up describing is much more epic than my actual tours ever are. I usually only go out for three or four weeks. The tour you've just read about would probably have taken at least three months if it really happened! And normally only one really crazy thing happens on each trip instead of a whole bunch, like I described in this book. Mainly between Zen gigs I just wander around quaint European cities looking for used-record shops.

Even so, pretty much all the events I recounted actually happened in some form. However, in many cases I've changed the details or locations or fudged the names of the people and organizations

241

involved. Sometimes I did this to make the narrative work out, and sometimes I did it because I didn't necessarily want to embarrass or otherwise call out the actual people or organizations.

Marky Moon, the dead friend I'm writing to in the book, is based mainly on two people that I knew since high school. Both of them were involved in the Northeast Ohio punk scene of which I was a part, and both of them died of cancer at around the same age and within just a few months of each other. One was in my first punk band in high school, and the other was a housemate of mine. I've also added in bits and bobs of other people I knew from that scene, some of whom are still alive, particularly the real Marky Moon, Mark Smith, who kindly lent his punk-rock name to this project.

I did this because I didn't think it was right to pick just one of those people and address him by his real name in this book. That could have drawn too much attention to his family and friends as well as to others who might not really want to be part of a book. It was better, I thought, to create a new character who wasn't exactly fictional but wasn't quite nonfictional either.

Therefore, in a sense this book is partly fiction. Yet I feel like it's one of those cases in which fiction can be truer than nonfiction. There are true things you can say about made-up characters that you couldn't say about actual people. There are also true things you can say about your own reactions to made-up characters that you couldn't say about your reactions to actual people. Fictionalizing the parts of this book that I did made it possible to go into aspects of this story that I couldn't have if I'd stuck to being rigorously factual.

It was really hard to write this book, but I'm glad I did it. It would have been much easier to write the kind of book I had initially intended to.

My initial idea for this book was for it to be called *Zen 101*. It was going to be a primer of basic Zen and Buddhist philosophy. For the past few years I've been writing books that went into great detail about very specific aspects of Zen. I wrote three books about the philosophy of Dogen, for example. I also wrote one about God as approached by the Zen tradition and another one about Buddhist ideas and practices around sexuality.

But when traveling around talking about those books, I noticed that a whole lot of people I encountered didn't have a basic understanding of what Buddhism or Zen is. So there I was talking about the intricacies of Dogen's unique take on Buddhist philosophical concepts to audiences often composed largely of people who weren't even quite sure who Buddha was. I figured it was time to get back to the basics.

But as I wrote chapters addressing those things to an imaginary audience, it just wasn't working for me. Frankly, I was bored!

Then I came across an entry I'd written in a diary I kept while on one of my European tours. In that diary entry, I addressed one of my friends who had just died as if I were writing a letter to him. That diary entry forms most of the first chapter of this book. I didn't change much. In fact, I went through several drafts in which I did rewrite it but then ended up discarding most of those changes and leaving a lot of the rawness of the original version directly from my diary.

After rereading that diary entry I thought, Why not just write the entire book as a series of letters to my dead friend? That way I could be much more intimate and much more real. I was no longer envisioning an anonymous, imaginary audience. I began writing about all of the same sorts of topics I'd planned to write in *Zen 101*, but now I was writing them to a specific person — or at least to a specific fictionalized composite person.

I tried to stay as true as I could to that approach. Although I was, of course, aware that I was actually writing for an audience of people I didn't know, I tried not to think about that too much. I tried to say what I wanted to say as if I were telling one of my now-deceased friends who I tried to imagine could somehow read what I wrote. I tried to write just the way I would really have written to one of those actual people.

The same passages that had initially been kind of boring to me when I was writing them to an anonymous audience now came to life. They took on a new kind of urgency. I started to remember why I'd gotten interested in Zen in the first place. I remembered what it meant to me when I first discovered a philosophy and practice that was so real, so true, and so fearless.

I hope a bit of this comes across. And I apologize for lying to you.

ABOUT THE AUTHOR

BRAD WARNER was born in Ohio, grew up in Africa, and lived in Japan for eleven years, where he got ordained as a Zen monk. He now resides in the Hipsterville part of Los Angeles. He began sitting zazen when he was eighteen years old under the instruction of Tim McCarthy and was made a dharma heir of Gudo Nishijima Roshi in the futuristic year 2000. He used to work for a company that made movies about giant radioactive lizards eating Tokyo, and now he writes books like this one.

He also travels the world showing people how to sit down and shut up. He has given talks and led Zen meditation retreats in the United States, Canada, England, Scotland, Northern Ireland, Finland, the Netherlands, Germany, France, Poland, Israel, Belgium, Spain, and Japan. His books have been translated into fewer languages than those of anyone you've ever seen on the cover of a meditation magazine, but there are editions in Finnish, Polish, German, and Greek. And supposedly there's one in Hebrew, but he's never seen a copy. Or maybe he has but doesn't know it because he can't read Hebrew. He wishes someone would point it out to him somewhere if the book actually exists.

He plays bass guitar in the hardcore punk band Zero Defex

(oDFx).* He has had major roles in several movies, including *Zombie Bounty Hunter M.D.* and *Shoplifting from American Apparel*. He also wrote, produced, and directed his own film, *Cleveland's Screaming*. Plus, he made five albums for Midnight Records under the semi-fictional band name Dimentia 13.

When he's not doing zazen, Brad can be found at record stores all over the world searching for obscure psychedelia and songs to add to his incredible cheesy seventies playlist. He enjoys bad science fiction movies and cats, though dogs are okay too. He's a vegetarian but tries not to be a total pain in the ass about it.

---

* Did you ever wonder where NOFX got their name? We were around well before them.

LETTERS TO A DEAD FRIEND ABOUT ZEN

THE PODCAST

Letters to a Dead Friend about Zen is also a podcast! In each exciting episode, Brad Warner reads a newly composed letter to his dead friend Marky about Zen before a live audience. These aren't the letters from the book, but brand-new ones specially written for the podcast. Then the audience is invited to discuss the letter or any other subject they like, and hilarity ensues! Actually, the discussions get pretty profound sometimes. If you're interested in Zen or Eastern philosophy in general, but you don't like the way they're usually discussed either as dry, academic subjects or flowery, new-agey nonsense, you'll enjoy the *Letters to a Dead Friend about Zen* podcast.

Find the *Letters to a Dead Friend about Zen* podcast
wherever you look for podcasts!